Black Box Casino

Black Box Casino

How Wall Street's Risky Shadow Banking Crashed Global Finance

Robert Stowe England

 PRAEGER

AN IMPRINT OF ABC-CLIO, LLC
Santa Barbara, California • Denver, Colorado • Oxford, England

332.042 ENGLAND 2011

England, Robert Stowe.

Black box casino

Library of Congress Cataloging-in-Publication Data

England, Robert Stowe.
    Black box casino : how Wall Street's risky shadow banking crashed global finance / Robert Stowe England.
    p. cm.
    Includes bibliographical references and index.
    ISBN 978–0–313–39289–4 (hbk. : alk. paper) — ISBN 978–0–313–39290–0 (ebook)
1. Global Financial Crisis, 2008–2009. 2. Mortgage backed securities—United States. 3. Investment banking—United States. 4. Financial crises—United States. I. Title.
HB37172008 .E54   2011
332'.042—dc23   2011028748

ISBN: 978–0–313–39289–4
EISBN: 978–0–313–39290–0

15 14 13 12 11   1 2 3 4 5

This book is also available on the World Wide Web as an eBook.
Visit www.abc-clio.com for details.

Praeger
An Imprint of ABC-CLIO, LLC

ABC-CLIO, LLC
130 Cremona Drive, P.O. Box 1911
Santa Barbara, California 93116-1911

This book is printed on acid-free paper ∞

Manufactured in the United States of America

To the American people,
who wonder what went wrong

Contents

Acknowledgments

The eyewitnesses to the events that shaped the financial crisis have spoken to few journalists and authors. Some of them were interviewed by the Financial Crisis Inquiry Commission. Many were not forthcoming in those interviews, and the commission did not publish all the interviews it conducted and redacted others. Therefore, those who have been willing to be sources for this book are all the more important for making it possible to tell the story of the crisis. A number of deep background sources were willing to talk to me frankly. The sources are inside the banking regulators, current and past Administrations, Fannie Mae, Freddie Mac, and Congress. They also come from banks, investment banks, and the worlds of private mortgage-backed securities and collateralized debt obligations. Most sources talked to me on the record and are cited in this book. Even so, much remains unknown and much remains to be written about the crisis.

A number of colleagues and experts have also provided invaluable assistance. Edward Pinto, former chief risk officer for Fannie Mae and a key source for this book, also went the extra mile and reviewed the manuscript for accuracy and clarity, an invaluable contribution. Kenneth Cline, managing editor of *BAI Banking Strategies*, reviewed parts of the manuscript and made suggestions on how to improve them, for which I am grateful. Auburn Faber Traycik did yeoman's service in copyediting the original manuscript and pointing out where the text needed clarification and definitions of financial terms for the general reader.

I am grateful to friends who provided encouragement and advice as I plowed through mountains of information, studies, reports, and books, trying to sort my way through them all and separate the wheat from the chaff. Timothy Stuart Warner, in frequent phone conversations, was my New York sounding board who listened patiently through my explanations of what I was discovering and what I made of it, and offered helpful comments in return. A special thanks to Lorraine Gagliardotto Garry of Old Jersey City, New Jersey, who prepared graphic designs for the figures in this book. I greatly appreciate the support I received from a number of other dear friends, including especially Don Voth and Nelda Holder.

Finally, I am deeply grateful to my brother Randy for his enduring faith in me as a journalist and author.

1

The Mortgage Meltdown

As the New Year dawned in 2007, the $11 trillion American residential mortgage market stood like a colossus striding the globe.

It was the envy of the world. It was the most liquid market of its type anywhere. It drove financial innovation on Wall Street. It turned illiquid loans that might otherwise be stuck on a bank's books into tradable bonds. It did this by gathering a pool of loans into a trust and issuing mortgage-backed securities against them—a process known as *securitizing the loans*.

The loan payments from the homeowner flowed to mortgage servicers though the trust and then out to the investors. Fannie Mae and Freddie Mac, the two giants that dominated the industry, guaranteed timely payment of the coupon on mortgage bonds for loans they had purchased and securitized. With an assumed implicit government backing, bonds backed by Fannie and Freddie are AAA credits—just like U.S. Treasury bills and bonds—due to their "agency" status. In the case of Ginnie Mae, the government guarantee is explicit.

Private-sector financial institutions issued their own private-label mortgage-backed securities. These private-label bonds were also able to win AAA ratings by offering credit protection through structured finance. Tiered tranches, or slices, of private-label bonds allowed lower-rated classes to absorb losses from delinquencies and defaults.

The American mortgage market had long given the consumer the advantages of the 30-year fixed-rate mortgage. More recently, it had begun offering consumers an even wider range of other mortgage products as well. There were jumbo prime mortgages for borrowers whose mortgage balances were too high to qualify for Fannie and Freddie guarantees. There were also products for the self-employed with good credit who "stated" their income without fully documenting it. These were part of a class of loans known as Alternative A, or Alt-A—A as in good credit. Additionally, subprime loans were offered to borrowers with poor credit histories and little cash available for a down payment.

The AAA ratings made mortgage-backed securities a prized investment. Institutional investors, insurance companies, and pension funds in America, Europe, and Asia plunked down trillions of dollars to get a piece of the American mortgage pie. They earned a premium return above government bonds on what was seen as among the safest of investments. Wall Street had turned the American dream of homeownership into a modern gold rush for the financial engineers of structured debt.

The financial architecture of this most sophisticated of financial markets was widely seen to be strong and resilient and built on a rock-solid foundation.

It was not. It was about to come crashing down.

SHADOW BANKING

The American mortgage market was in the vanguard of a broad movement of financial activity away from the traditional regulated banking industry into the shadow banking system, or, as it is sometimes called, the parallel banking system. The traditional banking system in its simplest form is a business of taking in deposits and making loans. In the shadow banking system, the loans are converted into securities. The banking regulatory regime that oversees the safety and soundness of banks does not oversee shadow banking. The degree to which mortgages became securitized is the same degree to which the mortgage market moved into shadow banking.

And it was not just mortgages that inhabited the world of shadow banking. The process of securitizing loans, which began in earnest in the 1980s, had increasingly been used to move all sorts of loans off the balance sheets of banks. Securitization was used to "liquefy" car loans, student loans, small-business loans, and credit card receivables. These became the basis for issuing asset-backed securities, or ABS, that were backed by pools of these consumer and business loans. Commercial real estate was also increasingly being financed by commercial mortgage-backed securities, or CMBS. Corporate loans, too, had also been securitized through a creation known as *collateralized loan obligations*, or *CLOs*. Corporate bonds could be securitized via collateralized debt obligations, or CDOs.

Wall Street firms got increasingly inventive and creative with their securitizations and came up with a way to securitize the securitizations. That is, they began to securitize mortgage-backed securities and asset-backed securities. These new instruments were known as *CDOs of ABS*, and they became a centerpiece of the financial crisis. Over time, the share of the collateral made up of mortgage-backed securities—especially subprime—rose, until many of the CDOs of ABS were mostly CDOs of subprime mortgage bonds.

The CDOs of ABS were created in some of the darkest reaches of shadow banking and were black boxes to most of the financial world. Black boxes are financial instruments and institutions so lacking in transparency that outsiders cannot see any of what's inside and can only hazard a guess about their safety and soundness. Moreover, outsiders might not even be aware of all the black boxes hidden in the corners of the shadow banking system.

SUBPRIME COLLAPSE

The first dent in the architecture of mortgage finance did not seem all that alarming. On January 3, 2007, one of the larger subprime lenders, Ownit Mortgage Solutions of Agoura Hills, California, filed for bankruptcy protection.

Ownit, more sensible in earlier years, had come to specialize in making loans equal to 100 percent of the value of homes to borrowers with poor credit. The mortgage lender was 20 percent owned by Merrill Lynch and served as a conduit for loans, the raw material for Merrill's mortgage-backed securities and CDO businesses.

Ownit hit the wall when J. P. Morgan pulled its $500 million credit line in November 2006. Next, Merrill Lynch cut off its funding, forcing the mortgage lender to cease operations. Merrill had been demanding Ownit buy back an ever-increasing volume of delinquent loans. Ownit was out of cash and unable to warehouse loans.

The rising tide of new loans from Ownit that did not last through the first payment should have prompted a stronger response from Merrill, according to Janet Tavakoli, founder and president of Tavakoli Structured Finance, Inc., a Chicago consulting firm. Merrill should have been looking to see if Ownit had engaged in any fraud or predatory lending.[1]

There were certainly some powerful clues. For example, William Dallas, Ownit's founder and president, had famously quipped, "The market is paying me to do a no-income-verification loan more than it is paying me to do the full documentation loans."[2] No-documentation loans were those in which borrowers could state any income or state they held any amount of assets and not have to verify any of the information. What Dallas was saying is that Ownit could improve its profits by originating loans with weaker credits—loans that might actually be bad for the borrower.

Merrill had the means to delve into Ownit's problems. Michael Blum, the head of Merrill Lynch's global finance, sat on the subprime lender's board of directors. "When Ownit went bankrupt, in the post Sarbanes-Oxley world, you might think he might have asked for a fraud audit," suggested Tavakoli. "Instead he faxed in his resignation" as a member of Ownit's board.[3] The Sarbanes-Oxley Act of 2002[4] passed Congress after the implosion of Enron and WorldCom and other companies. It set new and stricter accounting oversight and auditing standards for the boards and senior management of publicly traded companies, and for public accounting firms.

"Now, a fraud audit doesn't mean you are accusing anyone of fraud. It just means that if fraud is present, you will uncover it," Tavakoli explained. Merrill's failure to order a fraud audit, in turn, should have raised red flags with the regulators. "Based on public information like this, the [Securities and Exchange Commission] should have taken immediate action and asked Merrill and other investment banks why they did not write-down losses on mortgage loans and their securitization business," Tavakoli contended.[5]

Ownit had not always been so reckless a subprime business. Back in 2003, Dallas had asked Ownit's wholesalers—the brokers who originated loans for Ownit—to reduce the volume of Alt-A and subprime loans when he began to see a decline in credit quality.[6] In response, Vincent Mora, head of the mortgage desk at Merrill Lynch, pressed Dallas to reverse course and ramp up subprime lending because those were the loans with the higher interest rates that made the mortgage bonds and related CDOs work. After first resisting, Dallas caved in to Mora's request. Four years later, the bill came due. Merrill Lynch, J. P. Morgan, and Credit Suisse were demanding Ownit buy back $165 million in bad loans, according to the bankruptcy filing.

While Ownit was slipping towards its implosion, Merrill Lynch was so determined to continue its subprime money train, it bought subprime lender First Franklin for $1.3 billion in September 2006. First Franklin, co-founded by Bill Dallas, was owned at the time by National City Bank. Merrill's chairman and CEO Stanley O'Neal, who earned

$91 million in compensation in 2006, was vigorous in his support of the acquisition, claiming the purchase would provide "revenue velocity." Indeed. A year later, Merrill had to take an $8.3 billion write-down on its mortgage assets and O'Neal was fired, walking away with another $151 million.[7] Lose megabucks and walk away rich—it was a theme that would prove all too common in the financial crisis.

By early 2007, many stories had begun to emerge of outlandish subprime lending practices that defied logic and seemed farcical. One of the more remarkable is the story of Naira Costa, a 27-year-old woman who cleaned houses. She earned $24,000 a year but managed in 2005 to get two mortgages to cover 100 percent of the cost of buying a $713,000 house in South San Francisco, California.[8] Costa had a credit score of 585—among the worst one could have and still qualify for a subprime mortgage. The industry standard for prime credit is a score of 660 or above. Costa was an illegal immigrant from Brazil who overstayed the student visa she had obtained as a teenager. Her husband, Samir Abdelnur, was a taxi driver who earned $4,000 a month. His credit was weaker. So the mortgage broker suggested Costa apply for the mortgage. Costa got the loan from WMC Mortgage Corp., a unit of General Electric. It was a 2/28 adjustable-rate mortgage, the bête noire for subprime borrowers, with a fixed low-interest rate for two years, which adjusted sharply upward in the third year. Costa also walked away from the closing with an $8,000 cash-out, according to mortgage broker Soario Santos.[9] She and her husband lived in the house for only three weeks before realizing they could not afford even the first monthly mortgage payment.

There were increasingly thousands of borrowers like Costa, especially after mid-2006, who qualified under circumstances that suggest both fraud and predatory lending. For example, at a Chicago office for Countrywide Home Loans of Calabasas, California, the nation's largest mortgage lender, an employee admitted that in September 2006 about 90 percent of the loan applications the local office originated had fake incomes.[10]

Mark Zachary, a former regional vice president of Countrywide, wrote in a February 13, 2007, e-mail to one of his supervisors that "it seems to be an accepted practice for [Countrywide] to have a full doc loan and then if it can't be approved . . . we flip to a stated [income loan] and send to [Full Spectrum Lending, Countrywide's subprime mortgage affiliate] under non-prime."[11] Once in the stated-loan process, Countrywide employees would coach applicants to lie about their income by as much as doubling it, Zachary wrote.

Zachary also said that Countrywide's loan origination was plagued by "outright misrepresent[ation of] loans to the secondary markets, to end investors, and to buyers." Home appraisers were pressured to raise their appraisal of homes by 6 percent to cover the practice of rolling the closing costs into the value of the loan.[12]

By early 2007, the chickens from a reckless abandonment of prudent lending practices were flocking home to roost and, in the process, revealing further weakness in the architecture of mortgage finance.

Some of the chickens came home to roost at New Century Financial Corporation of Irvine, California, the second-largest subprime lender and the largest independent subprime company. On February 7, 2007, the company announced it would have to restate its earnings for the first three quarters of 2006. This set off a death watch for New Century.

As of January 1, New Century employed 7,200 and had a market capitalization of $1.7 billion. Market capitalization is the aggregate value of a company's shares. The subprime giant had originated $60 billion in mortgages in 2006 and earned $276 million for the first nine months of that year before restating its earnings. The image of financial strength portrayed in these numbers was about to be shattered.

New Century, like Ownit, was seeing sharply rising delinquencies for new mortgages and was having to buy back more of the loans it sold to securitizers. By March 9, New Century had breached the terms of its $17.4 billion warehouse line of credit. The warehouse line, usually provided by a bank, provides funding up to 90 days, so a mortgage originator can advance the funds to close on a home sale before it receives the funding for the loan from investors. New Century also reported it was under a criminal investigation by federal authorities. On March 14, Fannie Mae terminated its contract with New Century, and the New York Stock Exchange delisted the firm from its exchange. By the next day, its market cap had fallen to a mere $55 million. On April 2, New Century filed for bankruptcy protection. The company had imploded in less than 60 days.

Subprime lending had not always been so precarious. In the early 1990s, subprime lenders focused on A-minus credits, borrowers with credit scores between 620 and 660. But by 2007, nearly all subprime mortgage originators focused mostly on the B and C credits—borrowers with credit scores below 620. In 2006, mortgage bankers originated $600 billion in B and C credits.[13] That represented 20 percent of the $2.98 trillion in mortgage originations that year.

Private subprime lenders had long been pushed out of the better A-minus subprime credits by Fannie Mae and Freddie Mac. These shareholder-owned but government-sponsored enterprises, or GSEs, could underprice any player in the private sector in any market they entered. This is because investors who bought debt issues from Fannie and Freddie assumed they had the implicit backing of the federal government and were willing to buy their securities at a lower rate, thus reducing the funding costs of the two giants.

Apparently to keep volumes up during 2006, New Century and other subprime lenders had been gathering in lower and lower credits with greater levels of fraud and misrepresentation, luring unsophisticated borrowers into loans that would explode in their faces in as soon as two years. A bankruptcy judge, Michael Missal, would conclude a year later that New Century had engaged in "accounting irregularities" to camouflage losses.

New Century had been covering up the fact that it was forced to repurchase an increasing share of the mortgages it was originating because they did not meet underwriting guidelines or because borrowers quickly defaulted on them. Instead of increasing its reserve for these losses, New Century lowered its reserves. Without the improper change in accounting, New Century would have reported a loss rather than a profit for the second half of 2006, Missal concluded.

The implosion of Ownit and New Century was quickly followed by other implosions of subprime mortgage lenders, revealing widespread weakness in subprime lending. A common pattern of business activities was emerging.[14] Demand from Wall Street securitizers for more subprime mortgages—the "money train," as Tavakoli calls it—had flowed to lenders who, wanting to keep the profits rolling, sometimes to cover up losses coming into the system from recent loans, had to scrape the bottom of the barrel of credits to generate more business. In this way, the frenzy of subprime lending by 2005 and 2006 was like a Ponzi scheme, Tavakoli has argued.

Throughout the first quarter of 2007, the pace of subprime failures continued to rise as lenders lost their warehouse lines of credit and could no longer originate new loans. Surviving mortgage lenders were initially pleased at the demise of irrational pricing from their former competitors. Adding to the notion that the rough patch might be ending, Federal Reserve Chairman Ben Bernanke told the Joint Economic Committee in Congress on March 28 that "the impact on the broader economy and financial markets of the problems in the subprime markets seems likely to be contained."

What should have been an alarm was seen by the mortgage industry as only a market correction and by regulators as a passing worry. The assumption was that the market would bounce back and, with subprime lenders wiped out or acquired, there would likely be no further major hits from the excesses in the subprime market. Some even thought it was a buying opportunity to snap up subprime mortgage bonds, whose prices had been beaten down.

TWO HEDGE FUNDS AT BEAR STEARNS

The fate of two investment funds at Bear Stearns would quickly snuff out any hope for a rebound in the mortgage market. The trouble began at Bear Stearns's Enhanced fund,[15] which had taken in $638 million in investor capital and invested $11.15 billion mostly in subprime CDOs with borrowed money. To buy its assets, the fund used overnight financing and a credit facility at Barclay's Bank. It had a high 17.5 leverage ratio, the gauge of borrowed funds to capital. Ralph Cioffi managed the Enhanced fund, along with its older companion, the High-Grade fund, which was launched in October 2003.[16] This older fund had $925 million in investor capital and $9.7 billion in gross long or investment positions. That gave it a lower leverage of 10.5 to 1. Cioffi's portfolio manager for the two funds was Matthew Tannin.

Most of the investments acquired by the funds were financed through overnight funding that had to be rolled over every day. In its repurchase or repo contracts, Bear Stearns agreed to sell and repurchase some of its subprime collateral, transferring it overnight to another party, usually a large Wall Street firm. In return, the counterparty placed a sum of cash equal to the value of the collateral on deposit at Bear Stearns. The funds were used to purchase investment assets in the two hedge funds. Bear Stearns, in a practice that is typical for a repo, agreed to pay more for the repurchase of the assets than the price for which they were sold. That difference in the sale and repurchase price represents the interest earned by the counterparties to the repo transaction.

By agreeing to the repo contract, the counterparty has, in effect, placed an insured deposit at Bear Stearns, and is holding collateral equal to 100 percent of the value of the deposit. Thus, the counterparty is insured against its losses and can sell the collateral if Bear is unable to return the cash the next day.

The hedge funds, in turn, profited because they could earn more from the investment they made than it cost to borrow the funds. It was not exactly robbing Peter to pay Paul. It was more like paying Peter to park his cash with you in order to buy assets from Paul that would earn far more money than you would have to pay Peter to park his cash with you.

In addition to net earnings margins represented by the difference between the cost of getting the deposit and the income from the investment, the fund itself and its investors also gained big returns because the fund was so leveraged. Moreover, the collateral that you temporarily handed over to Peter was taken from the stash of investments you bought from Paul and that provide the income for the shareholders in your hedge fund.

It was clever, to be sure. But it was too clever by half. The investments you bought from Paul—tranches or slices of subprime CDOs—and the method of funding you got from Peter—repos—would turn out to be the weakest links in the entire shadow banking system. But, for as long as it worked, it was like financial manna from Heaven.

The repo funding method employed by Cioffi's two funds was a common way of financing investments in leveraged investment funds.

The first sign of trouble for Cioffi's hedge funds came in February 2007, as subprime lenders began to implode. The subprime CDO assets in the fund were cratering in value. Because of its thin capital base, the Enhanced fund reported its first loss in February and began to lose value.

On March 15, Cioffi wrote to a colleague, "I am fearful of these markets. Matt [Tannin] said it's either a meltdown or the greatest buying opportunity ever, I'm leaning more towards the former. As we discussed it may not be a meltdown for the general economy but in our world it will be."[17]

The Enhanced fund was facing margin calls from repo lenders throughout March, forcing Cioffi to start selling assets at unfavorable prices. Margin calls from counterparties are made to demand cash or securities to bring a margin account up to the minimum posting requirement. "We do need to take positions down. We are getting loads of margin calls," he wrote on March 14 to a team member for the Enhanced fund.[18]

The results for March were worse than February. The Enhanced Fund returned minus 5.4 percent, while the High-Grade fund had a return of minus 3.7 percent. Despite Cioffi's reassurance, a major investor decided to withdraw its entire $57 million investment.

On April 19, a report by a member of the portfolio management team showed the CDOs held by the fund had suffered much higher losses than originally calculated. This prompted Tannin, who had been wavering between being very aggressive with the funds versus shutting them down, to decide it was time to close the funds. An e-mail, sent via a private account and not on Bear Stearns's e-mail system, concluded that "caution would lead us to conclude the [CDO report] is right—and we're in bad bad shape."[19]

On a conference call on April 25 to investors, Cioffi and Tannin painted a rosy view of the funds. "[W]e're very comfortable with exactly where we are," Tannin said. "[I]t is really a matter of whether one believes that careful credit analysis makes a difference, or whether you think that this is just one big disaster. And there's no basis for thinking this is one big disaster."

When investors asked about redemptions, Cioffi omitted telling them about redemptions scheduled for April 30 and May 31, and did not report the full amount slated for June 30—avoiding entirely any mention of a $57 million redemption from a major investor.[20]

The pricing committee at Bear Stearns questioned the net asset values Cioffi had assigned to some assets in the fund for April returns. Cioffi's method would have yielded a minus 6.5 percent for April, which was reported in May by the Enhanced fund. The pricing committee later rejected Cioffi's method and calculated instead a minus 19 percent return for April, with an overall year-to-date loss of 23 percent.[21]

News on June 7 of the sharp decline in the value of the Enhanced fund prompted a flurry of redemptions or requests for cash-outs from investors and a series of margin calls from creditors. Meanwhile, Cioffi told a repo lender, both funds had more than enough liquidity to meet any likely need.

To meet the redemptions and margin calls, Bear Stearns sold a whopping $8 billion in assets from its less leveraged High-Grade fund to generate cash. The fund had $11.5 billion in assets. Investors were stampeding for the exit doors with whatever they could salvage before everything collapsed.

The internal struggle to rescue the Enhanced fund went public when Bear Stearns suspended redemption payments to investors in the fund. On June 15, Merrill Lynch, a major creditor of the funds, said it would sell $400 million of its collateral held against the loans it had made to the Enhanced Leveraged Fund. Bear Stearns persuaded Merrill to wait until it had time to hear its proposal for recapitalizing the funds.

On Monday, June 18, Bear Stearns told Merrill Lynch it was injecting $500 million of equity and providing $1.5 billion in credit from the parent company.[22] Merrill was unimpressed, and decided to raise the ante by announcing it would sell at auction the next day at least

$850 million worth of collateral assets, mostly mortgage-related securities. The position taken by Merrill Lynch was, in fact, reckless, given the huge stash of subprime assets it held in its own accounts. Fire sales of subprime collateral that Merrill held from Bear could force Merrill to mark down its own assets. This, in turn, could lead to write-downs at all Wall Street firms and banks that held similar assets.

On June 22, more than a week after the crisis went public, Bear Stearns released a statement announcing a $3.2 billion deal to rescue the less leveraged High-Grade fund. At the same time, the firm revealed it was in the process of de-leveraging the Enhanced fund. Lower leverage would mean less dependence on repos. A hopeful Jimmy Cayne, Bear's chairman and CEO, seemed convinced the crisis was over. "By providing the secured financing facility, we believe we have helped stabilize and reduce uncertainty in the marketplace," he said. "We believe the repurchase agreements are adequately collateralized, and we do not expect any material adverse effect on our business as a result of providing this secured financing."

Bear Stearns's reassurances proved less than convincing to market observers. "The public unwillingness of the broker-dealer to assume the hedge funds' debts for ... two weeks fueled lively speculation about the severity of the losses by them and the prospects that other hedge funds may have incurred similar losses," said Michael Youngblood, managing director of asset-backed securities research at FBR Investment Management Inc., Arlington, Virginia.[23]

Fears about the value of subprime assets began to nibble away at confidence internationally because, thanks to the efficiencies of the shadow banking system, pieces of subprime mortgage-backed securities and CDO deals were sitting in funds and banks around the world. Market fears were enhanced June 25 when Cheyne Capital Management (UK) LLP in London announced it was writing off 400 million euros from one of its hedge funds, Queen's Walk Investment Ltd. The fund had invested only 4.2 percent of its portfolio in U.S. subprime mortgage bonds, but that was enough to cause a panic.

This was an early sign of how interlinked the financial system had become, and how spreading the risk around the globe in the shadow banking system meant spreading losses in the event of a systemic crash involving widely dispersed assets that appeared safe and sound but that were, in fact, poorly understood and loaded with high risk. Events at Bear Stearns and Cheyne Capital raised more speculation that the U.S. subprime meltdown had "contaminated" the primary and secondary markets for subprime mortgage-backed securities.

The slow-motion train wreck at Bear Stearns ultimately could not be stopped, despite the intense and costly efforts of the firm. In a July 17 "Dear Client" letter,[24] the company revealed that "preliminary estimates show there is effectively no value left for investors in the Enhanced Fund and only 9 cents on the dollar for investors in the High-Grade fund as of June 30, 2007." It was New Century all over again. Value utterly and swiftly vanished.

The letter told investors the funds had lost value due to "unprecedented declines" in the valuations of a number of highly rated (AAA and AA) securities. The hedge funds had been struck by lightning and set ablaze. All that was left were the charred remains. Investors lost $1.6 billion.

On July 31, the two funds filed for bankruptcy protection. On August 1, as the company's stock continued to plummet as doubts grew about Bear Stearns, Cayne unexpectedly ousted the firm's co-president, Warren Spector, leaving Alan Schwartz as president and likely successor to Cayne.[25] The sudden evaporation of $3 billion into the black hole of the two hedge funds revealed to the markets the soft underbelly of subprime mortgage-backed securities and their financial cousins, the CDOs of ABS heavily invested in subprime bonds. It also demonstrated the susceptibility of parties in the repo system to panic-induced runs.

SUBPRIME AND CREDIT RATING AGENCIES

The next blow to the mortgage infrastructure hit when credit rating agencies, after reviewing the latest casualties from sharply rising delinquencies, began the process of downgrading their ratings of mortgage-backed securities and CDOs of ABS. The actions began July 10, 2007, when Moody's Investors Service lowered credit ratings on $5.2 billion in 399 subprime mortgage bond classes and placed an additional 32 bond classes on negative watch. Moody's also downgraded 52 subprime second-lien mortgage bond classes.[26] Not to be outdone, Standard & Poor's announced it had placed on watch 612 classes of subprime mortgage bonds totaling $7.35 billion.

On July 11, Moody's placed 184 classes of CDOs on negative review because of their exposure to the subprime mortgage bonds the agency had downgraded the prior day. Then, on July 12, S&P downgraded 498 classes of the 612 it had put on watch, and left 26 classes on negative watch.

A few days later, New York-based Fitch Ratings Ltd. placed 170 subprime bonds and 19 related CDOs on negative watch. "These actions are unprecedented," wrote Youngblood in *Structured Finance Insights*.[27] "Never before has either S&P or Moody's downgraded or placed on watch so many classes of RMBS [residential mortgage-backed securities]—a grand total of 1,095."

According to FBR Investment Management's analysis, issuers owned directly or indirectly by Wall Street firms accounted for 7 of the top 10 issuers with classes downgraded by the credit-rating agencies between July 10 and 12. The list of issuers with downgraded mortgage bonds was a virtual who's who list of mortgage securitization: American Home, Bear Stearns, Citigroup, General Electric-WMC, J. P. Morgan, Lehman Brothers, Merrill Lynch, Morgan Stanley, New Century, and Option One.

S&P, Moody's, and Fitch scheduled telephone conference calls to discuss the downgrades. The credit rating agencies made it clear that losses would likely continue to rise as the 2006 vintage of subprime loans aged and housing continued to be in recession. David Wyss, S&P's chief economist, predicted that property values would decline 8 percent on average, nationally, between 2006 and 2008, reaching the bottom in the first quarter of 2008.

S&P told investors it had modified its approach to reviewing the ratings on senior classes of mortgage bonds in a transaction in which the subordinate classes had been downgraded. Going forward, S&P said, "There will be a higher degree of correlation" assumed to exist between asset classes, meaning that a downgrade in a subordinate class is more likely to lead to a downgrade in a senior class. As events would soon demonstrate, the single most pernicious misperception in the financial crisis, and one that led to widespread investment mistakes, was the failure to see the extent to which losses in lower mezzanine classes of a CDO would immediately lead to losses in the AAAs.

The agency warned that in future securitization deals for subprime mortgages, the default expectations for the 2/28 hybrid adjustable-rate mortgage would increase. For the subprime industry, the 2/28 had become an engine of growth, getting people into houses they could otherwise not afford—at least initially. The subprime mortgage-backed securities market began to grind to a halt, removing opportunities to refinance for homeowners holding adjustable-rate mortgages.

Moody's announced August 2 it had altered its method of rating subprime mortgages. Among other things, the agency adjusted modeling assumptions to anticipate that mortgages that have simultaneous second mortgages would be expected to have 25 percent higher rates of defaults than previously expected. These arrangements represented the biggest miscalculation in prior ratings, Moody's conceded.

The rating agency had also revealed other weak spots in its computer model. "Loans where the borrower's income is not fully documented (especially where the borrower is a wage earner rather than self-employed) have, in general, a higher probability of default than fully documented loans," Moody's stated in its explanation of its revised methodology. This included stated-income, stated-asset loans, or SISAs, and no-income, no-asset loans, or NINAs.

Mark Zandi, chief economist at Moody's Economy.com, was predicting that home prices would fall 10 percent, peak to trough, in the housing recession he said had begun in late 2005. "The decline in credit quality that is occurring today is the worst the U.S. economy has seen since the mid-1990s in Texas, Louisiana and Oklahoma," he said.[28] The potential damage from deteriorating credit had been exacerbated because the subprime market had become so much larger, reaching 40 percent of all originations in 2006.

MELTDOWN HITS NON-SUBPRIME LENDERS

During a brief interlude in mid-July, the financial markets in the United States stabilized as investors seemed to believe that the damage had been contained after the Bear Stearns episode. Yet as July moved toward a close, more and more firms were being impacted by subprime failures. Worries expanded from subprime to include prime second liens, Alternative A, and even jumbo prime, loans greater than $417,000 in 2007. Such loans were too large to qualify for guarantees from Fannie or Freddie.

Any lingering notions of damage containment were dashed on July 24, when Countrywide reported unexpected losses in its prime home-equity business during the second quarter. Delinquency rates rose sharply to 4.56 percent from a level of 1.77 percent a year earlier. Countrywide took a $388 million charge or write-down in value on residual securities collateralized by prime home-equity loans. These were the pieces of deals the company could not sell off to investors and that it felt would be safe to hold on its books. Countrywide also set aside $293 million for held-for-investment loans, including a loan-loss provision of $181 million on prime home-equity loans in the banking segment of the company. Shares in Countrywide fell 10 percent.

In a conference call with analysts and investors, Countrywide's chairman and CEO Angelo Mozilo assured analysts and investors that Countrywide had "excess capital in the near term—the next quarter or so" that it intended to put to use by investing in the balance sheet until market conditions normalized. John McMurry, the company's chief risk officer, reported that Countrywide had been actively modifying mortgages in places where interest rates were resetting, when appropriate, in order to keep homeowners in their homes and thereby reduce the potential level of defaults.

Like so many other players, Countrywide failed to grasp the severity of the situation. Mozilo said that a recovery in the housing market would first require a clearing of the oversupply of homes, which would not happen until prices fell further and supply and demand came into balance. "My experience is that it just takes a long time to turn a battleship around," Mozilo said. "This is a huge battleship, and it is turning in the wrong direction. It's going to take 2007 to get this thing slowing down; 2008 to get it to stop; and 2009 to head in the other direction." For Countrywide, the battleship was about to start sinking.

American Home Mortgage Investment Corporation, Melville, New York, became the first major non-subprime mortgage company to fall victim to the subprime mortgage meltdown. American Home Mortgage's borrowers generally are considered prime or near prime credits. The company had originated $59 billion in mortgages in 2006 and $35 billion in the first half of 2007, making it the tenth-largest originator in the first six months of the year.[29]

At the end of June, American Home warned it would likely report a loss for the second quarter. On July 27, the company announced it was suspending payment of its dividend in order to have more cash to fund current operations. Trading in its shares was suspended July 30, as the company was swamped by margin calls on $4 billion in warehouse lines of credit from lenders. The next day, the company reported it had already paid "very significant" margin calls in the prior three weeks and had "substantial" unpaid margin calls pending. Shares in the company fell 86 percent.

Without access to additional funds from its warehouse lines, American Home said it had failed to provide $300 million in mortgages to homebuyers scheduled to close on July 30. Further, it did not expect to be able to finance $450 million in mortgages due to close July 31. On

August 3, American Home laid off all but 750 of its 7,047 workers. On August 5, the company filed for bankruptcy. Its implosion was as quick and dramatic as that of New Century. Obviously, the crisis bubbling up into the financial system was not just about subprime.

The contagion spreading out from U.S. subprime mortgage securities soon showed its ability to infect continents as far away as Australia, where it hit several leveraged funds, including those with no ties to U.S. mortgages. Sydney's Basis Capital Group, which was not invested in mortgage securities, announced in July it was defaulting on margin calls and suspended redemptions on two hedge funds, valued at A\$656 million. The fund told investors they could receive less than 50 cents on the dollar for their investments.

As the contagion continued to spread around the globe, nervous lenders monitored loans to leveraged funds, and investors clamored for more information on the value of their investments. "We are to some degree shooting in the dark here," said Charles Dumas, chief economist for Lombard Street Research Ltd., London.[30] "We haven't got real information. One of the reasons is, of course, people don't mark to market and people aren't on top of this in terms of how to handle it."

Investments in CDOs and hedge funds, for example, are typically marked to model—not marked to market, Dumas explained. The accounting principle of marketing to market requires firms to raise or lower the value of an asset on their books to conform to prices of similar assets recently sold. In a period when there are few or even no sales, firms may mark to model, using a model tied to other asset values, such as corporate bonds, to determine current values. The ability to mark to model can camouflage losses.

Dumas said that panic in the market was being generated by the fact no one knew who owned what amount of assets that might have lost most of their value. "There comes a moment when the stone is lifted up and everyone rushes for their little holes in the ground. Then you ask yourself, 'What, in that context, is the value of all this paper?' Unfortunately, the paper has proliferated in such an extraordinary way on the back of all these various forms of asset-backed securities and collateralized stuff; we don't have the first idea of who owns this stuff, really, at this point," he said. "No one's prepared to admit they own it, because at the moment, the value in the game is trying to muddle it out."

Dumas found it ironic that the world markets were roiled by a liquidity crisis when, in fact, there is "a grotesque excess of liquidity, which to some extent is why this market has been created—because it is a means of parking excess appetite for investments out of range of scrutiny, really," he said.

MORTGAGE SECURITIZATION GRINDS DOWN

As defaults rose above expected losses and the subprime meltdown demonstrated that it could trigger other financial flare-ups, one previously obscure market indicator became the focus for measuring investor sentiment on subprime loans. That indicator was the ABX Index, which is made up of credit default swaps, or CDS, some of which tripped up Cioffi at Bear Stearns. Market observers around the world began to follow the ABX daily, sometimes in fascinated horror, as an indicator of the ongoing collapse of the U.S. mortgage securitization market.

As earlier noted, credit default swaps are derivative transactions in which one side sells credit protection against losses on designated assets and the counterparty in the deal buys credit protection. This market, which was $919 billion in 2001, had mushroomed into a behemoth $62.2 trillion market by 2007.[31] With these swaps, a piece of regulated insurance activity had slipped into the world of shadow insurance. Credit default swaps were not only private contracts—so no outsiders knew much about their terms and which counterparties were at risk—they were also completely unregulated. So aside from derivatives surveys conducted by the Office of the Comptroller of the Currency, which only captured part of the swaps activity, regulators knew next to nothing about them.

There were separate ABX indexes for the different classes of residential mortgage-backed securities against which the credit default swaps had been placed. Pricing is reported on classes from AAA to BBB-minus and by four different quarters: the first and second quarters of 2006 and the first and second quarters of 2007. The various ABX indices had daily pricing, and the credit default swaps made trading on those prices very liquid. These contracts gave fund managers an efficient way to short or bet against the subprime market and win big as it continued to fall. Meanwhile, the mortgage-backed securities that were the reference collateral for credit default swaps were hardly trading at all.

On July 2, 2007, the ABX.HE Index (subprime first mortgages and home equity loans) for swaps placed on AAA-rated residential mortgage-backed securities from the first quarter of 2007 stood at 99.48. This meant that those buying contracts thought such bonds were worth close to full value or par, which is 100, reflecting great confidence in the highest-rated tranches of subprime mortgage bond issues of some of the most recent CDO deals. Similarly, AA tranches stood at 98.74, while the single-A, which is the high end of the mezzanine tranches, was somewhat weaker at 82.12. The lower mezzanine tranches, however, had already suffered enormous declines. The BBB tranches stood at 60.77, while BBB-minus stood at 54.06.

Since most of the subprime CDOs were structured from mezzanine tranches, but mostly BBB and BBB-minus tranches, these prices captured what was essentially a free fall in this enormous $895 billion CDO of ABS market.[32] About $700 billion of those CDOs had some mortgage-backed securities as part of their collateral.[33] There was also a very large unrated single-tranche CDO market, also known as *bespoke* or *customized tranches*. Plus, there were CDO tranches from credit default swap indexes, also usually unrated, according to Tavakoli.[34]

By July 16, all credit class tranches of the ABX indexes except AAAs had declined appreciably.[35] The AA index slumped to 88.17, while the A had plummeted to 69.35 percent. The BBB class had fallen to 47.72, while BBB-minus was down to 45.28.

Similar changes in investor sentiment could be seen in changes in the spreads between floating-rate mortgage bonds, on the one hand, and the one-month London Interbank Offered Rate, or LIBOR, on the other. In mid-June, the single-A bond of a residential mortgage-backed security traded at a premium spread of 50 basis points over LIBOR, which meant that the markets viewed it as a somewhat safe investment. However, BBB's spread was a hefty 200 and BBB-minus an even heftier 400, according to the FBR Investment Management.[36] Sentiment had turned strongly against the lower-rated tranches.

A month later on July 14, single-A spreads rose sharply to 110 points. Spreads ballooned for BBB to 425 and BBB-minus to 700. The subprime CDO market was crashing, with the potential to bring down the financial system with it.

As July 2007 came to a close, more and more lenders announced sharp declines in earnings and cutbacks in mortgage product offerings. Countrywide said it would no longer offer 2/28 and 3/27 subprime mortgages. GMAC Financial Services, Detroit, reported that its Minneapolis-based Residential Capital LLC, or ResCap, subsidiary had been sharply reducing both originations and holdings of subprime mortgages since the end of the first quarter, when it reported a $910 million loss. In the second quarter, ResCap trimmed its losses to $254 million, and GMAC injected $500 million in new capital. ResCap reduced subprime originations from $3.3 billion in the first quarter to $700 million in the second quarter.

The company also reduced its subprime portfolio of $5.4 billion at year-end 2006 to $1.9 billion at the end of the second quarter. GMAC reported that ResCap had lowered its overall exposure to the subprime market through asset sales in its held-for-sale portfolio, a steady asset run-off in its held-for-investment portfolio, plus loan restructuring and sales in its warehouse lending receivables. Mortgage lenders were finding it increasingly difficult to securitize other mortgage products beyond subprime, such as Alt-A and even jumbo prime.

On August 2, Mike Perry, chairman and CEO of Indymac Bank in Pasadena, California, sent out a frank e-mail that opened a window into the dilemmas facing companies that rely on the private-label secondary market to finance a significant share of their mortgage loan originations.

The e-mail commentary came on the heels of an announcement that Indymac's earnings had declined 50 percent. The communication was sent out to explain to investors how Indymac planned to cope with the difficulties it faced. "Unfortunately, the private secondary markets . . . continue to remain very panicked and illiquid," Perry wrote.[37] "By way of example, it is currently difficult . . . to trade even the AAA bond on any private [mortgage-backed security] transaction," he noted. Private-label securitization had shut down.

Perry indicated that the disruptions apparent in the private-label secondary market appeared likely to last longer than those in the past, such as in 1998, when the interruption lasted only a few weeks. Perry warned that Indymac faced a difficult dilemma. It would not be able to continue funding $80 billion to $100 billion of loans a year with a $33 billion balance sheet. It would now have to rely more and more on originating loans that could be sold to Fannie or Freddie or through a Ginnie Mae security.

Perry informed investors that Indymac had sold 40 percent of its second-quarter originations to the GSEs, up from 30 percent in the first quarter and 19 percent in 2006. Perry further stated that it was Indymac's goal to increase the portion of loans sold to Fannie and Freddie "up to at least 60 percent, ASAP."

In a postscript, he wrote: "We will still originate product that cannot be sold to the GSEs . . . just less of it; and we will have to assume we retain it in [Indymac's] portfolio [until the private-label market recovers]."

Hopes for a rebound in private-label securitization would soon enough have to be abandoned, though, as market conditions failed to improve. Indeed, the mortgage crisis was about to set off a panic in shadow banking that would imperil global finance.

2

The Panic of 2007

The cratering private mortgage bond market in the United States was creating financial jitters around the world. Investors were increasingly unsure who held any U.S. securitizations of almost any type, not just residential mortgages. The steady march of investors to the exit doors at all sorts of funds and financial institutions was about to turn into a stampede. On Thursday, August 9, a panic wave of selling in world bond and stock markets erupted after BNP Paribas, France's largest bank, announced it was suspending redemptions in some of its funds with ties to U.S. subprime mortgages.

A week earlier, the Paris-based bank had publicly denied that there were any problems in its holdings. This denial came after IKB Deutsche Industriebank AG, Dusseldorf, Germany, said on July 30 that it would be hurt by losses on U.S. subprime loans.[1] On August 8, WestLB Mellon Asset Management, also based in Dusseldorf, suspended redemptions in one of its funds that had invested heavily in mortgage securities. The fund failures at two of the biggest banks in Dusseldorf embarrassed the city's mayor, Joachim Erwin, who had been trying to lure overseas banks to the city. "I'm appalled by both banks," he said. "WestLB was acting like a gambler, and IKB is a boring old bank that has no business investing in subprime. It's bizarre."[2]

The panic selling around the globe that began August 9 was rumored to come from hedge funds and other leveraged funds. For hedge funds, the risks of higher leverage were made painfully clear by the growing number of fund freezes, rescues, and meltdowns. Higher leverage meant greater profitability in good times. However, the flip side of the coin is that higher leverage leads to greater losses when markets turn. If the ratio of borrowed money to equity capital is very high, accelerating losses can quickly exceed the capital in the fund, wiping out investors and threatening creditors, counterparties, and corporate affiliates. Thus, overleveraged hedge funds can collapse almost overnight.

As hedge funds moved to de-leverage, many sought to do so in a steady way so as not to send asset values plummeting. But as fear rose and a drumbeat of negative news hit the markets on a daily basis, hedge funds stepped up the pace of selling, dumping any assets they held that they felt they could dispose of to raise cash and reduce leverage. This included dumping Fannie and Freddie securities and highly rated shares of companies that were performing well in the current economy. The irrationality of the sell-off could be seen in some of the market anomalies. For example, spreads of Ginnie Maes over Treasuries at one point were higher than the spread for corporate AAA bonds, in spite of the government guarantee behind Ginnie Mae securities.

Share prices plunged first in Europe and then in the United States, where the Dow Jones Industrial Average fell 385 points after more bad news from two major U.S. mortgage companies.

Countrywide warned in its quarterly earnings report filing with the SEC: "We have significant financing needs that we meet through the capital markets, including the debt and secondary mortgage markets. These markets are currently experiencing unprecedented disruptions, which could have an adverse impact on the company's earnings and financial condition, particularly in the short term."

Seattle-based Washington Mutual, the nation's largest savings and loan association, gave a similar warning. WaMu's SEC filing stated: "While these market conditions persist, the company's ability to raise liquidity through the sale of mortgage loans in the secondary market will be adversely affected."

The European Central Bank (ECB), Frankfurt, Germany, moved quickly to settle the markets there, injecting nearly 95 billion euros (about $131 billion), the most the bank had ever provided in a single day. ECB said it was prepared to meet all the requests for funds from banks. "The ECB move shows that interbank financing is drying up. The banks don't trust each other anymore," commented Heino Ruland, a strategist at Stebing AG in Frankfurt.[3]

"Essentially no trades are taking place" since noon of August 9 in private-label securities, said Douglas Duncan, chief economist for the Mortgage Bankers Association.[4]

The Federal Reserve Bank injected $12 billion in one-day repurchase agreements. The Fed followed up the next day, Friday, August 10, with three injections of cash—all three-day repos over the weekend:

$19 billion before the markets opened, $16 billion in the morning, and $3 billion in the early afternoon, for a total of $38 billion. The Fed was accepting mostly mortgage-backed securities in return for cash.

The market for new issues of private-label residential mortgage-backed securities had already come to a complete halt before BNP Paribas set off a global panic. "There has been a complete flight of investors from the market, with the exception of the agencies, Freddie, Fannie and Ginnie," said Duncan.[5] "They've lost confidence in the rating agencies and their ability to accurately assess the collateral," he added. "There is a fundamental question in the mind of investors about the value of mortgage-backed securities: How can they be certain about the value? Because they are uncertain, they've simply left the market."

There was still widespread hope that the private-label securitization market could be resurrected. Yet private-label bonds would continue to suffer blows in the marketplace as panic spread. The drama was captured again by declines in the ABX Indexes, which are based on a basket of 20 first and second subprime mortgages. On August 10, on the ABX.HE for the first quarter of 2007, the AAA tranches showed the first signs of real distress, falling to 89.78 (100 is par). The other credit tranches sank lower. AA fell to 69.56, while A dropped to 48.25. The BBB tranches were down to 37.58, with BBB-minus slightly lower at 36.69.

Given the declines in the full range of mezzanine tranches, rated A to BBB-minus, it was becoming clear that the CDO of ABS market was finished not only for 2007, but maybe forever.

During the week of August 13, markets were hit daily in response to a steady diet of bad news. A flight to quality lifted U.S. Treasuries. Troubles emerged in the commercial paper market, especially asset-backed commercial paper, or ABCP. This part of the shadow banking is short-term corporate debt that is backed by real estate, autos, and other commercial assets. There were even concerns about a few money market funds.

On Tuesday, August 14, the president of the ECB, Jean-Claude Trichet, foolishly said the financial turmoil was largely over. Later that day, U.S. markets fell sharply on more anxiety about mortgages. Thornburg Mortgage Inc., a Santa Fe, New Mexico, real estate investment trust that invested in prime jumbo mortgages, announced it was postponing its dividend after worries about its liquidity led to a 47 percent drop in its share price.

On Thursday, August 16, the Federal Reserve injected $17 billion into the markets and issued a statement that it stood ready to inject more funds as needed. Yet the Dow Jones Average sank 300 points on news that Countrywide had drawn down its entire $11.5 billion bank credit line as the global liquidity squeeze hit the commercial paper market upon which the bank relied. This had curtailed its access to short-term cash. Investors breathed a sigh of relief, however, as the market surged back to close near where it had opened.

Only three weeks earlier, Countrywide's Angelo Mozilo had been confident the firm had enough liquidity to get through a crisis; now it was out of money. The next day, a crisis atmosphere resumed at Countrywide as depositors lined up to take out savings.

The roller-coaster markets in the first two weeks of August 2007 were enough to confound pundits and observers, but one observer was not rattled—former Fed governor Lyle Gramley, then senior economic adviser at the Stanford Group, Washington, D.C. Gramley blasted the irrationality of mortgage bond investors in an interview on CNBC on August 17. "A year ago they were buying garbage, and buying it avidly," he said. "Mortgage products that are being churned out by the mortgage market today are of much better quality. And investors don't want to have any part of them, because they are scared," he added. "Now, if we can get the panic situation turned around, and if investors will begin to think more rationally about their decisions, we'll come through this."[6]

EFFORTS TO CONTAIN THE CRISIS

As the trading day began on Friday, August 17, Asian stocks began to plummet as investors sold shares to unwind their yen carry trades. The carry trade is an investment strategy where a fund borrows at virtually no cost—in this case in yen—and invests in any number of assets. At trading day's end, the Nikkei was down a sharp 5.4 percent.

Worried investors in the United States who rose early Friday were pleasantly surprised to hear that the Federal Reserve had unexpectedly announced a cut of 50 basis points in its discount rate for loans, from 6.25 percent to 5.75 percent. The higher rate had acted as a penalty and kept potential institutional borrowers who needed to shore up liquidity away from the discount window.

The Federal Reserve also said it would continue to accept a broad range of collateral for discount window loans, including home mortgages and related assets. Further, the Fed would allow loans up to 30 days to be renewable at the discretion of the borrower. This decision, in effect, allowed mortgage lenders that are also depository institutions, such as Countrywide, Washington Mutual and Indymac, to borrow to meet their short-term liquidity needs.

The Federal Open Market Committee, or FOMC, sought to reassure the markets by saying its members were "prepared to act as needed to mitigate the adverse effects on the economy arising from the disruptions in the financial markets." The FOMC sets monetary policy goals for the Federal Reserve System. The policy is carried out through market interventions by the New York Fed, usually executed by buying or selling Treasuries to move rates up or down toward a specified goal. The move raised expectations that there would be one or more federal funds rate cuts during the remainder of the year. The Dow Jones rose 225 points. It was the first real break in the ongoing panic that began August 9.

On August 20, Countrywide placed ads in newspapers assuring its depositors their funds were safe and federally insured, and the panic by depositors subsided. On August 23, depositors and markets were further relieved when Bank of America announced ahead of the stock market opening in New York that it was investing $2 billion in Countrywide.[7] The bank, headquartered in Charlotte, North Carolina, was one of the few major mortgage lenders that had stayed away from subprime mortgages.

By Labor Day, "subprime"—once an obscure term—had become a household word synonymous with global financial meltdown. The panic in the mortgage industry did subside, but the private mortgage market did not come back. The market for new mortgage originations was captured almost entirely by the players with explicit or implicit backing by the federal government: Fannie, Freddie, and the Federal Housing Administration. Fannie and Freddie had saved the mortgage market from total collapse. Yet more than half the origination capacity of the mortgage market had been wiped out, along with scores of mortgage companies and a raft of investment funds around the globe. Far more damage was yet to come, not just for the mortgage market, but also for all of global finance.

In mid-September 2007, the feel of panic was once again in the air, as the crisis claimed its first major European victim. Depositors in the United Kingdom began an old-fashioned run on Northern Rock[8] after the bank was forced to ask the Bank of England for emergency funds. Northern Rock, Britain's third-largest mortgage lender, was having trouble raising funds in the money market to replace prior borrowings that were maturing and needed to be rolled over. It was

Britain's first run on a bank in 150 years. An estimated £2 billion in funds were withdrawn in two days, Friday, September 14, and Monday, September 17.[9]

Northern Rock, which was highly leveraged and relied on short-term debt funding, was caught in a squeeze when the cost of its debt rose sharply. On September 17, the Chancellor of the Exchequer, Alistair Darling, announced the government would guarantee 100 percent of all deposits at the bank.[10] The government already protected 100 percent of the first £2,000 and 90 percent of the next £33,000 with a maximum protection of £31,000. The full guarantee of deposits ended the run, but Northern Rock's financial condition would continue to worsen.

On September 18, the U.S. Fed surprised financial markets ahead of the stock market opening by lowering both the federal funds rates and the discount rate by 50 basis points each to 4.75 and 5.25 respectively. The Dow Jones Industrials Average roared its approval with a 330-point gain. It was the biggest one-day boost since October 15, 2002, when the Dow rose 387 points. Also, by the second week of September, there were reports that new private-label jumbo prime deals were being securitized "on a very limited basis," indicating that "things had stopped getting worse," Gramley said.

It was not, however, the beginning of a rebound. A few deals would emerge here and there, but there would be no real revival. Except for a single deal in 2008,[11] there were no private-label securitizations of newly originated mortgages until April 27, 2010. That's when Redwood Trust of Mill Valley, California, closed a $237.8 million transaction on 255 prime jumbos. In late 2007, despite the hopes of some market players, the private-label mortgage business was dead, and its resurrection was at least five years away.

In the deluge of news after a panic began August 9, it was scarcely appreciated that this panic was not like those from the 1990s. The world was not experiencing something as simple as a contagion spreading from a single crisis based on the meltdown of values in the U.S. mortgage market. The world was witnessing a panic within the shadow banking system. This was being missed because, among other reasons, the world had not seen anything like this since 1933, according to Yale professor of finance Gary Gorton, who has described parallels between the Panic of 2007 and the Panic of 1907.[12]

The 2007 shadow banking run began as a run against Structured Investment Vehicles, or SIVs. The assets of the SIVs featured tranches of mortgage-backed securities deals and subprime mortgage bond

CDOs that could not be sold to investors. Many SIVs held tranches of securities backed by auto loans, credit card receivables, and student loans, and not just securities backed by subprime loans. SIV activity was driven partly by the fact that banks could reduce capital requirements by moving assets off their books to the SIVs. If a tranche of a mortgage-backed security or CDO were held on the balance sheet, both commercial and investment banks would have to set aside from 1.6 percent to 4 percent capital for those assets.

Off balance sheet, banks needed only to set aside capital for any residual interests the banks retained in the mortgage assets. The mortgage assets parked in SIVs often earned only a small premium above the cost of funding, sometimes as few as 8 or 9 basis points. As assets vanished into SIVs, it made these corners of the shadow banking system into black boxes in which potentially troublesome assets could be hidden away from public and regulatory scrutiny. Neither the Federal Reserve, nor other federal banking regulators, nor the Securities and Exchange Commission, or SEC, had authority to inquire about and monitor assets held in SIVs by commercial and investment banks. Therefore, they could not fully know what risks and activities were occurring in the SIVS.

The SIVs financed the acquisition of assets by issuing asset-backed commercial paper to institutional investors who were looking for a slight premium over Treasuries on short-term returns. ABCP typically turns over in 90 days or less and sometimes 30 days or less.[13] The first SIV to hit the fan was at Toronto's Coventree Inc., Canada's largest nonbank sponsors of ABCP. On Friday, August 10, the crisis erupted when institutional investors began demanding 40 to 60 basis points premium over Government of Canada bonds to roll over existing ABCP funding for Coventree's SIVs.

Coventree's galactic-themed SIV conduits had names such as Aurora Trust, Comet Trust, Gemini Trust, Planet Trust, and Rocket Trust.[14] As recently as a month earlier, Coventree could attract investors by offering a premium of just eight basis points over interest rates on government debt. Since the company did not disclose what was in each pool of assets backing the commercial paper, it spooked investors who worried the pools were laden with U.S. subprime mortgage assets. On Monday, August 13, Coventree announced it had no bids or buyers for its commercial paper. Without funding, Coventree's SIVs could not survive. When the collapse finally came, it was the largest insolvency in Canada's history, with C\$32 billion in notes in the SIVs that filed for bankruptcy protection.[15]

In the ensuing weeks, similar runs occurred in SIVs linked to other financial institutions. As rollover dates arrived for various issues of asset-backed commercial paper, they were not renewed. The total amount of ABCP began a steady and dramatic decline as the run on SIVs advanced.

LIBOR rates, which had been steadily rising, hit 6.7975 percent on September 4, the highest level since 1998. This spelled more trouble for SIVs and asset-backed commercial paper. Total ABCP outstanding stood at $1.225 trillion on August 8, before the run on the SIVs began.[16] By September 5, ABCPs outstanding had fallen to $1.005 billion. A total of $220 billion, or 18 percent, of the market in paper had not turned over in four weeks. The run on SIVs claimed its first victim when the $8.8 billion Cheyne Finance, an SIV sponsored by the London-based Cheyne Capital Management, was forced into receivership[17] because it could no longer turn over its commercial paper funding.

It was beginning to look like 1998 all over again. That's when the New York Fed organized a $3.6 billion rescue and eventual wind-down of the storied hedge fund Long-Term Capital Management in the global financial crisis that followed Russia's default on its bonds. Plans for a rescue effort for the SIVs got started the third week of September 2007, when Treasury Secretary Hank Paulson, former chairman of Goldman Sachs, called a meeting in Washington for representatives of Citigroup, Bank of America, and JPMorgan Chase.[18] More meetings were coordinated by Robert Steel, undersecretary for domestic finance and a former Goldman Sachs executive, and Anthony Ryan, assistant secretary for financial markets.

Treasury officials wanted a bank industry-led bailout of the SIVs before what they saw as a liquidity squeeze or credit freeze turned into a broader panic.[19] The idea being suggested was to transfer all the troubled assets in individual SIVs to a Super SIV. Major financial firms would be asked to finance the cost of acquiring the assets by the Super SIV.

Super senior tranches of subprime mortgage bond CDOs were the thorniest of the assets. They were originally thought to be extremely safe but they were now effectively "toxic assets." These were seen to be more troubling because banks had not yet fully accounted for them. A rescue of the toxic assets before they were forced back on the banks' balance sheets, it was hoped, would reduce the potential for systemic risk. The fear was that once the troubled assets went back to the banks, it would greatly weaken them or even push some of them toward insolvency.

Citigroup, despite putting on a stoic public face, was the most vulnerable. The Super SIV effort was designed to forestall a crisis there as much as anywhere, given that the assets in SIVs created by Citigroup were estimated to be in excess of $40 billion and possibly much more. The proposed Super SIV, by contrast, was expected to need $75 billion to $100 billion in funding to set up. The Super SIV would issue short-term notes to finance the assets in the SIVs. It was not clear, however, whether banks would be expected to invest in the notes for the Super SIV or buy the assets in the SIVs directly.

The Super SIV was to carry the unwieldy name of the Master-Liquidity Enhancement Conduit, or M-LEC. Treasury leaked news on Friday, October 12, that plans for M-LEC would be unveiled the following Monday. Worries by healthier banks that were being coaxed into supporting the industry bailout delayed that announcement. Underscoring the importance of the M-LEC endeavor, another SIV moved closer to its demise on October 18 when its sponsor, IKB Deutsche Industriebank AG, determined that their Rhinebridge SIV was unable to repay its debt.[20]

As Super SIV discussions limped along, criticisms of the bailout began to mount. It was seen as essentially an end-run around the accounting rules, even though it was potentially limited to only industry players paying for the Super SIV. Former Fed Chairman Alan Greenspan faulted it because it was not a market-based solution and warned it might undermine rather than strengthen market confidence.[21] The blogosphere's critics did not approve. "Desperate measures are being taken so that banks do not have to bring this garbage onto their balance sheets," blogged Mike Shedlock, an investment adviser for SitkaPacific Capital.[22] The Super SIV was dying the death of a thousand cuts.

Meanwhile, the biggest potential beneficiary, Citigroup, was running out of time. On November 4, the board at Citigroup fired its chairman and CEO, Chuck Prince, for failing to understand the risks in subprime securitization. Not having a permanent replacement for Prince, the bank announced that former Treasury Secretary Robert Rubin would be chairman while Sir Win Bischoff would serve as interim CEO. Citi, which had earlier announced a $3 billion write-down on its $55 billion subprime portfolio, revised that upward to a range of $8 billion to $11 billion. On November 13, the fallout hit money funds that had invested in asset-backed commercial paper. Bank of America, Legg Mason, SEI Investments, and SunTrust Banks had to prop up money market funds that had invested in ABCP issued by SIVs.

Absent any rescue, SIVs began to fall like dominoes. On November 26, HSBC Finance Corporation had to take back onto its balance sheet $41 billion in SIV assets. Then West LB and HSH Nordbank bailed out $15 billion from their SIVs on December 3. At Paulson's urging, Citigroup sought and landed a $7.5 billion investment from Abu Dhabi's sovereign wealth fund.[23] On December 10, Bank of America said it was shuttering a $12 billion money-market mutual fund after losses on subprime-related instruments, including investments in SIVs. Then Citigroup ran out of time completely. On December 15, it said it would take $49 billion onto its balance sheet from seven SIVs it had set up. On Christmas Eve, the Treasury-coordinated plan to set up a Super SIV was abandoned entirely.[24]

By year's end, because ABCP rolls over every 90 days or less, the run had collapsed the vast majority of SIVs funded by asset-backed commercial paper. Total ABCP outstanding had fallen to $774 billion, a $451 billion decline and a 36 percent slide since August 8. For former Freddie Mac senior economist Arnold Kling, it was evidence of deep flaws in the rules governing capital requirements for banks. Given the fact that banks had to bring the assets back on their balance sheets, "it is clear in retrospect that the banks had not [really] off-loaded the risk of those mortgage securities," Kling said.[25]

THE REPO RUN

While the fall of the SIVs was playing out in the spotlight, something far larger and more significant was occurring in the darkest corners of the shadow banking system. A run was under way on broker-dealer banks that had been attracting low-cost overnight deposits to fund their operations by offering purchase for repayment or repo transactions to institutional investors and firms.

Yale's Gary Gorton was among the first to identify a pattern in the events surrounding SIVs and repos. His conclusion was that both were part of a broad panic that caused a run on the banks in the shadow banking system. A year later he would write: "[The] run started on off-balance sheet vehicles and led to a general sudden drying up of liquidity in the repo market, and a scramble for cash, as counterparties called collateral and refused to lend."[26]

For shadow banking, repos were the other side of securitization. Like any banking system, the shadow banking system has both a long-term asset side—the securitizations—and a short-term liability side, which included repos, one form of "deposits" in the system.

The sell-side of the repo entered the transaction to obtain funding or deposits and paid interest to the buy-side. The interest was not paid strictly as interest, but as the difference between the sale and repurchase prices.

No one knew then or now for certain the exact size of the repo market. Gorton estimated it to be $12 trillion in 2007. It was thus equal in size to all the deposits in regulated commercial banks and thrifts.[27] Since repos are overnight lending agreements, the daily volume is enormous. It was estimated to be $7.1 trillion in 2008,[28] far exceeding the $80 billion daily turnover in the stock market.

What's scary in hindsight is that the size of the market was also unknown to monetary authorities, as well as banking and securities regulators. Few in Congress and the media, including many in the business press, knew very much about this huge part of the parallel banking system. Repos have been compared to checks[29] from checking accounts in that they are another form of money. In this case, they are another form of money for institutional investors and firms with large sums of cash that would not be covered by the FDIC if they were deposited in checking accounts at a bank.

Gorton contends that the very essence of banking, both today and in the past, is creating short-term trading in securities backed by long-term assets.[30] A financial institution can provide funds, usually overnight, to another party, on a short-term basis. In banking, loans are assets and deposits are liabilities. Consumers have checking accounts—or as they are known in the business, demand deposit accounts. Since the Great Depression, the Federal Deposit Insurance Corporation, or FDIC, has guaranteed demand deposit accounts. Just before the financial crisis, the FDIC guarantee covered amounts up to $100,000 per account. There was no such guarantee for large commercial and institutional accounts at banks.

A Wall Street firm that enters in a repo contract sells an amount of securities overnight, say $100 million, and transfers those securities to another party, usually an institutional investor or firm. In return, the Wall Street firm receives $100 million in cash, or "deposit," from the party that temporarily purchased the assets overnight with the right to resell the next day. The buyer or counterparty in the repo takes custody of the collateral to protect the cash they have advanced to the Wall Street firm. The collateral thus substitutes for the FDIC guarantee that protects smaller checking accounts in commercial banks and thrifts. Repos, to the extent they were regulated, were under the oversight of the Securities and Exchange Commission.

The implicit and explicit federal government guarantees behind Fannie, Freddie, and Ginnie kept a portion of the mortgage securitization markets functioning after August 2007. There was no back-up guarantee, however, for the ABS part of the market that did not involve mortgages. The private-label ABS market, just like the private-label mortgage-backed securities market, was wiped out, a bystander casualty of the run on the bank in the shadow financial system. There was a run on SIVs holding ABS and funded with ABCP. The ABS market by itself was enormous. In 2004, non-mortgage ABS issuance of just under $800 billion was already equal in size to corporate debt issuance. In 2005 and 2006, the ABS issuance market surged ahead of the corporate debt issuance market. In 2006 total ABS issuance passed $1.2 trillion. It fell back and collapsed in August 2007. It would not begin to restart until 2009, when the Federal Reserve intervened to create a funding facility to get it moving again.

The mechanism by which a run occurred in the repo system has garnered little attention in analyses of the financial crisis. So how did the repo run occur? Gorton has argued that the run on Wall Street firms occurred when the firms and institutions on the buy side, who had advanced cash to the broker-dealers, began to demand and receive a "haircut" on the collateral that the sell-side had to provide.

It was no longer enough that the sell-side of the repo was repurchasing the assets at a price higher than they were sold. Now the buy-side wanted more than 100 percent collateral as a guarantee against the cash advanced to the sell-side of the deal. They wanted a haircut on the deal—usually expressed as more collateral for a given amount of cash.

Before the panic, the haircuts on assets were all set at zero. As the crisis began to unfold, the buyer of assets began to demand an amount of collateral that was greater than the amount of the cash being deposited in the broker-dealer bank. For example, for a $100 million cash transfer to a Wall Street firm, the party receiving the collateral might demand $120 million in assets for a $100 million deposit. This was a 20 percent haircut. In effect, it was a $20 million withdrawal from the broker-dealer bank.

"Massive withdrawals" via haircuts "are a bank panic," Gorton has argued. "That's what happened" beginning after August 9, 2007. It continued and steadily escalated until it peaked in late 2008.[31] Gorton has contended that the amount of assets that provided the shock to the financial system—total subprime loans outstanding—was small relative to the size of the meltdown that ensued. It was the run on the broker-dealer banks that led to mass withdrawals that turned the subprime crisis into the Panic of 2007 and later, as the run continued to steadily grow, the financial crisis of 2008.

Gorton, along with fellow Yale economics professor Andrew Metrick, have calculated the magnitude of the haircuts and thus have given some guidance on the potential amount of the withdrawals and run on the broker-dealers, which was in effect a run on the financial system.[32] Thanks to data on actual haircuts that occurred on specific collateral at a large broker-dealer, whose identity is concealed, Gorton and Metrick have been able to open a window into the black box of repo financing.

The data from the large anonymous broker-dealer show that the percentage of haircut required by the buy-side on repo deals varied by the credit rating and type of collateral. Average collateral haircuts were different at any given point in time for all types of asset-backed securities. Within each product category, there were differing haircuts based on credit ratings of various tranches of deals.

From their rich data set, Gorton and Metrick have provided overall averages along a timeline for two broad buckets of assets—subprime related and non-subprime related. Haircuts for subprime-related assets had already reached 20 percent by the end of 2007. By contrast, haircuts for non-subprime-related assets were averaging under 5 percent around the same time.

By late 2008, the haircuts on subprime-related assets had risen to 100 percent, meaning no one would take the collateral for cash and all broker-dealers who held cash for these assets were required to return it. At the end of 2008, the haircut for non-subprime-related assets had risen into the teens. Overall, all structured finance products as a group had an average haircut in the high single digits at the end of 2007, which rose to a calamitous mid-40 percent range at the end of 2008.

The volume and pace of increase in the collateral haircuts for repos captured the degree to which subprime assets contaminated non-subprime assets. This contamination occurred because when no one is sure whether a given securitization contains toxic assets, all securitizations became suspect. Even repos based on corporate debt collateral—not an instrument of the dreaded structured finance group—faced haircuts at the peak of the crisis.

The run on the broker-dealer banks was not unlike classic runs on a bank during a panic. From the broad sketch provided by Gorton and Metrick, one can see that the run on broker-dealer banks was mammoth in scale. If you assume that $10 trillion of the estimated $12 trillion in repos involved securitized assets, then the level of haircuts from the anonymous large broker-dealer can be calculated against the entire market.

"It's a travesty—but none of this data was collected," said Metrick.[33] "We don't know what the size of the market was. We don't know what different types of collateral were used for different things. We suspect that outside of general collateral—like Treasuries and agencies— mortgages were the most significant part of the market. But, we don' t have any hard evidence." The only solid data is the percentage of haircuts on specific assets that Gorton and Metrick found at one large anonymous investment bank.

If one makes a wild guess that asset-backed securities and private-label bonds make up half the collateral in the estimated $12 trillion repo market, then by the end of 2007, it meant that institutions "might have to find a couple hundred billion dollars somewhere," Metrick suggested. By the end of 2008, however, that number might have been "five or six times higher," pushing it above $1 trillion, he added. Those numbers give a ballpark estimate of the orders of magnitude of the repo run.

As broker-dealer banks had to provide more collateral to a given amount of cash, they had to sell other assets in order to raise cash. Thus, nearly all assets except safe-haven Treasuries experienced declines as they were dumped on the markets to raise cash. "[O]ne hopes that by the time of the next crisis, we will be following these numbers," Metrick said.

The crash in securitizations and the repo run on Wall Street firms provided strong evidence that the shadow banking system was capable of endangering and even crashing global finance. While the crash of private-label mortgage securitization and asset-backed securitizations was dramatic and public, the same cannot be said for the repo run on the bank. This was potentially an even bigger financial event in terms of the amount of assets involved and the order of magnitude of the losses incurred. Yet there was no dramatic visible evidence that could be reported in the press, such as people lined up taking deposits out of a bank.

"The panic of 2007 was not observed by anyone other than those trading or otherwise involved in the capital markets because the repo market does not involve regular people, but firms and institutional investors," explained Gorton.[34] That made this panic unlike earlier panics in American history. "The fact that the run was not observed by regulators, politicians, the media, or ordinary Americans has made the events particularly hard to understand," Gorton argued. "It has opened the door to spurious, superficial and politically expedient 'explanations' and demagoguery."

The crash of the mortgage-backed and asset-backed securities and CDOs of ABS showed the vulnerabilities on the asset side of the shadow banking system ledger. The run on SIVs and the repo run showed the vulnerability of the liability side. Bad mortgages were at the center of both phenomena. Thus, the story of how mortgages went from being among the most safe and sound to being tarnished by substantial levels of toxic assets is central to understanding how the panic and crisis came about.

Tragically, federal officials did not take to heart the vulnerabilities they witnessed in the financial system with the mortgage meltdown and the panic that ensued. James Rickards, who was general counsel at Long-Term Capital Management in 1998 and negotiated the terms of its rescue with the New York Fed, sought to warn Treasury about the increased vulnerability of the financial system and tell them they needed to take steps to prepare for more severe outcomes.

Rickards, senior managing director for Tangent Capital Partners, a merchant bank based in New York, said the panic he saw after August 9 convinced him the global financial system was headed toward a crisis far greater than the one of 1998. In early September 2007, he went to visit an unnamed assistant Treasury secretary and spelled out step by step what they should do to prepare for the crisis.

"I pleaded with them—you need to [have the President] issue an executive order," Rickards recalled.[35] The order would be to gather information on all the holdings of all financial institutions and hedge funds. If any hedge fund or institution refused to cooperate, then it should be shut down, he advised. The information obtained could be classified top secret under national security laws to protect private-sector interests. The next step would be "to hire big brains from IBM" to pull all the data together to ascertain the full extent of risks across the financial system and how they were interrelated. Rickards spelled out the steps in a two-page white paper he handed to the Treasury official.

"You have to understand what you have here. You need to look inside the bubble and see what you've got. Your biggest handicap is you don't understand the complexity," he said.

The response from Treasury was a polite "thank you very much." Apparently, Treasury had forgotten the Boy Scout motto, "Be prepared."

3

Seeds of the Disaster

"Never believe anything in politics until it has been officially denied," Prussian leader Otto von Bismarck advised back in the 19th century. This paradox of political bombast was illustrated yet again in the 21st century, with blustery denials that federal housing policy had any role in the housing and mortgage bubbles. Such claims were made after the government seized failing mortgage giants Fannie Mae and Freddie Mac and placed them in conservatorship in September 2008. The electorate, not surprisingly, was skeptical, given that the taxpayers' tab for bailing out these two government-sponsored enterprises, or GSEs, tops by far any of the other of the many bailouts of the financial crisis of 2008.

The Treasury Department first set a cap of $400 billion—$200 billion each—on how much money it would inject into the two GSEs. On Christmas Eve 2009, however, Treasury removed the caps entirely, leaving no limit on how much taxpayer funds could be injected into Fannie and Freddie through the end of 2012. Beginning on January 1, 2013, any further support from the government is limited to an additional maximum of $274 billion—$125 billion for Fannie and $149 billion for Freddie. A 2010 Congressional Budget Office study estimated that the tally could rise as high as $380 billion.[1] Some estimates have run higher, including one from Standard & Poor's for an astonishing $685 billion.[2]

As for the official denials, there's the one by Shaun Donovan, Secretary of Housing and Urban Development (HUD), who, in testimony before Congress in April 2010, vigorously defended the affordable housing goals. Under the first goal set for Fannie and Freddie in 1996, 40 percent of the loans and securities they purchased had to represent mortgages from borrowers with moderate or low incomes. That goal was 10 percentage points higher than the 30 percent level of such activity in 1992. Once hiked to 40 percent, the goal was frequently raised. It was never lowered. As the housing bubble gained momentum in 2000, the two GSEs were required to purchase mortgage loans and securities equal to 50 percent of new business each year from borrowers whose incomes were low or moderate. The goal was raised to 52 percent in 2005 and stood at 56 percent in 2008 when the two giants failed.

There are actually three affordable housing goals. The broadest one is for a population segment made up of low- and moderate-income households. There is a second goal for targeted rural and urban neighborhoods and communities that are underserved. Finally, there is a more narrowly focused goal for households with very low incomes.

Where did these goals come from, and how did they come to be imposed? They were the result of a long struggle and ultimate victory by community organizations and housing activists. Their triumph came when affordable housing provisions were incorporated into the Federal Housing Enterprises Financial Safety and Soundness Act of 1992 or, as it usually called, the GSE Act.

Chief among the community leaders who lobbied Congress for affordable housing goals was Gale Cincotta, a feisty Chicago neighborhood activist who staged disruptions at banks to pressure them to lend in poorer neighborhoods. She co-founded the National People's Alliance in 1972 with her long-time ally Shel Trapp, who also headed a coalition of churches, civic associations, and neighborhood groups known as the Northwest Community Organization, "one of Chicago's most powerful Alinsky-style groups."[3] Alinsky, in this case, is the famous mid-20th-century radical Saul Alinsky. Trapp was affiliated with the Industrial Areas Foundation that Alinsky had founded in 1940. The foundation began its methodical training of community organizers in 1969, after Midas Muffler founder Gordon Sherman gave the foundation a sizable grant.[4]

Another key player in GSE reform in 1992 was the Association of Community Organizations for Reform Now or ACORN, which was co-founded in 1970 in Arkansas by former Students for a Democratic Society leader and 1960s radical Wade Rathke, who hailed from New Orleans.

Community organizers were frustrated at the time because when they pressed local banks to make loans to minorities and low-income households in economically depressed neighborhoods, Fannie and Freddie were rejecting the applications. The loans did not meet their underwriting standards, then the gold standard for the industry.

Imposing housing goals on the two GSEs would help transform the mortgage lending process from one based primarily on prudential standards to one increasingly subject to political pressure to meet designated loan approval outcomes.

This is where the Home Mortgage Disclosure Act of 1975, or HMDA, began to pay off for the activists. That law required banks to collect data on the income, racial characteristic, and zip code of borrowers. An initial study[5] by the Boston Fed of mortgage lending patterns in Boston between 1982 and 1987, based on HMDA data, was released in early 1989. "Racial Pattern Is Found in Boston Mortgages," was the story's headline in the *New York Times* on September 1, 1989.[6]

This was the first of a series of studies from the Boston Fed that concluded that there were racist motives behind bank lending patterns, all done when Richard Syron[7] served as president of the Boston Fed. The studies were designed to determine how well banks were doing in complying with the Community Reinvestment Act, or CRA. That law was passed in 1977 to combat the practice of denying loan applications to poor inner-city neighborhoods with heavy concentrations of minorities—or, as it was better known, redlining.

Another study of Boston area HMDA data in 1990 showed that loan approvals were lower in minority census tracts, 57 percent, compared to 76 percent for non-minority census tracts, even when adjusted for income. This study, among others, prompted hearings on racial bias in mortgage lending in March 1991 by Democratic Illinois Senator Alan J. Dixon. Bruce Dorpalen, head of the Philadelphia office of ACORN, testified that his office had negotiated agreements with local lenders to use more flexible credit criteria for properties in low-income or inner-city neighborhoods—only to be told that "these loans are not acceptable to the secondary market," to which they are sold and securitized.

Of course, local lenders had more options than just selling mortgages to the GSEs. They could also originate loans that would qualify for guarantees from the Federal Housing Administration, or FHA and these loans could be securitized with guarantees from Ginnie Mae, a government agency. The reason this was not seen as an attractive option for the activists is that in 1990 Congress enacted a law that placed limits on discretionary spending and adopted a deficit-neutral, pay-as-you-go approach to taxes and spending. FHA programs are part of the federal budget.

"Congress had to find another means to fund low- and moderate-income housing," according to Edward Pinto, a former chief risk officer at Fannie Mae and an industry consultant. "Fannie and Freddie filled the bill perfectly. Both were not included in the federal budget and both could raise virtually unlimited sums in the capital markets. As an added bonus, this also would meet the demands of community groups," he said.[8]

At Senator Dixon's hearings, Freddie Mac chairman and CEO Leland Brendsel came armed with focus group studies of 147 loan officials in 12 cities that showed that bias can influence credit decisions. The studies put the blame on the loan originators (and not Freddie Mac). One obstacle was "cash on hand" provided at closings. Cash on hand is a source of funding that was previously not listed among the assets of the borrower at the time of the loan application. Under Fannie Mae guidelines, cash on hand is not acceptable since there is no way of verifying where the money came from. A person who saves up his or her own funds to buy a house is a better credit risk than someone who is provided funds from a grant or unknown source.

ACORN's Philadelphia office reported that one-fifth of the loans done with agreements they negotiated with lenders are based on cash in hand as opposed to identifiable sources of funding ahead of the closing.

So far, studies of lending practices in Boston had not delivered a knockout punch that convincingly showed that banks were discriminating, but that was about to change. The Boston Fed conducted a study[9] of 1990 and 1991 HMDA data for the Boston area and published its findings in 1992. Because the data provided under HMDA are limited—and do not include all relevant credit criteria—the Boston Fed had to seek out additional data from financial institutions in the Boston area in order to conduct a broader test of credit criteria.

This included information on the debt burdens of applicants, the ratio of the value of the mortgage to the value of house, credit histories, and neighborhood characteristics, all of which can influence decisions on loan applications.

The Fed authors asked for information on all 2,340 applications in the Boston area for whites but only 722 of the 1,143 applications from blacks and Hispanics. The study had two findings, which seemed at odds with one another. First, the study found no evidence of redlining by Boston banks. However, the study did find evidence of what the authors called "subtle" discrimination against minorities living across the Boston area in different loan rejection rates for blacks compared to whites. The authors found the ratio of loan approval for whites compared to blacks and Hispanics to be nearly 1.6 to 1.

The methods and conclusions of the study were criticized, most importantly by David Horne, an economist at the Federal Deposit Insurance Corporation. And the study continued to generate controversy among academics for years to come.[10] Yet the dissenting views were seen to be of no consequence in Washington, where this single study was viewed as definitive and the final word in scientific analysis by most in the political and policy arenas.

A HOUSING MISSION FOR THE GSEs

The provisions that would ultimately make their way into the GSE Act were largely decided behind closed doors and without a public debate. Housing advocates had already achieved success when they won a key battle over provisions in a 1989 savings and loan bailout bill that also had new rules governing the Federal Home Loan Bank System.[11] Their winning strategy was for community and housing organizations to meet and negotiate a consensus on what they wanted in a new law and then present that consensus to friendly members of Congress, who, in turn, would insert the desired provisions into the new law. This was the insider strategy. At the same time, activists could disrupt hearings, occupy rooms, and otherwise make an impact as outsiders. This dual insider/outsider strategy packed a political wallop.

The idea of bringing that strategy to bear in order to influence the provisions that would become part of a new safety and soundness regime for Fannie Mae and Freddie Mac came from the Center for Community Change. This umbrella organization urged the National Low Income Housing Coalition to convene a working group of affordable housing advocates, which included the National People's Alliance, ACORN, and the Consumers Union. It also included other participants from state governments and nonprofits involved in community development.

House Banking Committee chairman Henry Gonzalez, a Texas Democrat, "informally deputized" the alliance of housing advocates to come up with an affordable housing provision, which he would then champion in the House.[12] ACORN wanted to require Fannie and Freddie to set aside a share of earnings every year to support low-income housing, a "tithing" approach similar to the Community Investment Program imposed on the Federal Home Loan Bank System in 1989.[13]

The National People's Alliance under Gale Cincotta preferred to codify into law existing requirements for affordable lending already in place informally at HUD. Since 1970, HUD had established a goal that 30 percent of mortgages guaranteed by Fannie Mae should be made to low- and moderate-income people, and also that 30 percent of mortgages should be on homes in urban areas. These were known as the *30/30 goals*.

The working group at first was divided over whether to support the approach recommended by Cincotta or ACORN. As disagreement lingered, the GSEs, having seen the power of this coalition against the Federal Home Loan Banks, were determined to limit the damage and had become involved with the efforts to help the alliance of housing advocates reach consensus.[14] Fannie and Freddie sided with Cincotta and were able to convince others not to support the ACORN proposal.

ACORN put forth another proposal that the GSEs be subject to a new third housing goal targeted at borrowers with incomes under 80 percent of an area's median income, with some of that directed at very-low-income (under 60%) households. This became known as the special affordable housing goal, and this goal, like the others, was to be expressed as a percentage of the overall mortgage activity of Fannie and Freddie.

The coalition was divided over the issue of the special affordable goal. Cincotta and the National People's Alliance wanted the existing informal 30/30 goals in the GSE Act because they thought the GSEs would substitute the new, lower special affordable goal for the old 30/30 goals. This time, however, ACORN's view prevailed, and the working group agreed to support the special affordable goal in addition to the other two goals HUD was already following.

The coalition extracted a pledge from Fannie and Freddie to purchase $3.5 billion in special affordable mortgages[15] during 1993 and 1994. With this victory in hand, the compromise was shipped to Gonzalez, who introduced it, and it was incorporated in the final GSE Act of 1992.[16]

The importance of what the housing advocates had just accomplished was missed by most at the time but not by Fannie Mae's chairman and CEO Jim Johnson. He was a man on a mission when he arrived at the agency in 1988 as a consultant from Lehman Brothers, where he was a rainmaker for the investment banking firm. Fannie's chairman and CEO David Maxwell tapped Johnson in 1990 to be the firm's vice chairman. "Maxwell saw Fannie Mae's charter as its most valuable asset," said Pinto, and, thus, "political risk its greatest risk."[17] Johnson was moved into his position in 1990 for what Maxwell intended to be a one-year transition before Johnson's elevation in January 1991 to chairman and CEO of Fannie Mae.

Johnson came to Fannie Mae with an enormous influence within the Democratic Party. Born in 1943, he was a graduate of the University of Minnesota, and had earned a master's degree in public affairs from Princeton University, where he went on to became a faculty member.

After a stint as director of public affairs for the Dayton-Hudson Corporation (later known as Target Corp.), he served as executive assistant to Vice President Walter Mondale during the Carter Administration. He founded and ran Public Strategies, a private consulting firm, from 1981 to 1985 (running Mondale's failed bid for the presidency in 1984).

Johnson left his firm to work for Lehman Brothers in 1985. With a career path that had enabled him to keep one foot in Washington and the other in Wall Street, he was in many ways the perfect candidate for a public-private hybrid like Fannie Mae, at a time that the agency was increasingly willing to wage battle on the political front.

It was no surprise, then, that after Johnson became chairman and CEO at Fannie Mae in 1991, he did not hesitate to meet with the housing advocates, including ACORN, which had extensive ties with the Democratic Party. "Johnson probably thought Fannie Mae could capture its regulator, HUD," and control how the affordable housing goals were set and implemented so that they did not undermine the profitability of the firm, Pinto said.[18]

No doubt Johnson was able to persuade some of the affordable housing advocates of his willingness to bend Fannie Mae to their vision when he announced a commitment to do $10 billion in affordable housing, "a sizable figure for Fannie at that time," according to Pinto.[19]

In time, these goals would not only lead Fannie and Freddie to build up a mountain of risky loans that remained mostly hidden from view—but also to become the chief buyer of private-label mortgage securities put together by Wall Street and backed by risky mortgage products and weak credits that helped the GSEs achieve their housing goals and made them more profitable.

DESIGNED TO FAIL

What is forgotten today is that the purpose of GSE legislation in 1992 was not to inaugurate an era of credit allocation and affordable lending, but to prevent Fannie and Freddie from suffering the fate of the failed savings and loan industry. In the quest to set up a system of prudential regulation to ensure that Fannie and Freddie were operated in a safe and sound manner, there were two key issues in play, one involving capital standards and the other relating to the independence of a safety and soundness regulator for the GSEs.

The Administration of President George H. W. Bush called for a new arm's-length safety and soundness regulator to oversee Fannie and Freddie. But instead of asking Congress to give that regulator real independence, Bush's Treasury Department, under Secretary Nicholas Brady, implausibly called instead for the regulator to operate inside of HUD.

Senator Jake Garn, Utah Republican and ranking minority member on the Senate Banking Committee, wanted a completely independent regulator to ensure that the two GSEs would face serious oversight. Without any support from the Administration, he, like John the Baptist, was just a voice crying in the wilderness.

In the end, the GSE Act as enacted represented a complete policy reversal from its original intent. "The way the bill got through was that the safety and soundness got watered down" and the affordable housing goals became the price paid for the watered-down protections, according to Pinto.[20] Those who supported strong prudential regulation "were rolled" by the advocates for affordable housing, he added.

There was little skepticism in Congress about the intent and impact of the affordable housing goals, which many thought at the time were there merely to insure equal lending standards for all, which was not its intent at all, according to Pinto. "They didn't see the HUD affordable housing mission for what it was, to completely recast underwriting standards for the entire industry in an effort to spread wealth to get equal outcomes," he said.

Not only did the final legislation place a weak safety and soundness regulator within HUD—known as the Office of Federal Housing Enterprise Oversight, or OFHEO—lobbyists for Fannie and Freddie were able to stop any effort to establish strong explicit capital requirements for the GSEs.

In the final law, the amount of capital that Fannie and Freddie were required to have available against loans purchased and held on their books was 2.5 percent of the value of the assets, representing a high 40 to 1 leverage ratio of capital to assets. In contrast, banks have an 8 percent minimum capital requirement, which represents a prudent

12.5 percent to 1 leverage ratio. Furthermore, banking regulators can adjust the capital requirement higher—but OFHEO had no similar authority. With leverage so high and cast in stone, it would not take much in the way of losses for either Fannie or Freddie to slip into insolvency.

It gets worse. The capital requirement for mortgage-backed securities guaranteed by Fannie and Freddie was a tiny 0.45 percent. That translates into an astronomical 222 to 1 leverage ratio. Thus, Congress basically created the framework for what would become the world's two largest hedge funds.

Few appeared to understand that such minimal capital requirements would drive Fannie and Freddie to accumulate ever-larger quantities of mortgage-backed securities, thereby pumping more funding into the mortgage markets.

The capital levels at Fannie were also a huge incentive for banks to securitize mortgages, since holding them required 4 percent capital at the banks, but selling them required no capital. Plus, banks could buy some of the mortgage-backed securities and hold them for a capital charge of only 1.6 percent, thereby boosting the profitability of the assets. The combined effect of the capital requirements at the GSEs and favorable treatment for mortgage-backed securities at banks generated a gusher of funds for mortgage finance at the expense of competing loans and investments.

In retrospect, the GSE Act was a watershed event for mortgages. It established a prominent government role in allocating the flow of mortgage credit to designated segments of the population. HUD was free to set and increase the affordable lending goals and underserved area goals on its own authority, outside any prudential oversight of those goals.

The law failed to create even the semblance of a sufficient regulatory infrastructure to adequately oversee the safety and soundness of the GSEs. Fannie and Freddie walked off with everything on their wish list but the keys to Fort Knox.

The law did not require Fannie and Freddie to file quarterly reports with the Securities and Exchange Commission, settling instead on periodic audits by the Government Accountability Office.

The GSE Act gave regulators only limited authority to rein in what turned out to be runaway compensation arrangements for senior management.

Given the susceptibility of the GSEs to political interference, especially with their new emphasis on affordable housing goals, the law did not restrict or prohibit Fannie and Freddie from lobbying and from making campaign contributions.

Politically connected people went in and out of the revolving door of patronage and political influence at Fannie and Freddie, racking up millions in compensation on each round trip.

The GSE Act also left Fannie and Freddie free to set up charitable activities and provide funds for the myriad housing and community organizing groups, including ACORN. The doors were flung open wide for Fannie and Freddie to wield enormous political clout with Congress, while regulators had little or no way to restrain their financial and political activity.

While there was authority to put the GSEs into conservatorship, there was no authority to put them into receivership and shut them down should they fail.

In what was done and what was left undone in the GSE Act, Congress failed to serve the best interests of the nation. As Pinto has put it, "The GSE Act set Fannie and Freddie on the road to the mortgage meltdown."[21]

The GSE Act became the vehicle for putting forth a philosophical view that housing is a "civil right," meaning people are entitled to housing, including owning a house, making it a form of entitlement, according to Pinto.

Fannie and Freddie were politically unassailable fortresses of power and influence. No one could hold them to account. As a result, any effort to reform them, to strengthen capital requirements, to scale back affordable lending goals, was doomed to failure. Reform would not be possible, in fact, until both were on the edge of collapse in the summer of 2008.

With the passage of the GSE Act, housing activists expected that the GSEs would now be forced to do more minority lending and more lending to low-income neighborhoods. Yet thanks to HMDA data, we know that did not immediately happen. Any hopes that the new affordable housing goals would lead to something approaching equal credit allocation by neighborhood or race were quickly dashed.

In 1993, mortgages made to African American borrowers accounted for only 2.3 percent of Fannie's purchases and 1.7 percent at Freddie. There were similarly low numbers for Hispanics: 2.7 percent for Fannie and 2.9 percent for Freddie.

Affordable-lending advocates soon began to pressure HUD to make progress by putting in place specific racial and ethnic credit allocations instead of the broader goals in the law. "HUD's proposed rules [for affordable housing goals] do not address this issue [of racial and ethnic credit allocation]. We think they should," wrote Allen Fishbein, general counsel for Center for Community Change, and Dana Wise of the Low Income Housing Information Service in 1995.

STRONG-ARMING THE BANKS

Housing advocates would soon, however, find their most important ally yet—President Bill Clinton, who took office in January 1993. Clinton's initial focus, though, was not on Fannie and Freddie but on pressuring banks to do more lending to minorities. With the appointment of Henry Cisneros at HUD, Eugene Ludwig to the Office of the Comptroller of the Currency (OCC), and Janet Reno as Attorney General, the Washington regulatory establishment was ready to close ranks behind an effort to end what they saw as discrimination in mortgage lending.

By the spring of 1993, the political rhetoric was in full bloom. At his confirmation hearings, Ludwig said he intended to eliminate discrimination, "root and branch," from the financial system. Senate Banking Committee chairman Don Riegle, Michigan Democrat, lobbed a few rhetorical grenades. "They talk about how the free-enterprise system is supposed to work, but it's sophistry, as we all know."[22] For the new Washington political establishment, the end of discrimination could only occur when loan rejection rates were no longer higher for minorities than for whites. The anti-establishment had become the establishment.

President Clinton, in a speech on the South Lawn of the White House on July 15, 1993, claimed that the Community Reinvestment Act had not lived up to its potential. He called for better enforcement of CRA's provisions and for banking regulators to rewrite and strengthen the rules implementing the law to emphasize results instead of efforts. His administration engineered a crackdown by reinterpreting the Fair Lending Act of 1968 and the Equal Credit Opportunity Act of 1974.

Ludwig at OCC increased from 330 to 530 the number of compliance officers who examine banks and thrifts for fairness in lending and consumer protection. In short order, Ludwig's shock troops had managed to send four referrals to the Department of Justice for further investigation. Two of the initial four referrals publicly revealed their identity: Shawmut National Bank of Boston, the largest mortgage lender in New England, and Barnett Bank of Jacksonville, Florida.

Reno, meanwhile, chastised the Federal Reserve Board before the Senate Banking Committee for failing to join the crackdown. A contrite Fed chairman Alan Greenspan said ending discrimination would boost the economy. Two weeks later, the Fed, setting aside the question of safety and soundness on which its merger decisions are usually made, prevented Shawmut Bank of Hartford, Connecticut from acquiring New Dartmouth Bank of Manchester, New Hampshire, claiming Shawmut had discriminated against minorities.

The vote by the Federal Reserve Board was tied at three for and three against the application for the merger. The tied vote prevented the merger. Chairman Greenspan, Vice Chairman David Mullins, and Fed Governor Lawrence Lindsey voted no.[23] Shawmut had been under investigation by the Department of Justice as a result of the controversial Boston Fed study.

The Clinton Administration had already set the course of its crackdown before the Shawmut decision in a case against Decatur Federal Savings & Loan of Atlanta. That case was referred to Justice during the Bush Administration, and, under the threat of litigation, Decatur Federal agreed to a settlement in 1992 that included, among other things, sensitivity training for Decatur's loan officers and bonuses for those who bring in minority loans.

The Justice Department's case against Decatur was not based on individual complaints and contained no proof that any single minority loan was rejected without just cause. It relied entirely on a computer model that attempted to duplicate the factors that banks consider when making loans—a process most bankers say is an art, not a science.

A leading mortgage expert in Congress, Representative Bruce Vento, Minnesota Democrat, was alarmed at the reliance on computers to reach a decision on racial discrimination. "We can't take away the judgment of individual financial institutions about what is a good credit risk. You can't put that into a computer because there are too many uncertainties. You have to have a market test at some point," he said.[24] Nevertheless, Justice's computer concluded that Decatur Federal had discriminated.

Taking a cue from Justice, the Federal Reserve adopted its own computer program to determine if banks were discriminating. Governor Lindsey revealed the existence of the program in Senate testimony.[25] The Fed apparently used a computer analysis to make its case against Shawmut Bank and was planning to continue using it to find more cases to refer to Justice.

Under the new examination process at both OCC and the Federal Reserve, compliance examiners could look through applications until they found a single case of an approved white loan applicant whose qualifications are close to those of any rejected minority applicant, which includes blacks, Hispanics, Asian Americans, and Native Americans. This one close match would establish that the bank had discriminated.

Stephen Cross, deputy comptroller for compliance management at OCC, said that perhaps as few as four examples a year would lead to a finding of a pattern of discrimination. Since no two applications are ever identical, this approach allowed considerable latitude for a subjective conclusion.

One person inside the regulatory maze, however, did raise a red flag: Vern McKinley, an attorney who had served as a financial regulatory policy analyst at the Federal Reserve Board and the Federal Deposit Insurance Corporation.

McKinley specifically faulted the Fed and Greenspan for vetoing Shawmut's proposal to acquire New Dartmouth in 1992 in an article[26] published in 1994. "Rather than being a positive trend, these recent actions allow government and special interest groups to influence and even dictate lending decisions," he wrote. "Instead of being expanded, the CRA should be repealed," he argued.[27] Not long afterward, the Fed reversed its earlier decision and allowed Shawmut's acquisition of New Dartmouth to go forward.

"VOLUNTARY" ENLISTMENT OF MORTGAGE BANKERS

HUD Secretary Cisneros, like community organizers and affordable housing advocates, believed banks discriminate by such means as telling white applicants, but not black applicants, how to fill out their applications to get loan approval. The truth was, however, that by the early 1990s, most banks routinely reviewed all rejected minority applications, sometimes passing the loan file to the president's office. For example, the Consumer Bankers Association found in 1993 that 88 percent of banks responding to its annual "affordable housing" survey reported that they automatically reviewed all mortgage rejections.

Nevertheless, HUD set out to weed out "subtle discrimination." Cisneros's target: mortgage bankers—lenders like Countrywide Home Loans, then based in Pasadena, California—that originated mortgages for sale into the secondary market. Such firms were not closely regulated like banks and thrifts. They were, in fact, more aggressive in filling in the gaps in the mortgage market. Ironically— in view of HUD's decision to target them—mortgage bankers at the time originated 80 percent of government-guaranteed Federal Housing Administration loans, which disproportionately benefited minorities.

Cisneros tapped Assistant Housing Secretary Roberta Achtenberg, a civil rights attorney, to lead the campaign to forcefully enlist mortgage bankers. She hired an independent testing firm to send out phony black, white, Hispanic, and Asian American mortgage applicants to see if minorities are treated differently from whites. If a single loan officer or other employee in any way treated a single minority applicant less favorably than a white applicant, then it would be considered a case of discrimination. Discrimination can be something as simple as not smiling at the black tester, having smiled at the white one, under the rules for these tests.

Achtenberg had considerable leverage against mortgage bankers, since HUD is the regulator for Fannie and Freddie's affordable housing goals. If HUD denied a mortgage banker the right to sell its mortgages to Freddie Mac or Fannie Mae, it would force the banker out of business.

Mortgage bankers had, for years, been trying to improve their lending to minorities without sacrificing good underwriting principles. They had discovered along the way that education and counseling could increase the pool of potentially credit-worthy minority homebuyers, although not everyone then or now agrees on the value of such programs.

Mortgage bankers had claimed that many minority applicants had been rejected because they applied for a larger mortgage than they could afford or because they had failed to clear up past delinquent loans. Under "affordable housing" programs devised without Washington's help, lenders found that many rejected applicants can pass muster as early as a year after initial counseling and remedial action. The cost of the education is generally absorbed by nonprofit organizations that provide it free to would-be homeowners. Such organizations receive grants for these programs, often from settlements against lenders they have targeted. ACORN was a major recipient of such grants.

Beginning in 1989, under new flexible underwriting standards at both Fannie Mae and Freddie Mac, mortgage bankers were qualifying minorities for loans without conventional credit criteria. For example, they counted regular rent and utility payments as proof of credit-worthiness. Fannie Mae, Freddie Mac, private mortgage insurers, and mortgage lenders worked together to develop programs that combined counseling with lower down payments (as low as 3% of the applicant's own money).

The lack of a down payment had traditionally been the leading obstacle to greater minority homeownership, and community organizations and ACORN were in the forefront of efforts to pressure Fannie and Freddie to lower the down payments. Similar low down payment programs before 1985 led to disastrous results for Fannie Mae—but all that had been deleted from corporate memory banks.

Mortgage lenders were unable to locate sufficient numbers of minorities or of poor or very poor applicants. So they increasingly relied on community organizations and specifically ACORN to find such applicants for them.

Finding minorities and low-income borrowers was proving to be costly, however. The Consumer Bankers Association, for example, reported in 1993 that 69 percent of banks in its affordable housing survey subsidized their minority outreach programs, usually by offering lower interest rates, but also by incurring higher operating costs to administer the loans.[28] Among banks that subsidized, 76 percent of the subsidies were coming from bank profits, while the remaining subsidies were coming from government programs and nonprofit organizations.[29]

Mortgage bankers were a difficult prey for ambitious Washington regulators. For one thing, they were not subject to the Community Reinvestment Act. Forcing them to do more lending to the poor and minorities would seem to be a challenge if they decided to fight back. The solution? Achtenberg threw down the gauntlet. Agree to lower the underwriting standards to do more lending to the poor and minorities—or else HUD would persuade Congress to impose CRA on them.

This was no idle threat, and the mortgage bankers realized it would take little to transform this proposal into law, given the fact that the Democratic Party controlled both houses of Congress.

Capitulation came quickly and completely. In September 1994, the Mortgage Bankers Association of America (MBA) signed a three-year agreement with HUD to support the department's Fair Lending Best Practices Initiative. This program came with a model best practices agreement for individual mortgage banking companies to sign. The "best practices" were not, of course, the best practices in good underwriting. Instead, they were weakened or "flexible" underwriting guidelines.

Countrywide, the nation's largest mortgage banker, signed the first Fair Lending Practices and Principles Agreement with HUD. Despite HUD's use of threats to impose its will, HUD Secretary Cisneros and Assistant Secretary Achtenberg repeatedly pitched the best practices agreements as "voluntary" in nature. Countrywide President Angelo Mozilo towed the new party line, stating that his agreement was not "a forced march at all."[30]

Mozilo became the face of the mortgage banking industry as the head of Countrywide, a firm that defied the odds to survive and thrive as an independent company for 40 years, from its founding in 1968 until it was rescued by Bank of America in January 2008.

Mozilo was the son of a Bronx butcher who went to work at 14 in 1952 in his father's shop, where he was admonished by Papa Ralph Mozilo to get a college degree or be stuck in the Bronx as a butcher for the rest of his life. Mozilo went to work at 15 for United Mortgage Servicing in New York, where he processed loans and learned the business as he worked his way through Fordham University to earn a bachelor's degree in 1960.

In a 1988 profile in *Mortgage Banking*,[31] Mozilo recalled how he and fellow New Yorker David Loeb together founded[32] Countrywide in 1968 with only $800,000 in capital.[33] Short of funds, Loeb shut down the New York office, and he and Mozilo moved to Southern California, where Countrywide set up shop in Pasadena.

In 1974, Countrywide, in an effort to keep down costs, ditched the entire sales force that worked out of its eight branches and closed all the branches. Overnight the firm was reduced to three people: Angelo, Loeb, and a secretary. Countrywide would be reborn to focus on loan pricing as the ticket to growth and expansion to become a national firm.

Countrywide sent out mailings to real estate agents to tell them about their lower loan pricing and willingness to lock in interest rates from origination until closing. Real estate agents ignored them, and the whole new strategy looked like a big mistake. So Mozilo hit the streets to convince them it was a good idea. His efforts paid off, and Countrywide opened its first loan processing office in Whittier, California, with a staff of two. Whittier was so successful, Mozilo said, it almost collapsed from the high volume of business.

Countrywide, by standardizing the process, reduced the cost of originations below the 1 percent origination fee allowed by the FHA—the focus of Countrywide's originations. By comparison, the business model for other mortgage lenders was to view originations as a loss leader to be made up by servicing fees allowed by Ginnie Mae on the mortgages.

Countrywide's loan price discounting and standardization of the origination process allowed it to expand from its West Coast base to become a nationwide lender. By 1988, Countrywide had become the nation's second-largest mortgage lender. When number-one mortgage banker Lomas and Nettleton of Dallas was hit by losses from the deep recession in the oil patch, Countrywide became the nation's largest independent mortgage banker.

With fair lending requirements now imposed on them, mortgage bankers became enthusiastic backers of affordable lending. Mozilo cultivated a valuable and profitable political alliance with Washington that helped Countrywide become and remain the dominant mortgage lender in the country. Cisneros, for example, became a member of the board of directors at Countrywide.

Even before HUD pressured mortgage bankers into agreeing to its best practices agreement, Countrywide had in 1992 launched its own House America program that relied on flexible underwriting, community outreach, and counseling to expand lending to minorities. By 1994, Mozilo was hailed a hero of the fair lending revolution.

Countrywide, however, was more than just politically astute. The company hired the best and brightest people in the business and developed the best technology for originating and servicing loans, making it a consistent exemplar of excellence. It was not surprising, then, that in 2000 Countrywide could be both the biggest lender to minorities as well as earning the highest customer satisfaction rating among mortgage lenders from J. D. Power and Associates.[34]

In 2000, Countrywide was the first to renew its Declaration of Fair Lending Practices and Principles. "We continue each year to devote our tremendous resources toward reaching out to thousands of prospective homeowners to help them understand that the dream of home ownership is within their grasp," Mozilo said. "This mission is a cornerstone of Countrywide and something I'm incredibly proud of."

Unlike virtually everyone else associated with the reckless mortgage lending practices hatched in Washington, Mozilo possessed charisma. He was such a good advocate he made you want to believe that this whole idea of fair lending and affordable lending was a good one and that it would work. And for a long time, it appeared to work.

Countrywide was able to be the number-one lender to minorities as well as the number-one lender overall. The Fannie Mae Foundation, in a report issued in 2000, touted Countrywide's lending virtues. "Countrywide tends to follow the most flexible underwriting criteria permitted under GSE and FHA guidelines," the Fannie Mae report stated.[35]

Fannie Mae Foundation was particularly impressed that Country-wide would use unconventional factors, such as paying your electric bill on time, to gauge creditworthiness in its underwriting of mort-gages. "Because Fannie Mae and Freddie Mac tend to give their best lenders access to the most flexible underwriting criteria, Countrywide benefits from its status as one of the largest originators of mortgage loans and one of the largest participants in the GSE programs," the foundation stated.

This accolade reveals not only that Countrywide could enjoy better pricing because it was such a big client of Fannie and Freddie, but that the two GSEs gave Countrywide more latitude in originating loans with the weakest underwriting criteria the two agencies could allow. What that meant, as we can see in hindsight, is that—paradoxically— Countrywide could grow dramatically and become increasingly profit-able by weakening underwriting standards.

Fannie Mae was extremely grateful for the role played by Country-wide, as its dynamic growth was a boost to the agency's efforts to meet its very ambitious affordable lending goals.

GIVING CRA SOME TEETH

After it had brought the mortgage banking industry on board the fair lending bandwagon and quashed a series of proposed mergers and acquisitions of banks, the Clinton Administration was ready to meet another key demand of the housing activists. That would be to give CRA examiners greater ability to pressure banks into adopting "inno-vative and flexible"—that is, looser—underwriting standards that would help more minorities qualify for mortgages.

The method of conquest was to change CRA regulations from a soft emphasis on outreach into the hard instrument of measurable out-comes. The process got under way in 1993 when Clinton asked the banking regulatory agencies to "improve CRA performance evalua-tions and institute more effective sanctions against institutions with consistently poor performance."[36] In short order, regulators, led by Comptroller of the Currency Ludwig, proposed a new rule on CRA regulations that required lenders to meet certain numerical guidelines in total minority loans. Ludwig called them "performance-based standards." The "fairness" examiners would judge institutions not on their efforts, but on the results of those efforts.

Democratic Congressional supporters of the performance-based CRA standards—Senators Paul Sarbanes (Maryland) and Carol Moseley-Braun (Illinois), and Representatives Joseph Kennedy (Massachusetts) and Maxine Waters (California)—denied that the performance-based standards constituted quotas. Nevertheless, some CRA consultants and Wall Street banking analysts said that banks having trouble finding qualified minority candidates would simply approve the minimum number of bad loans and consider them, as one put it, "blood money for the politicians."[37]

Instead of the previous checklist of 12 factors that measure the efforts of banks in reaching out to low- and moderate-income neighborhoods, the proposed new rule offered a three-part test measuring lending, service, and investment to targeted populations and neighborhoods.

The banking regulators held hearings with over 250 witnesses and 50 written comments, and issued the "final rule" revising CRA regulations in May 1995.[38] The new rule adopted "performance tests" and "performance criteria" as the benchmark for judging the degree to which financial institutions comply with CRA. Previously, the regulation had stated "assessment tests" and "assessment criteria."

A rating system was established to pressure banks to engage in various forms of lending. Political science professor Helena Yeaman has explained how it works.[39] "If a bank was rated 'needs to improve,' then it would have two exam cycles to improve its rating. Or it would fall into the category labeled 'substantial non-compliance,' and be unable to open new branches or acquire other facilities," she noted.[40] "In essence, banks would have to prove their market share in low- and moderate-income areas was equal to their market share in their general service area," she added.

Financial institutions did win on one point. The regulation stopped just short of requiring bank examiners—instead of the banks themselves—to assess the needs of the communities where their branches are located and measure the degree to which banks are able to meet those needs.

With the final CRA rule in place, banks faced more and bigger hurdles to potential mergers and acquisitions. The banking regulators, for their part, enhanced the role of community organizers and housing advocates by holding public hearings when there were "highly contested applications,"[41] as Ben Bernanke would later call them.

The opportunity to turn up the heat on banks arose in the wake of the passage of the Riegle-Neal Interstate Banking and Branching Efficiency Act of 1994. The increased merger and acquisition activity, along with the higher demands from community organizers and housing advocates, fueled a dramatic rise in CRA commitments by banks.

The new final CRA regulation, in fact, turned out to be the jackpot for CRA lending. The CRA commitments that banks made with activists began to skyrocket.

Prior to the adoption of the new regulation, CRA commitments had amounted to $59.4 billion. Following the new CRA regulation, the commitments began a steady rise. By 1998, CRA commitments hit $812 billion in a single year, pushing the total commitments since 1977 to $1.17 trillion.[42] In 2004, banks made $1.63 trillion in commitments in a single year. By the end of 2006, on the eve of the mortgage meltdown, CRA commitments had reached $4.55 trillion. While one would have to find a way to measure the extent to which commitments were actually fulfilled, clearly this is a substantial level of affordable lending.

To argue that the volume of CRA lending was not material enough to have an impact on the mortgage meltdown and financial crisis, as some defenders of the Community Reinvestment Act have done, defies the evidence. To contend that the timing of the CRA was not relevant also defies the evidence—given that the commitments reached their highest levels during the peak of the housing boom when lending standards were the weakest.

NATIONAL HOMEOWNERSHIP STRATEGY

In June 1995, with all the regulatory power in place to force more bank lending, President Clinton announced a National Homeownership Strategy[43] that was designed to achieve a goal of having 67.5 percent of households own their own homes rather than rent by 2000.[44] "Our home ownership strategy will not cost the taxpayers one extra cent," he boasted. "It will not require legislation. It will not add more federal programs or grow federal bureaucracy."

Clinton's strategic plan targeted the 10 percent and 20 percent down payment requirement as a "barrier to home purchase" and promised to pursue efforts to lower down payments as a major way of increasing homeownership. The strategic plan also called for more "flexible underwriting criteria," and more public-private partnerships to help potential homeowners accumulate the cash needed to make a down payment.

Washington should have been cautious about a bold new federal housing policy, given that past federal efforts to increase homeownership in poor and minority urban neighborhoods, such as the FHA program, had instead been blamed for destroying those neighborhoods in the 1960s and 1970s.[45]

With the collapse of the savings and loan industry, Fannie and Freddie were able to grow rapidly and take more and more of the mortgage origination market. In fact, from 1990 to 2003, they nearly doubled their market share from 25 percent to 46 percent,[46] its pre-crisis peak in market share.

During the 1990s, in fact, the GSEs took control of the mortgage market and kept expanding their share of mortgage originations. In 1990, for example, they had a $138 billion portfolio of whole loans and managed a $604 billion portfolio of mortgage-backed securities—at a time when the total outstanding residential mortgage market was $2.9 trillion. By 2003, the GSEs held $909 billion in mortgages and $2 trillion mortgage-backed securities with the total residential mortgage market at $7.8 trillion.

Over time, every type of competitor of the GSEs was routinely swept aside when Fannie and Freddie entered a given market niche. They could beat the private sector, as well as government-backed FHA loans, on pricing. Their funding cost and capital advantages were so huge, they could undercut loan pricing on all comers. This did not leave enough spread in the cost of funding and the interest rates that could be charged for mortgages to allow for the private sector to invest and make a profit.

Gains in market share posed their own set of financial risks for Fannie and Freddie, as well as potential systemic risks and exposure for taxpayers, even without factoring in the lowering of lending standards.

In 1994, Fannie Mae's Jim Johnson announced a $1 trillion commitment to affordable lending. It was a staggering sum for 1994—a decade and a half before Washington made trillion-dollar numbers a routine affair. No program of any sort in the history of the United States had involved such a pledge.

The market for mortgage-backed securities with guarantees from Fannie and Freddie—so-called agency mortgage-backed securities—was on target to exceed the size of the U.S. Treasury market. Such bonds were AAA credits, although they were not formally rated. The AAA came from the presumed implicit backing of the U.S. government. When Fannie Mae announced its $1 trillion in affordable lending, it had only $15 billion in regulatory capital to support that ambitious program. The announcement of the commitment was universally applauded. No one raised any red flags or asked any hard questions.

For Fannie Mae, the $1 trillion pledge was a political home run with Congress and was seen to preserve its unique franchise. Fannie played hard and by its own rules. Johnson earned a reputation for invincibility. "The old political reality was that we always won, we took no prisoners, and we faced little organized opposition,' recalled Daniel Mudd years later, after he was handed the reins of Fannie as chairman and CEO following the government takeover in 2008.[47]

Within a decade of the launch of Johnson's initial program to advance homeownership, Fannie and Freddie together had announced $5 trillion in commitments to affordable housing goals, an unimaginable figure for a market and population segment that was nowhere near large enough to absorb that much funding. The entire mortgage market, for example, was $11 trillion on the eve of the financial crisis. The leverage of all assets at the GSEs was rising, too, with more and more assets in its investment portfolio. Overall leverage, including securities guarantees, moved toward 60 to 1 and then higher.

When George W. Bush became president, he was, during his first term, as enthusiastic and supportive of the housing goals of the GSEs as anyone had been during the Clinton Administration. Increasing the number of homeowners would advance his hopes for an "ownership society." In 2004, HUD Secretary Alphonso Jackson proposed to raise the broadest affordable housing goal from 50 percent to 56 percent by 2008.

Outside a few furrowed brows at OFHEO and the Federal Reserve, few were aware or concerned that the GSEs were building a mountain of mortgage bonds with ever-growing risk, all with the implicit guarantee of the same government that enabled the constant expansion of these programs without regard to the underlying risk. It seemed that just about everything was moving higher—the level of lending, the level of assets in the investment portfolios, homeownership rates, profits, share prices, salaries, and bonuses. Life was good. What could possibly go wrong?

4

The Race to the Bottom

Over the years, ever-rising affordable housing goals set Fannie Mae and Freddie Mac on a path toward accumulating hidden amounts of subprime and other risky nontraditional mortgages and securities.

Everyone knew the underwriting standards for the government-sponsored enterprises (GSEs) had weakened. Practically no one, even people well acquainted with Fannie and Freddie, had the foggiest notion of just how much "flexibility" had been employed to reach affordable housing goals—which by 2008 represented 56 percent of all lending. In 1992, when the GSE Act[1] was passed, the affordable housing goal was 30 percent of all loans from low- and moderate-income borrowers.

It was only after the accounting scandals at Freddie in 2002 and Fannie in 2003 that their regulator, the Office of Financial Housing Enterprise Oversight (OFHEO), extracted concessions from them requiring that they begin releasing key financial data on a quarterly basis. Fannie and Freddie began to voluntarily report financial data similar to what is required for all publicly traded corporations when they file quarterly income statements with the SEC. These reports were often late and incomplete. They were not required under the their charters. Nor were they subject to audits.

Once Fannie and Freddie were placed into conservatorship in September 2008, they were required to release even more information. Only then did it become clear what had been going on inside these two financial giants.

The efforts of a single forensic researcher—former Fannie Mae risk officer Edward Pinto—unearthed the facts on risky lending and investing by Fannie and Freddie and made them public. Pinto, who worked at Fannie in the 1980s, had since then worked as a mortgage industry consultant.

Pinto poured over the data that was emerging from the GSEs, including information on the amount of lending to borrowers with credit scores below 660—the dividing line between prime and subprime—and the amount of lending done with little or no money down. He found that from 1997 to 2007, Fannie and Freddie had bought or guaranteed $4.1 trillion in nontraditional mortgages and securities, a staggering amount of risky lending activity that apparently few imagined had been done. (See Table 4.1.)

In one of several compilations of data sets, Pinto looked at the level of subprime and Alt-A lending in the financial system as of June 30, 2008, just before Fannie and Freddie had to be taken over by the government. At that point, the two GSEs owned or guaranteed more than $1.8 trillion, or 40 percent of the $4.6 trillion in total outstanding mortgages that were either subprime or Alt-A.[2] (See Table 4.2.)

Pinto included in the Alt-A category a wide variety of nontraditional mortgages with low or no documentation, plus exotic loan products such as interest only, option adjustable rate, and no income, no asset, no job (NINJA) mortgages. In actual numbers of mortgages, Fannie and Freddie owned or guaranteed 12 million or 44 percent of 27 million subprime and Alt-A mortgages.[3]

Pinto also counted $600 billion in 5 million subprime and Alt-A mortgages that were guaranteed by the Federal Housing Administration (FHA), Veterans Administration (VA), or made by the Federal Home Loan Bank System. He calculated that outstanding Community Reinvestment Act or anti-redlining loans and other programs from the Department of Housing and Urban Development (HUD), such as a best practices initiative for mortgage bankers, represented $300 billion in 2.2 million mortgages.

The private-label mortgage-backed securities market—the epicenter of the mortgage meltdown of 2007, and the assets that wreaked havoc on the shadow banking system and helped precipitate the 2008 crisis—represented $1.9 trillion in 7.8 million subprime and Alt-A loans.

Thus, the government share of risky mortgage loans outstanding on the eve of the financial crisis was 19.2 million out of 27 million. The principal balance for these mortgages was $2.7 trillion, or 59 percent out of $4.6 trillion in subprime and Alt-A loans outstanding.

Pinto's work also revealed just how bad overall mortgage credit in the system had become by mid-2008. It was not just bad. It was horrendous.

Table 4.1 Fannie Mae's and Freddie Mac's Annual Purchase Volume of Subprime, Alternative-A, and Very High Loan-to-Value Mortgages and Securities (in Billions of Dollars)

	1997	1998	1999	2000	2001	2002	2003	2004	2005	2006	2007	1997–2007
Subprime Private-Label Mortgage-Backed Securities (PMBS)	$3[a]	$18[a]	$18[a]	$11[a]	$16[a]	$38	$82	$180	$169	$110	$62	$707
Subprime Loans[b]	$37	$83	$74	$65	$159	$206	$262	$144	$139	$138	$195	$1,502
Alt-A Private-Label Mortgage-Backed Securities[c]	Unknown	Unknown	Unknown	Unknown	Unknown	$18	$12	$30	$36	$43	$15	$154
Alt-A Loans	Unknown	Unknown	Unknown	Unknown	Unknown	$66	$77	$64	$77	$157	$178	$619
High Loan-to-Value Mortgages[d]	$32	$44	$62	$61	$83	$87	$159	$123	$126	$120	$226	$1,124
TOTAL[e]	$72	$145	$154	$137	$259	$415	$592	$541	$547	$568	$676	$4,106

[a]Total purchases of private-label mortgage-backed securities (PMBS) for 1997–2001 are not known. Subprime purchases for these years were estimated based upon the percentage of subprime PMBS that existed in total PMBS purchase in 2002 (57%).

[b]Loans in which the borrower's credit score is less than 660.

[c]Fannie and Freddie used their various affordable housing programs and individual lender variance programs (many times in conjunction with their automated underwriting systems, once these came into general use in the late 1990s) to approve loans with Alt-A characteristics. However, they generally did not classify these loans as Alt-A. Classification as Alt-A started in the early 1990s. There are an unknown number of additional loans that had higher debt ratios, reduced reserves, loosened credit requirements, expanded seller contributions, etc. The volume of these is not included in this table.

[d]Loans with an original LTV or original combined LTV >90% (given industry practices, this effectively means >=95%). Data to estimate loans with CLTV >90% is unavailable prior to 2003. Amounts for 2003–2007 are grossed up by 60% to account for the impact of loans with a CLTV >90%. These estimates are based on disclosures by Fannie and Freddie that at the end of 2007 their total exposures to loans with an LTV or CLTV >90% was 50% and 75% percent, respectively, higher than their exposure to loans with an LTV >90%. Fannie reports on p. 128 of its 2007 10-K that 15% of its entire book had an original combined LTV >90%. Its Original LTV percentage >90% (without counting the impact of any 2nd mortgage simultaneously negotiated) is 9.9%. Freddie reports on p. 60 of its Q2:2008 10 Q that 14% of its portfolio had an original combined LTV >90%. Its OLTV percentage >90% (without counting any simultaneous 2nd) is 8%. While Fannie and Freddie purchased only the first mortgage, these loans had the same or higher incidence of default as a loan with an LTV of >90%.

[e]Since loans may have more than one characteristic, they may appear in more than one category. Totals are not adjusted to take this into account.

Source: Financial Crisis Inquiry Report.

Table 4.2   All Outstanding Subprime and Alt-A Loans in the United States on June 30, 2008

Entity	Number of Subprime and Alt-A Loans	Unpaid Principal Amount
Fannie Mae and Freddie Mac	12 million	$1.8 trillion
Federal Housing Administration, Veterans Administration, Federal Home Loan Banks, and others	5 million	$0.6 trillion
Community Reinvestment Act and HUD Programs	2.2 million	$0.3 trillion
Total Federal Government	**19.2 million**	**$2.7 trillion**
Private-label mortgage-backed securities backed by subprime, Alt-A, and all others	7.8 million	$1.9 trillion
Total	**27 million**	**$4.6 trillion**

Source: Edward J. Pinto, Exhibit 2. See Edward Pinto's analysis in Exhibit 2 to the Triggers Memo, April 21, 2010, p. 4. http://www.aei.org/docLib/Pinto-Sizing-Total-Federal -Contributions.pdf. Edward Pinto, "Triggers of the Financial Crisis," March 15, 2010. http:// www.aei.org/paper/100174.
Source: Financial Crisis Inquiry Report.

The subprime and Alt-A category combined had become a majority of all outstanding mortgage loans—27 million out of 55 million. In dollar figures, it was $4.6 trillion, or 43 percent of the $11 trillion in mortgages outstanding.

What is hard to recognize in retrospect is that, from the market's perspective, the vast majority of the risky loans were not even on the radar. Only the FHA and related programs ($600 billion) and private-label mortgage-backed securities ($1.9 trillion) were known by the markets and regulators to represent subprime and Alt-A lending. Thus, only these loans and balances were being taken into account in assessing the risks in the overall mortgage market and the broader housing sector.

The markets and regulators were assuming there was $2.4 trillion in subprime and Alt-A mortgages in the system, but instead there was $4.6 trillion.

Thus, the $11 trillion U.S. mortgage market was not a tower of strength at all, but perhaps the largest mountain of weak and bad credit in the history of the world. The federal government, in turn, represented by far the largest part of that weakness, $2.7 trillion, or 59 percent of the $4.6 trillion in nontraditional mortgages. It was a disaster waiting to happen, with the biggest part of the problem hidden away in the world's two largest black boxes—Fannie Mae and Freddie Mac.

WHEN MORTGAGE CREDIT WAS GOOD

The credit underwriting regime of 2008 was far different than the one that existed in 1989, before credit standards began their steady march downward.

In 1989, individual credit risk, or FICO scoring, had just been invented as a product for credit bureaus. The individual score was not invented for mortgages, but for consumer debt such as credit cards and auto loans.[4]

FICO stands for Fair Isaac and Company. Engineer Bill Fair and mathematician Earl Isaac founded this Minneapolis-based company in 1956. A year later, the new company was hired by Conrad Hilton to design, program and install a complete billing system for one of the first credit cards, Carte Blanche, for the Hilton hotel chain.

The FICO-developed individual credit risk score saw its 1989 debut at Equifax in Atlanta, where it was released under the brand name of BEACON. When Pinto heard that Equifax was introducing an individual credit score, he wanted to know more. "I met with them in Atlanta and asked them to do a run on all single-family mortgages, which they did," he recalled. As a result, Pinto obtained "the first-ever run of FICO scores on mortgages."[5]

The data revealed that the average median FICO score in 1989 for individuals with mortgages was 730,[6] considerably higher than the minimum of 660, the cut-off point between prime and subprime borrowers.[7]

Only 18.3 percent of individuals with mortgages had a FICO score that was below 660. Of this group, 8.4 percent had FICO scores between 620 and 660—a designation that roughly corresponds to A-minus subprime credit in the broad mortgage market, while 9.9 percent were below 620, which would roughly translate into B, C, and D subprime mortgages. From this period of gold underwriting standards, one can measure the extent of decline.

There is also evidence from more than a dozen years before the financial crisis that Fannie and Freddie were very well aware that the bad loans in their portfolios were experiencing sharply higher delinquency rates, but these were camouflaged in the overall averages.

A landmark 1996 Federal Reserve study looked at the predictive value of credit scores and, in the process, revealed that loan performance had declined significantly from the gold standard in the 1989 Equifax data. Credit scores had become increasingly important after first Freddie, then Fannie, in the prior year had issued letters to lenders strongly encouraging them to consider using credit history scores in their loan underwriting from one of three providers—Equifax's Beacon, TRW-FICO, or Empirica.[8]

One of the studies discussed in the Fed report was Freddie Mac's experience with its Affordable Gold program. The Freddie Mac study looked at loans originated in 1994 and found delinquency rates higher for loans that had allowed third parties to meet part of the minimum down payment, when measured against a peer group. Freddie Mac used a separate Gold Measure Worksheet to help evaluate a variety of additional flexible lending factors that could adversely affect loan performance. For borrowers who had more flexible lending factors in their loan underwriting for 1994, loan delinquencies were 5.6 times higher than for the peer group.

In a 1989 Equifax study, 13.4 percent of people who had taken out a mortgage recently had a credit score below 660, making them subprime.[9] By 1994, the subprime share for first-time homebuyers had risen to 14.5 percent.[10] By 2008, about 25 percent of all mortgages went to borrowers with a FICO below 660, with 7 percent in the 620 to 660 range, and 18 percent below 620.[11] Clearly, weaker credits over time became an ever larger share of the mortgage pool.

Fannie and Freddie steadily increased their share of subprime through both the purchase of whole loans and the acquisition of mortgage-backed securities, including private-label securities. The decision to allow Fannie and Freddie to purchase subprime mortgage-backed securities was made in 1995 by William C. Apgar, Jr., assistant HUD secretary. Apgar later regretted his decision. "It was a mistake," he said. "In hindsight, I would have done it differently."[12]

The steady increase in leverage (or decline in down payments) was an even more dramatic contributor to the decline in mortgage credit standards. In 1989, only one in 230 homebuyers made a down payment of 3 percent or less. Plus, virtually none of the 1989 homebuyers with a FICO below 660 made a down payment of less than 3 percent. Thus, there appeared to be a near-universal appreciation of the wisdom of avoiding the layering of risks—low FICOs plus low down payments—in mortgage underwriting practices. By 2003, one in seven mortgages at Fannie Mae had a down payment of 3 percent or less. By 2007, it was one in three.[13]

As the role of Fannie and Freddie expanded in the 1990s, they began to come under more criticism. Doubts were raised about subsidies they received, such as the implicit guarantee of their debt by the federal government, and the potential for a taxpayer bailout. There was also growing concern that the GSEs were becoming too large.

For example, Fannie Mae had already become the largest financial institution in the nation with $351 billion[14] in assets, higher than Chase Manhattan's $336 billion.[15] Congress ordered federal agencies to conduct studies on the costs and benefits of Fannie and Freddie and the potential effects of privatizing them.

The Congressional Budget Office (CBO) estimated that the GSEs received about $6.5 billion a year in various subsidies from the implicit government guarantee and other favorable treatment, but retained $2.1 billion of that for itself rather than pass it on to home-owners.[16] CBO found that "scant evidence exists of public benefits from the GSEs that would justify a retained taxpayer subsidy" of $2.1 billion. The Treasury Report, accompanied by testimony from Deputy Secretary Lawrence Summers, agreed with the CBO estimate of a $6 billion subsidy with only $4 billion passed on to homebuyers as lower rates.

A report from HUD argued against privatizing Fannie and Freddie.[17] A report from the General Accounting Office presented privatization as a viable option,[18] and calculated that if the GSEs were privatized, it would raise mortgage interest rates on a 30-year fixed-rate mortgage by 15 to 35 basis points (a basis point is 1/100th of a percent). GAO also specifically identified the implicit federal government guarantee for GSE debt and securities as 80 to 95 percent of the value of the subsidy they receive.

Vern McKinley, a former financial analyst for the FDIC, argued in 1997 that Fannie and Freddie should be privatized. He pointed to the success of the secondary market in automobile loans, which had grown from $18 billion in 1989 to $44 billion in 1995,[19] as evidence that the role of the GSEs could be played by the private sector.[20] McKinley claimed the GSEs were taking on increasing risk "that may threaten their viability in light of their comparatively more leveraged capital position."[21]

One worrisome trend spotted by McKinley was the rising share of mortgages that were being held on Fannie Mae's balance sheet instead of sold into the secondary market. The share of loans retained in port-folio reached 34 percent in 1996, up from 26 percent in 1991.[22]

McKinley pointed out that retaining the assets in portfolio exposes Fannie Mae to interest rate and credit risk, while securitizing them exposes them to only the credit risk. Fannie and Freddie had begun to hedge their risks with derivatives contracts, such as interest rate swaps, but the use of these derivatives increased the exposure of the GSEs to counterparty and other risks, McKinley noted.[23]

Finally, McKinley cited the growing political influence of the GSEs and the exorbitant salaries that were being earned by its executives.

In 1995, for example, Fannie Mae chairman and CEO Jim Johnson earned $5.1 million, president Lawrence M. Small earned $3.7 million, and vice chairman Franklin Raines earned $3.0 million, while Freddie Mac Chairman Leland Brendsel earned $2.2 million and Fannie Mae Executive Vice President Robert Levin earned $1.9 million. "Compensation packages such as those are not rare for private entities of a similar size, and purely private companies without government sponsorship should be free to pay any salaries they wish to get the talent they need. What is objectionable in the case of Fannie Mae and Freddie Mac is that public funds are in part underwriting such high salaries," McKinley wrote.[24]

CBO also objected to the compensation. "The problem with executive compensation at Fannie Mae and Freddie Mac is not necessarily that it is too high but that such a large share of it is paid by taxpayers and is awarded on the basis of management's success in securing ever-larger transfers from the government to the enterprises and their share holders," the CBO stated.[25]

It was already clear that the GSEs, under mandated affordable housing goals, could deliver public benefits that are hidden off budget, as McKinley noted. "In fact," he wrote in 1997, "the entire structure of the GSEs, whereby Congress offers special status in return for the government as a whole taking on a hidden, contingent liability as a *quid pro quo* for various housing programs that never hit the budget, acts as a back-door method to increase spending on housing without having to go through the appropriations process."[26]

Nothing came of the studies of Fannie and Freddie ordered by Congress. In this first major test of wills between the GSEs and a Republican-run Congress, Fannie and Freddie emerged unscathed and triumphant.

THE FANNIE AND FREDDIE CASINOS

The housing bubble in the United States is believed to have begun in 1997 and to have accelerated after 2000. The enormous flow of funds from the GSEs beginning in 1995 was a driving force in the inflation of this bubble, and a lot of the hot air came from risky lending. By 2001, the GSEs had already purchased or guaranteed $701 billion in subprime and Alt-A, according to Pinto's calculations. The private-label sponsors, by contrast, had from 1995 to 2001 issued $376.6 billion in subprime and $69.8 billion in Alt-A securities—a total of $446.4 billion.[27]

The GSEs, however, were also feeding the growth of private-label securities as the single largest purchaser of such issues. The subprime and Alt-A were "goals rich," Pinto points out. While many Alt-A borrowers do not state an income—and thus cannot be counted toward low- and moderate-income goals—the Alt-A category has a large share of minorities, which helps reach other affordable housing goals.

Pinto estimated that in the six years from 2002 to the end of 2007, Fannie and Freddie purchased $1.084 trillion in loans with credit scores below 660—or subprime.[28] In addition, over the same period, the GSEs purchased $641 billion of subprime private-label subprime securities, for a total of $1.725 trillion in subprime loans at the time the bubble was accelerating at its most rapid pace.

One can see how big the private-sector subprime market would have been without the GSEs by subtracting their role from the totals. That would leave $1.16 trillion in subprime private-label securities *not* purchased by Fannie or Freddie. The GSEs' total acquisition of all types of subprime from 2002 to 2007—both loan and securitized, guaranteed or purchased—was $1.725 trillion. (See Table 4.1.) Therefore, the subprime contribution of Fannie and Freddie in the peak bubble years was 1.5 times greater than the size of the part played by all other investors in the market combined. Clearly, Fannie and Freddie played an overwhelming and predominant role in driving subprime credit wherever it was originated.

The GSEs also loomed largest on the Alt-A side, based on Pinto's calculations. The $154 billion that Fannie and Freddie expended from 2002 to 2007 to purchase private-label Alt-A securities was nowhere near the $619 billion they shelled out to buy Alt-A loans. There was also $1.124 trillion in high loan-to-value mortgage purchased by the GSEs.

Thus, in the six years leading up to the mortgage meltdown, total risky lending at Fannie and Freddie hit $3.622 trillion, according to Pinto's calculations.

Fannie and Freddie acquired the huge portfolio of private-label subprime securities because it was so profitable to hold them on their balance sheet at very high leverage of 40 to 1. These purchases, in turn, helped the GSEs achieve a 25 percent rate of return for investors and drove the huge bonuses paid to senior managers.

Pinto's calculations show that the GSEs' big role in subprime and Alt-A predated the huge surge in private-label issuance that began

in 2004. It was the intervention of the regulator of Fannie and Freddie—
OFHEO—that reduced the volume of private-label purchases by Fannie
and Freddie after 2004.

Inside their GSE black boxes, the senior managers at Fannie and
Freddie became the biggest gamblers on the planet. One could hardly
call it investing when the leverage was so high and the assets were so
risky. This leverage and risk were higher than anything at Wall Street
firms or even at the major hedge funds. It would take only a small
move downward in the prices of assets to wipe out the tiny amount
of capital at both GSEs. A big movement in prices would lead to catastrophic losses. When house prices fell, the huge level of risky lending
pumped into the system by Fannie and Freddie made the force of the
crash all that stronger, flooding the system with far more delinquencies and defaults than anyone might have estimated even in the
worst-case scenarios. This, in turn, drove falling house prices much
lower than they otherwise would have been.

FREDDIE MAC IGNORES CHIEF RISK OFFICER

A window into the risk calculations inside Freddie Mac can be seen
from internal e-mails that have come to light about disagreements
over risky loan products being offered by the company. In September 2004, concerns about the no income, no asset (NINA) program
had prompted a review at Freddie Mac and David Andrukonis, chief
risk officer, decided to send a memo[29] to chairman and CEO Richard
Syron and other senior managers recommending that the program be
terminated.

Andrukonis objected to the fact that NINAs were being targeted to
lower-income salaried workers with weaker credits rather than self-
employed people with good credit who had traditionally relied on
NINA loans. The loans were also seeing very high first-year delinquency rates of 8 percent to 13 percent. In many instances, a spouse
with poorer credit was dropped from the loan application and mortgage note, he added. "This means that the borrower with the weaker
credit score was probably not adequately considered in the underwriting process," the letter explained. Finally, the chief risk officer said that
because the loans were being made disproportionately to target
Hispanics, it might give the "perception" or even the "reality" of fraud
or predatory lending. Freddie Mac should drop this loan program
entirely, he urged.

Chief operating officer Mike May, one of the managers who received the e-mail, was perplexed. "Wow," he wrote back to Andrukonis. "This seems a bit premature," he stated. "I would have expected you to wait until we had made a decision and a firm recommendation and then perform an oversight role on that decision." The chief risk officer replied that he understood that a review was going forward, but he wanted Syron to know "that he can approve of us doing these loans, but it will be against my recommendation."

After the review, May recommended Freddie Mac continue with the NINA program. Syron agreed.

There were also concerns within Freddie Mac about a new program, the stated income, stated assets, or SISA, loan program. The company was considering vastly expanding the product to many lenders. Don Bisenius, senior vice president for credit policy and portfolio management, raised questions about the program, as did Andrukonis.

In an e-mail to chief operating officer Paul Peterson, Andrukonis wrote, "In 1990 we called this product 'dangerous' and eliminated it from the marketplace." He said the program carried with it a considerable risk for fraud and put Freddie Mac out in front of the private sector with a risky new product. "Countrywide (who has reason to lie) swears no one else has their program," he pointed out. (Countrywide's SISA program was called Fast and Easy.) "Others say it's much more pervasive. It's hard to know who's telling the truth."

Andrukonis agreed with Bisenius, who had suggested there should be a formal airing of the issues in the SISA program. After a formal review, though, Freddie Mac dove deep into the SISA pool. In 2005, Andrukonis was fired.[30]

In 2005 and 2006, Freddie Mac's net income was stable at $2 billion, while top managers reaped huge financial rewards. Syron's compensation package for the two years totaled $23.2 million, while chief operating officer Eugene McQuade raked in $13.4 million.

Not surprisingly, similar conflicts occurred at Fannie. One conflict started after chief financial officer Robert Levin proposed to Fannie's board in January 2006 that the company expand its participation in the subprime market. The board approved the expansion.[31] In the summer of 2006, board chairman Stephen Ashley introduced Fannie's new chief risk officer, Enrico Dallavecchia. Ashley told the board of its plans to expand its subprime lending business and to "think differently and creatively about risk," assuring the board that Dallavecchia "was not brought on board to be a business dampener."[32]

Fannie, in fact, had expanded its riskiest business with vigor, ramping up loan purchases in 2006 to $516 billion. The majority—$289 billion or 56 percent—were risky mortgage products: $65 billion (13%) with loan-to-value ratios of 95 percent or more, $77 billion (15 percent) in interest-only loans, and $144 billion without full documentation, making them Alt-A loans.[33] In addition, Fannie purchased $36 billion in private-label subprime securities and another $12 billion in private-label Alt-A. That represented $337 billion in support of risky lending in a single year.[34]

While profits declined to $4 billion in 2006 from $6 billion in 2005, Fannie's top officials lined their pockets. Chairman Daniel Mudd reaped $24.4 million in two years. Levin, $15.5 million.[35]

In the summer of 2007, as the private-label market was starting to crash, Fannie Mae adopted a five-year strategic plan to regain its dominance of the market from private-label securitizers. This could be achieved by "moving deeper into the credit pool to serve a large and growing part of the mortgage market," according to the plan.[36]

Meanwhile, Dallavecchia was becoming more concerned about the cuts for the budget for overseeing risk that were occurring at the same time Fannie was moving ahead to take on more credit risk. He wrote on July 16, 2007, to chief operating officer Michael Williams to tell him that Fannie's risk controls were the weakest he had "ever witnessed." It was becoming clear that "people don't care about the [risk] function or they don't get it."[37] Dallavecchia also sent out a blistering e-mail the same day to Mudd, saying "I can only infer malice" from Williams and others who are slashing his budget by 16 percent as he is trying to ramp up credit risk oversight. "Do I look so stupid?"

Mudd, who was none too happy with the e-mail, shot back an e-mail message blasting Dallavecchia for using e-mail to "vent" and suggested Dallavecchia needed to address his concerns "man to man" with his peers rather than shoot complaints to Mudd to "carry messages" for him to his colleagues. "Please come and see me today face to face," Mudd wrote.[38]

Mudd's e-mail response would appear to be disingenuous if he was the one who ordered the 16 percent budget cuts for risk management, which is not an unreasonable assumption. Further, Dallavecchia, while violating protocol, would appear to have been right to go to the person he thought was the source of the cut, given that he considered the matter urgent. Thus, Mudd's impugning Dallavecchia's courage may have been an attempt to cloud the issue. Further, by asking

Dallavecchia to see him "face to face," Mudd was taking the entire conversation offline from e-mails.

The staff of the Financial Crisis Inquiry Commission (FCIC), who retrieved these e-mails, found no further evidence of concerns by Dallavecchia about having the resources to do his job of risk oversight. Dallavecchia downplayed the e-mails in an interview with the FCIC staff, saying he was tired and upset and that he overstated his concern in those e-mails.[39] The FCIC, which published audio recordings of hundreds of its interviews after releasing its final report, did not post the audio for its interview with Dallavecchia.

Fannie Mae's expanded risky lending in 2007 paid off for Mudd, who received $11.6 million in compensation, and for chief financial officer Levin, who pocketed $7 million. Fannie was not so lucky. It lost $2.1 billion.

GAMBLING

The $3.6 trillion hidden gamble in subprime, Alt-A, and lending with low or no down payments at Fannie and Freddie from 2002 to 2006 turned the already opaque GSEs into black boxes. Further, all this risky activity was occurring at high leverage ratios (40 to 1 for its retained loans securities investments and 222 to 1 for its securities guarantees); the two GSEs were not so much sound financial institutions as they were carefully orchestrated casinos where risky lending and leveraging led to handsome rewards for the people running the show. Fannie and Freddie were not the only black box casinos building up risks in the financial world that would threaten to bring it down; but they were the largest and had the most impact on the markets.

Could there have been $700 billion in subprime CDOs without Fannie and Freddie being the single largest buyer of AAA-tranches of the underlying subprime mortgage-backed securities? Clearly, that market would have been smaller. And would companies that took on trillions of dollars of risk by entering into credit default swaps as the protection provider have done so if they knew that the level of risky lending in the market was more than double what they thought it was? Presumably, less credit protection would have been sold.

The creation of so much additional risky lending by Fannie and Freddie—far more in volume than was originated for private label—also increased the weight of the correction as so many more homes ended up in default and added to the crush on home values. This, in turn, increased the losses in private-label securities and their derivatives.

One can make a powerful case that Wall Street bears more of the blame for the financial crisis than Fannie and Freddie because investment bankers ginned up fast-money schemes with CDOs that flooded money into subprime lending when any prudent player would have been pulling back. In the process, Wall Street put less sophisticated investors, CDO counterparties, taxpayers, and ultimately the entire economy at risk. Yet the size and scope of those excesses in private-label securitization and CDOs, described in subsequent chapters, would have been dramatically smaller without Fannie and Freddie as the largest driving force behind them.

Generating titanic risks in the system was not the only harm caused by the GSEs. The casinos of Fannie Mae and Freddie Mac fostered a culture of fraud that handsomely rewarded the managers at the top. When Brendsel was forced out as chairman at Freddie Mac in 2003 after OFHEO found the company had cooked its books to boost bonuses, he walked away with a compensation package of $24.35 million. Brendsel's political clout had saved him from a more disgraceful and less compensated exit. He had contributed a total of $30,500 to candidates in the 2002 election cycle.[40]

Compared to Fannie Mae chairman and CEO Franklin Raines, Brendsel was a piker. The OFHEO examination reports in 2004 and 2006 found that Fannie Mae had manipulated earnings to the penny to get the maximum amount of bonuses from 1998 to 2003. House Subcommittee on Capital Markets chairman Richard Baker, Louisiana Republican, revealed at a hearing on October 4, 2004, that this manipulation had contributed to $245 million in compensation for senior executives over a six-year period.[41] Of this total, $92 million (38%) went to Raines, $52 million of it in bonuses tied to the manipulation of earnings.

With the accounting scandals, the first glimmer of the massive calamity that was sown in the provisions of the GSE Act of 1992 had been revealed for all to see. The particular structure put in place was no accident. It was an intentional design with a specific purpose in mind—and it was not safety and soundness.

Given that the "house"—Fannie and Freddie—eventually went bust, the cost of these casinos was passed on to American taxpayers, with a peak at $151 billion and expected to rise higher.

A window into the "logic" behind the peculiar combination of low capital, weak regulation, and heavy-handed credit allocation contained in the GSE Act was opened inadvertently by the most visible defender of Fannie and Freddie in Congress—Barney Frank, the Massachusetts Democrat who for years was the ranking minority member and then the chairman of the House Financial Services Committee.

The revealing comments came at a hearing on September 25, 2003, after OFHEO had recently released the results of its examination of the accounting scandals at Freddie Mac. Maryland Republican Roscoe Bartlett had just suggested that Congress should allow the regulator of Fannie and Freddie to set capital standards for the GSEs just like bank regulators have the authority to raise and lower capital standards for banks and thrifts.

Frank objected to Bartlett's comparison of Fannie and Freddie with banks and thrifts, noting that the banking and thrift regulators do not have affordable housing as a mission. "I do not want the same kind of focus on safety and soundness that we have" with federal banking regulators, he said. "I want to *roll the dice* [emphasis added] a little bit more in this situation towards subsidized housing."

A string of top executives from Jim Johnson to Daniel Mudd at Fannie and Leland Brendsel to Richard Syron at Freddie had rolled and would continue rolling the dice.

In short, Frank was arguing that because Fannie and Freddie have affordable housing goals, they should have weaker safety and soundness regulation and lower capital standards so that they can maximize the amount of affordable lending they can accomplish on a given level of capital.

Of course, as everyone—even Frank—would eventually realize, the paltry statutory capital requirements at Fannie and Freddie—which OFHEO could not raise without new Congressional authority—hastened the GSEs' demise.[42]

In agreeing back in 1992 to thin capital requirements, a weak prudential regulatory scheme, a green light to run its own investment portfolios, and affordable housing goals that could steadily rise, Fannie and Freddie had inadvertently entered into a suicide pact. Along the way, however, a lot of people would get very rich greasing the skids for their demise.

5

The Rise of Private Label

As the financial world came tumbling down in 2008, crashing the economy and life savings in the process, the man and woman on Main Street were asking pointed and angry questions. What happened? Who caused it? Why did it happen?

The rise of private-label mortgage-backed securities provides some of the answers to those questions. These securitizations emerged as an extension of the expertise gained with the broader class of asset-backed securities. This class of credit assets includes auto loans, credit card receivables, student loans, and even small business loans. Wall Street investment banks began turning them into securities in the early 1990s.

The private mortgage-backed securities had a hard competitive market reality that the general class of asset-backed securities did not have. Private mortgage securitizers had two huge competitors by the names of Fannie Mae and Freddie Mac with an implicit government backing. These two government-sponsored enterprises, or GSEs, were not, in the beginning, the leviathans they later became. There was plenty of room for private mortgage securities to innovate, grow, experiment, fail, and start all over again. Most importantly, there were large segments of the population that could be reached with credit provided through private-label securitization, including subprime borrowers and self-employed borrowers.

Before there was securitization of subprime and Alt-A, there were specialty finance firms that entered this market. Typically they focused on borrowers with credit scores between 620 and 660—a segment of the credit market known as A-minus. There were also borrowers with credit (scores above 660) who could not document their income or who had irregular patterns of income. Alternative A mortgage products were developed to provide funding to households in this category.

In the early days, the subprime lenders were conservative in their underwriting. Finance companies like Household Financial, Avco Financial Services, Transamerica Financial Services, and Beneficial Finance required down payments of 20 percent, at a minimum, and usually only lent to borrowers who were A-minus or B-plus credits. "They were priced properly, at least 300 and typically 500 basis points above Fannie and Freddie, and we had essentially no problems with those loans because of the equity involved," according to Tom LaMalfa, a veteran mortgage industry analyst.

Subprime borrowers paid interest rates of 9 percent to 12 percent when Fannie and Freddie were offering 6 percent mortgages. With these higher rates, the lenders were pricing the higher risk of borrowers with poorer credit quality.

The loans financed by these early players were not securitized but held in the portfolios of the finance companies that originated them or sold to investors who were looking for higher-yield, lower-grade mortgages. LaMalfa looks back at this era as one built on the gold standard in lending to subprime borrowers. "There is no doubt in my mind that these lenders had it right and they weren't in competition with Fannie and Freddie to secure these types of loans," LaMalfa said.[1]

In the early 1990s, private-label securitization of subprime, Alt-A, and jumbo prime loans was just beginning. By 1995, it was still a very small market with issuances at $49 billion.[2] By contrast, the same year, Ginnie Mae, Fannie, and Freddie guaranteed $126.4 billion in mortgage securities.[3] Within the private-label segment in 1995, subprime represented $18 billion, while Alt-A was a mere $498 million, with jumbo prime completing the picture at $26 billion.

Subprime took off in the late 1990s with the advent of the subprime wholesale lender who originated subprime loans to be securitized and sold to investors. Subprime securitizations hit $57 billion in 1997, then $76 billion in 1998, before falling back in 1999 and 2000 as investors fled high-yield bonds in the aftermath of the Russian bond crisis and the collapse of the hedge fund Long-Term Capital Management.[4]

Fannie and Freddie entered the subprime market in 1996 with new mortgage products that, though they were not identified as such, were, in fact, subprime, according to LaMalfa. Fannie Mae introduced the Flex 97, a 3 percent down mortgage, and the Community Home Buyer's Mortgage, which was aimed at renters who had never owned a home, especially minorities and younger households. By the year

2000, both Fannie and Freddie had introduced zero down payment programs.

The strong push in this direction by Fannie and Freddie also led to the mispricing of subprime loans, both by the GSEs and by the wholesale subprime lenders, according to LaMalfa. By *mispricing*, he means that the interest rate charged the borrower plus additional points, fees and charges were all set too low to cover the delinquency and default risks that came with the loan.

"Fannie and Freddie got more aggressive as we moved into the [2000s]. They kept pushing the subprime lenders further out on the risk curve," LaMalfa said. As the two agencies took on more lower credit risks, moving down from A-minus to B-plus to B, private-sector lenders were driven lower on the food chain to B, B-minus and C credits.

The same evolution occurred with high loan-to-value mortgages, too. As Fannie and Freddie moved up the volume of loans they purchased that represented 100 percent of the value of the home, the private market moved into more exotic loan products, such as interest-only, or IO, loans. An ever-creative market greatly expanded the menu of nontraditional mortgage products, with the private sector leading the way and Fannie and Freddie one step behind (and occasionally in the lead) in a battle for market share and to meet their ever-higher affordable housing goals.

Stated income loans became very popular with investors who bought and flipped houses, as well as with second homebuyers. One product was called the stated income, stated asset, or SISA, where borrowers stated their income and assets and were not required to prove either with documentation—which often meant these were "liar loans." There were also no income, no-asset loans or NINAs, in which borrowers did not have to even state income or assets. Then there were the NINJA loans for borrowers who not only stated no income and no assets, but also who had no job.

Although it did not start out that way, perhaps the most lethal of all was the pay option adjustable-rate mortgage or option ARM—the specialty of Golden West Financial in Oakland, California. These loans permitted borrowers to choose between several payment choices. One was a minimum payment that, depending on the interest rate prevailing at the time, would not be sufficient to cover the interest costs for that month. These would increase the principal of the mortgage. The process was called *negative amortization*. A loan is said to amortize, or slowly pay off, when a portion of each payment goes to pay down the principal. Over time, the amount of the payment that goes to pay down the principal rises and the amount that goes to pay interest declines.

When Golden West began making these loans, they were to higher-income borrowers with a great deal of equity, and the minimum payment was not emphasized. Over time, as more competitors offered these loans, they were marketed to lower-income borrowers with less equity as an affordability product. It was difficult to securitize option ARMs, so they were generally kept on the books by their originators like Golden West, but also Washington Mutual and Countrywide and Indymac.

THE REFINANCE BOOM

Beginning in 2002, there was a wave of cash-out refinancing, along with a surge in second mortgage and home equity lines of credit (HELOCs) that began to wipe out the equity of homes all across the nation. While few noticed, prudent mortgages were being converted into non-prime mortgages and, in the process were making household finances and bank balance sheets more and more vulnerable to any sharp correction in home prices and almost any other economic shock. Fannie and Freddie led the way because of their advantage in 30-year fixed-rate mortgages.

The "refi" boom and rash of home equity lending took off after the Fed lowered interest rates during the recession of 2000 and 2001 and in the economic aftermath of 9/11 and kept the key target for the federal funds rate below 2 percent for more than three years. The federal funds rate is the interest rate at which private banks lend their balances held at the Federal Reserve to other banks, usually overnight. The pace of equity extraction was dizzying, according to a study by former Fed chairman Greenspan and James Kennedy.[5]

Starting at $613 billion in 2002, home equity extraction rose to $914 billion in 2005—that is, homeowners reduced the equity in their homes by borrowing more money against home values. There was a total home equity extraction of $3.08 trillion in only four years! This enormous amount of equity extraction was a factor in the pace of economic growth during those years. As underwriting standards eroded and credit became easier and easier to get, households showed little restraint in their accumulation of debt. The average equity extraction of $700 billion per year from 2001 to 2005 was nearly four times the annual average pace of $180 billion during the prior decade.

The home had become an ATM.

By 2009, the vast majority of Americans would see the equity they had in their homes either vanish or decline to a very low level, while people who bought at the top of the housing boom cycle would find themselves upside down in their mortgages, sometimes at such levels that some made the strategic decision to walk away from a home and mortgage even when they could afford to make the payments. Greenspan and Kennedy calculated that four-fifths of the increase in mortgage debt from 1990 to 2005 was for discretionary purposes and only one-fifth was to purchase a home.[6]

Lower interest rates were also a boon to the mortgage industry and led to a flood of mortgage credit that households had never seen before. The prior peak in mortgage originations was $1.45 trillion in 1998.[7] After the Fed lowered interest rates, the volume of mortgage originations doubled in 2001 to $2.2 trillion, then shot up to $3.9 trillion in 2003 at the height of the refi frenzy. After falling to $2.9 trillion in 2004, volume in 2005 rose to $3.2 trillion with the introduction of exotic new adjustable-rate mortgages. Originations fell back slightly in 2006 to $2.98 trillion. In 2007, volume fell to $2.4 trillion as the mortgage market melted down by mid-year.

It was a vicious circle. The flood of funds into mortgages brought in more buyers and speculators who drove up the price of homes, which made more securitizations more attractive, which, in turn, pushed up home prices. There was clearly the frenzy of a classic bubble.

The securitization of mortgages grew even more spectacularly during the housing and mortgage booms, as more and more funding flowed to homeowners through intermediaries from investors while less of the funding came from banks and thrifts that wanted to keep the mortgages on their balance sheets.

Fannie, Freddie, Ginnie and private-label securitizations mushroomed as the primary source of mortgage funding, pushing aside portfolio lending by banks and thrifts. The prior peak in securitizations was $930 billion in 1998.[8] In 2000, it hit $1.35 trillion. Overall securitization issuances peaked in 2003 at $2.7 trillion. Volume fell with the end of the refi boom in 2004 to $1.9 trillion, rising to $2.2 trillion in 2005 and remaining near $2 trillion in both 2006 and 2007.

In 2004, securitizations by Fannie, Freddie, and Ginnie Mae were outstripped for the first time by private-label mortgage-backed securitization. This was due to the shift away from fixed-rate mortgages to adjustable-rate mortgages, prompted by higher interest rates. Adjustable-rate mortgages typically offer lower initial rates.

The private-label industry began to take off in 2002 after new bank capital standards[9] made private-label securities just as attractive for banks to hold as Fannie, Freddie, and Ginnie securities. Thanks to new standards, banks only had to hold 1.6 percent capital against the AAA and AA tranches of private-label securities. Previously the regulated depository institutions were required to hold 4 percent capital against both whole mortgages and private-label mortgage-backed securities.

Fannie and Freddie adamantly opposed this change; but, in this case, their famed lobbying influence fell short with banking regulators.

Moody's Investors went on the record with its doubts about having credit rating agencies play a role in determining capital standards. In a comment letter in March 2000, the ratings agency recommended to the Basel Committee on Bank Supervision that any role for ratings agencies be done only on an "interim" basis—only until banks could fine tune internal ratings systems. "The credit rating agency industry is subject to moral hazard. Every rating agency has a business incentive to assign higher ratings to issuers, who are free to choose among agencies," Moody's stated.[10] "Pressure on issuers to 'shop' for the highest rating is increased by their use in regulation. Such practices undermine the reliability of ratings over time." This prophecy proved to be true.

The U.S. banking regulators ignored warnings and gave a role to the credit rating agencies in the new capital standard that went into effect at the beginning of 2002. In that first year, there was an immediate upsurge in the share of private-label securitizations from 9 percent to 22.3 percent. Total issuance of mortgage bonds rose from $267 billion to $414 billion.[11] Private-label issuance rose in 2003 to $586 billion.

While some have attributed the surge in private-label securitizations to the fact that banks could retain the highest-rated tranches of private-label securities at a lower capital risk weighting, the share of private-label securities held by banks actually declined in the years after 2001. As total outstanding issuances of private label securities tripled in size, from $414 billion in 2002 to $1.191 trillion in 2005, the share held by commercial banks and thrifts fell from 20 percent to 15 percent.[12]

A big chunk of these private-label bonds were being purchased by Fannie and Freddie to meet their affordable housing goals and to boost their overall profitability. Indeed, as private-label securities took off, Fannie, Freddie, and the Federal Home Loan Banks maintained a steady one-third share in total outstanding private-label securities from 2002 to 2005.[13]

The biggest driver for new private-label securitizations after 2002 was, in fact, demand for subprime and Alt-A collateral as the raw material for creating new issues of collateralized debt obligations, or CDOs. From 1998 to 2000, for example, single-family mortgage CDOs were only 8 percent, or $10 billion of a $120 billion market in CDOs, according to Moody's.[14]

By 2004, annual CDO volume totaled $100 billion, with single-family mortgage CDOs totaling 40 percent, or $40 billion. While CDOs and CDOs squared volume represented only 1.3 percent of the total mortgage market in 2004, they represented about 5 percent of private MBS issuance volume. More importantly, 78 percent of all private-label securities tranches rated below A made their way into CDOs.

Meanwhile, Fannie and Freddie were the chief buyers of the AAA tranches, while some banks placed CDOs in off-balance sheet Structured Investment Vehicles, or SIVs, where they did not have to have capital backing by the bank and where they were hidden in the shadow banking system.[15]

Fannie and Freddie acquired $530 billion in subprime private-label securities from 2000 to 2007, according to calculations by Edward Pinto, the former chief risk officer for Fannie Mae.[16] (See Table 4.1 in Chapter 4.) The purchases increased every year until 2006, and then fell in 2007. The GSEs showed a similar pattern of purchases for private-label Alt-A securities, shelling out $154 billion for them between 2002 and 2007.[17]

In 2004, the momentum shifted heavily in favor of private-label securitizations and away from Fannie and Freddie. That year, private issuance shot up to $864 billion, and the private-label market share jumped to 46 percent of $1.9 trillion in new mortgage bonds.

In 2005, the previously unthinkable occurred as private label garnered the dominant share with $1.2 trillion in securitizations, 55 percent of the $2.2 trillion securitization market. Then in 2006, private label's share rose to 56 percent, with $1.15 trillion in business compared to total securitizations of $2 trillion. With its collapse in mid-2007, private label reduced its share for the year to 38 percent, $707 billion of $1.9 trillion. There was virtually no private-label issuance in 2008.

MORE HELIUM FOR THE HOUSING BUBBLE

The housing bubble developed slowly over a long period of time. For example, national median prices for single-family homes languished for many years following the 1990–1991 recession. At the end of 1991, the national median home price index was $101,000[18] for conventional, conforming mortgages backed by Fannie Mae and Freddie Mac for either a home purchase or mortgage refinancing.

The government's median home price index was known as the OFHEO Home Price Index after the abbreviation for the name of the regulator of Fannie and Freddie—the Office of Federal Housing Enterprise Oversight.[19] In September 2008, it became the FHFA Home Price Index, reflecting the new name of the new regulator, the Federal Housing Finance Agency.

The OFHEO index has historically been less volatile than other indexes, such as the S&P Case-Shiller Index, which tracks only mortgages obtained to purchase a home (and not refinancings) and only for selected metropolitan areas, many of which have higher levels of jumbo loans with balances above the limits set by Fannie and Freddie.

By the end of 1996, the OFHEO median home price had risen to $116,000. From there, the pace accelerated to reach a median of $134,640 by 1999. The bubble gained more strength in 2000, jumping 7 percent in a single year to $143,960. By 2004, it was $194,490. In 2005, median prices soared 9.3 percent to $212,550. In 2006, the pace slowed but median still rose to $219,980.

While housing economists talked nervously about a soft landing for the housing market, the OFHEO median price rose to $224,000 in the second quarter of 2007, and then headed down as the mortgage meltdown curtailed the flood of mortgage financing that had driven the bubble. During the 10 years of the housing bubble—1997 to 2007—median home prices had nearly doubled.

During the 1990s, homes became increasingly affordable as prices rose slowly and incomes rose. In 1992, for example, 54 percent of the homes were affordable to a family earning the local median income, according to the Housing Opportunity Index developed by the National Association of Home Builders and Wells Fargo. This index measured how much of the median price home in a given area an average income household could afford if they provided a 10 percent down payment and took out a 30-year fixed-rate mortgage.

By early 1999, 70 percent of homes were affordable. Remarkably, the rise in home prices in the early part of the 2000s did not drive down affordability, mostly because interest rates fell and remained low.

During 2004, however, interest rates began a steady rise, and the impact on affordability, when combined with higher home prices, was striking. The share of affordable homes slipped from 61 percent at the start of the year to 52 percent at the end of 2004. This is also the year that homeownership rates stopped rising. By the end of 2005, the share of affordable homes fell to 41 percent, and then in the third quarter of 2006 to 40 percent, the lowest level in the NAHB-Wells Fargo series. This is also the point at which housing prices peaked and began to head down.

DICIER MORTGAGES

Low interest rates shared blame with weakening lending standards as a driver of the housing bubble from 2001 to 2003. But from 2004 forward, given that interest rates were rising, the blame shifts almost entirely to falling credit standards. Low interest rates were still a factor, however, as a range of new mortgage products offered low initial interest rates as teasers—the most notorious of which were known as *2/28s*. The borrower got a low teaser rate for two years, then the rate adjusted sharply higher in the third year. Increasingly, lenders qualified borrowers for a mortgage on the initial interest rate and not on the higher adjustable rate that would kick in later.

The federal banking regulators were slow to spell out the problems with new loan products and to set guidelines for lenders who offered nontraditional products. The first warning came in May 2005 on home equity lending by depository institutions.[20] The regulators warned that lenders might not fully understand the potential risks.

Yet the regulators did not issue proposed guidance[21] on nontraditional mortgages until December 2005, after these products became dominant in the marketplace. The regulators suggested that borrowers be qualified under nontraditional mortgages at the expected adjusted mortgage rate. The feds warned about layering risk for subprime borrowers, adding credit-weakening features on top of one another—for example, by allowing borrowers with low credit scores to state but not document their income.

As soon as the proposed guidance hit the streets, a chorus of opposition arose. Countrywide was among the stiffest of opponents, arguing in one investor presentation that if the guidance had been in place earlier, it would have had to refuse 89 percent of loan applications in 2006 and 83 percent in 2005, representing $138 billion in mortgages.[22] Some members of Congress, too, fiercely opposed the proposed guidance.

Fed Governor Susan Bies recalls that when she testified about the regulation on Capitol Hill, she was told "that we were going to deny the dream of homeownership to Americans if we put this new stronger standard in place."[23]

Final guidance was not issued until September 2006.[24] By then, millions of borrowers had already taken on the whole range of adjustable-rate mortgage products that would later blow up on balance sheets across the globe, and consumers were already moving away from what would become known just a year later as toxic mortgages. Among these were $255 billion in option ARMs in 2006 alone.[25]

The mortgage industry had slipped into a dream world in which hard realities dared not intrude. There was an inordinate level of confidence, not only in the quality of mortgages that had been underwritten but also in the modeling of potential defaults in a downturn.

Wall Street was confident that its sophisticated computer modeling and complex deals were engineered to withstand the highest level of historic losses. Unfortunately, the modeling did not take into account severe home price declines of the Great Depression. Importantly, there was very little data on the performance of the increasingly exotic mortgages that were being packaged into securities by Wall Street wizards.

Furthermore, everyone on Wall Street was relying on the same computer model. If it turned out to be flawed, they would all be equally unaware of lurking risks, and an unseen risk would bring them all down. The model of choice was the Gaussian copula model developed by David Li in 2000, when he worked at J. P. Morgan.[26] A *copula* model in statistics is designed to measure the behavior of two or more variables. In the case of structured finance, it is constructed to measure the degree to which one tranche or slice in a deal of mortgage-backed securities is related to the others. In an instance in which the lowest-mezzanine tranche of BBB-minus were to lose x amount of value, the model could predict how much in y value would be lost by the highest-rated AAA tranche.

Rather than rely on historical default data for loan performance by product type to gauge the relationships, Li instead used market data on the prices of credit default swaps tied to the loans. Credit default swaps, in this instance, are contracts between parties where one is selling credit protection and another is buying it on a referenced tranche of a mortgage-backed security. As it turned out, that correlation in a downturn was far greater than anticipated and closer to 100 percent in some instances. When lower-rated tranches of subprime securitization deals crashed, the highest-rated tranches were not far behind.

The ability of the private-label securitization market to eclipse Fannie and Freddie was seen by some as a game changer. "I do believe it is a permanent change," said Alec Crawford, head of agency mortgage-backed securities strategy at Greenwich Capital Markets in Greenwich, Connecticut. "There may continue to be a tug-of-war back and forth between agency mortgages and non-agency mortgages, but at this point what's happened is innovation on the non-agency side has accelerated to such a point that it's going to take the agencies a while to catch up."[27]

Super confidence in the future of private-label issuers was also the consensus view of the Council to Shape Change, a blue-ribbon mortgage industry panel of 19 experts that published a report[28] in August 2006. "It is unlikely that Freddie Mac and Fannie Mae will return to their former position of dominance within the industry," the report stated.

The newly achieved predominance of private label, however, rested on a rickety structure. Too much of the surge in private label was gained entirely from mortgage products that offered low initial interest rates. Most prominently, these included interest only or IO mortgages, which provided yet more traps for borrowers. These were originally designed for high-net-worth individuals but began to be marketed as affordability products for lower-income borrowers. When these began to flourish, some borrowers did not take much notice that the minimum payment was driving up the principal or that their payment and level of principal were tethered to an indicator that was obscure to most borrowers—the London Interbank Offered Rate.

The shift to dicier mortgage products was the underlying current that carried private label to the top.

Private-label securitized mortgages were gaining market share with mortgage products that, while they might be appropriate for some borrowers, were decidedly inappropriate for others. The mix of private-label issuance shifted dramatically from early 2003, when jumbo prime issuance was dominant, grabbing a 44 percent share of all private-label mortgage-backed securities.[29]

Subprime and Alt-A combined rose from 41 percent of private-label issuance in early 2003 to 56 percent in early 2006. Subprime's share of securitization increased from 8.5 percent to 22 percent. Alt-A's share rose from 12 percent to 34 percent.

The remaining increase in volume came mostly from second-lien mortgages.[30] Indeed, many second mortgages and home equity lines of credit (HELOCs) were, in fact, subprime in characteristics, and these mortgages proved eventually to be the weakest link in the mortgage chain.[31] The share of jumbo prime fell to 14 percent in 2006.

Jumbo prime mortgages represented a market that was tested over many years and one in which losses were historically extremely low. Although both subprime and Alt-A had more than a decade of delinquency and default performance to give comfort to investors, there was little historic performance data on the increasingly risky new loan products that were gaining market share and on the growing practice of layering risk in mortgage product offerings.

Private-label subprime and Alt-A in the first quarter of 2006 came close to eclipsing the total $204 billion in securitizations backed by Fannie and Freddie. What was not clear in the data, however, was that an increasing share of the loan purchases by Fannie and Freddie were not conventional prime mortgages but were also actually subprime or Alt-A.

While private-label issuers were pumping out lemons, so were Fannie and Freddie. The two GSEs were also going after adjustable-rate mortgages instead of sticking to the fixed-rate type on which they had a clear pricing advantage.

CENTRAL ROLE OF COUNTRYWIDE

At the height of the private-label market surge, a handful of issuers emerged as the dominant players, led by pacesetter Countrywide Financial Corporation, Calabasas, California. In 2006, Countrywide issued $76 billion in private-label bonds—far ahead of No. 2, Seattle-based Washington Mutual, at $39 billion.[32] "Countrywide is emerging as the private-sector alternative to Fannie Mae and Freddie Mac," said research analyst Mike McMahon at the time.[33]

Countrywide was not just the largest lender; it was still an independent mortgage company not affiliated with a major bank. Its survival as an independent has to be attributed to the unique drive and passion of Angelo Mozilo, its co-founder and chairman. In an interview for *Mortgage Banking* in 2002, Mozilo described his deep commitment to the company.[34] Is it fair, I asked him, to say that Countrywide has a passion for the mortgage banking business that does not seem to exist with the same intensity at its competitors?

"Yes," he replied. He continued:

> I think there's a reason for it. First of all, we gave birth to this business. This is our baby. Secondly, we were not caretakers. We created it, grew

it. Every brick that makes up this company, we set ourselves. So we have a sense of ownership and, as you say, passion for this company, for what it does. That is going to be difficult to replicate.

Every other mortgage company that we compete against was acquired. It was not incepted by the people who are running it now. They weren't there. They didn't go through the birthing process. I think your attitude toward your own children carries with it a greater degree of passion than does your attitude toward the children of others. I think what the competition has is the children of others. They bought company upon company, and that's why I think you sense a passion in this company. We call it concern. You can call it passionate concern or fire in the belly.

In 2006, Countrywide Financial was the largest issuer of mortgage-backed securities in the jumbo prime, Alt-A, and home-equity loan categories. The company, however, ranked fourth in private-label subprime issuance, behind subprime specialists Option One and New Century, both based in Irvine, California, followed by Washington Mutual.

The Securities and Exchange Commission (SEC) found Countrywide's subprime and Alt-A lending reckless and charged the company misled investors by not revealing the extent of risky lending it had done. The SEC also investigated Mozilo for insider trading because he was said to have frequently cashed out holdings for more than a year ahead of Countrywide's near-collapse in August 2007. In October 2010, Mozilo agreed to pay a record $22.5 million penalty for an individual to settle charges he misled investors and another $45 million to "disgorge" parts of his "ill-gotten gains" for insider trading and violating disclosure laws.[35] Even so, Mozilo paid only $20 million of the $67.5 million payment. This was only a fraction of the $521.5 million in compensation he earned from 2000 to 2008, when he left the company.[36]

The SEC charged that Mozilo knew Countrywide was being reckless and was trying to make sure he cashed out before everything crashed. In one e-mail on September 26, 2006, for example, after a meeting on the risks in the pay-option ARM loan portfolio, Mozilo confided, "We have no way, with any reasonable certainty, to assess the real risk of holding those loans on our balance sheet."

Mozilo pointed out that the only historical data on option ARMs came from World Savings (Golden West) of Oakland, California, which relied on higher levels of equity rather than higher credit scores as a bulwark against losses. "The bottom line is that we are flying blind on how these loans will perform in a stressed environment of higher unemployment, reduced values and slowing home sales."[37]

In an e-mail on April 16, 2006, Mozilo also faulted the practice of combining a second mortgage for 20 percent of the price of a home with a first subprime mortgage of 80 percent—a position completely at odds with his call in 2003 for 100 percent financing to expand home-ownership.[38] "In all my years in the business I have never seen a more toxic prduct [*sic*]. It's not only subordinate to the first, but the first is subprime. In addition the FICOs are below 600, below 500 and some below 400," he wrote. "With real estate values coming down . . . the product will become increasingly worse," he warned, and called for higher FICO scores to qualify for the product.

In a lawsuit filed in late 2010 against Bank of America, the acquirer of Countrywide,[39] Allstate sought to recover losses on $700 million in securities backed by Countrywide-originated loans.[40] Allstate charged that in 2003 Mozilo set the bar extraordinarily high when he decided the company would seek to capture 30 percent of the mortgage origination and was so determined to reach this goal that he cast aside virtually any concerns about credit quality. In 2003, Countrywide had 11.3 percent of national mortgage origination volume. The company's share of originations peaked at 16.8 percent in 2007.[41] David Sambol, who had been president and chief operating officer in 2004, became managing director for business segment operations and was given the task of sharply ramping up Countrywide's business.[42]

Countrywide also set a policy of matching products offered by competitors, according to Allstate's complaint. "To the extent more that 5 percent of the [mortgage] market was originating a particular product . . . then Countrywide would originate it," a former Countrywide finance executive has said. It was "the proverbial race to the bottom."[43]

Just like Fannie and Freddie, Countrywide began to classify loans as prime that were, in fact, subprime. According to the SEC, the lender included in the prime category loans with credit scores below 620— which was the lower segment of subprime.[44] The underwriting process stressed how to grant exceptions to approve loans under existing guidelines. Allstate charged that the exception processing system "was known to approve virtually every borrower and loan profile with a pricing add-on feature that increased the cost of the loan to cover the risk." The "Price Any Loan" system[45] of exceptions represented as much as 23 percent of Countrywide's origination volume, according to the SEC.

The Allstate complaint reported that more than 30 percent of the loans backing some of the certificates it bought as long-term investments were delinquent or had already defaulted. Some loan pools had delinquencies approaching 60 percent.[46]

The excesses at Countrywide were mirrored in one way or another at many of the other companies that were among the top 10 originators in 2006. The list included Washington Mutual, Seattle; GMAC-RFC, Minneapolis; Wells Fargo Home Mortgage, Des Moines, Iowa; and Indymac,[47] Pasadena, California. Wall Street investment banking firms—Bear Stearns, Lehman Brothers, and Goldman Sachs—occupied most of the remaining top positions.

The Wall Street firms, not content with obtaining originations from other parties, had acquired mortgage origination and servicing platforms.

EARLY INSIDER WARNINGS

As early as mid-2005, as a boom in credit transfer was roiling across the globe and reports of increasingly reckless lending began to surface, some investors began to worry about the quality of mortgage originations and the potential for another derivatives catastrophe like the one that brought down Long-Term Capital Management in 1998.

In a phone conference with investors, top executives at Saxon Capital, a real estate investment trust, or REIT, based in Glen Ellen, Virginia, talked openly about their expectations that excessive risk taking then occurring was creating "a perfect storm" that would likely lead to a "credit event" that could rattle global markets like they did in 1998.

Saxon originated mostly subprime mortgages, kept some in their portfolio, and sold others into the secondary market—but was growing increasingly wary about keeping loans on its balance sheet, according to notes of the conference call taken at the time by Mike Shedlock, then an advisor for SitkaPacific Capital Management in Sonoma, California.[48]

A Saxon official explained that the company had previously offered stated income loans only to borrowers with a down payment so they would have skin in the game. But now Saxon was going to offer 100 percent loan-to-value stated income loans, or "liar loans," because that was what customers were demanding and what the competition was offering.

"As long as the market is willing to provide that credit" then Saxon will offer it, the official said. "We have no intentions of putting those loans in our portfolio," he said. "We are going to pass them through to other investors." Thus, Saxon would only originate such loans if they could be sold to either Fannie Mae, Freddie Mac, or into pools for private-label securitization.

By not retaining the loans in portfolio, Saxon officials felt the company was putting itself in a position to weather the storm without neglecting profit opportunities. One unidentified analyst on the call was perplexed. "Since I have known you, you have been bearish on the [mortgage] industry," the analyst said. "Now you are saying I want to be more like people offering products that are unsustainable. I am struggling with that."

The Saxon official reassured the analyst. "The only difference is that I do not intend to put those in my portfolio. And the day that I can't sell these to someone else is the day I stop offering them."

While mortgage lenders talked openly and cavalierly of a "perfect storm" for bad credit, the Federal Open Market Committee (FOMC) of the Federal Reserve System was holding one of its periodic meetings on June 29–30, 2005, to consider the direction of monetary policy. At the meeting, there was a presentation[49] by senior economists from the Fed on the extent to which there might be a housing bubble in the economy and what the Fed might do about it.[50]

Fed economist Joshua Gallin told the FOMC that home prices were overvalued by 20 percent compared to rents, based on the historical relationship between the two. San Francisco Fed economist John Williams pointed out that a 20 percent correction could reduce household wealth, then at $18 trillion, by $3.6 trillion—or 30 percent of the gross domestic product.

Fed economist Andreas Lehnert reported that interest-only mortgages, or IOs, had been suddenly popular, with origination increasing sixfold to $300 billion. When queried about the extent to which Fannie and Freddie were involved with new risky loan products, such as IOs, Lehnert assured the FOMC that IOs represented only a tiny portion of the portfolio at Freddie Mac and none whatsoever at Fannie Mae.

Governor Bernanke revealed later that he took these comments to mean that the GSEs were not purchasing private-label securities,[51] although it does not appear that that is what Lehnert intended to say. What the Fed researchers apparently did not know was that, in fact, the GSEs were the single largest purchasers of both subprime and Alt-A loans and securities. In 2004, for example, the GSEs purchased $180 billion in loans with credit scores below 660, while not identifying them as subprime. They also purchased $144 billion in private-label subprime securities. That's $324 billion in subprime risk in a single year. The same year the GSEs also purchased $30 billion in Alt-A loans and $64 billion in private-label securities. (See Table 4.1 in Chapter 4.)

FOMC alternate member Janet Yellen (who became vice chairman in 2010) was concerned about the increase in "creative financing." She asked whether Fannie's and Freddie's books may only reflect an existing first mortgage—and thus be too rosy—while not reflecting the increasing prevalence of piggyback loans up to 125 percent of a home's value.

Fed Governor Susan Bies, who was chairman of the Fed Board's committee on supervisory and regulatory affairs, as well as being a member of the committee on consumer and community affairs, raised red flags over the dramatic increase in adjustable-rate mortgages to half of all home loans originated in 2004.

"This is happening in a period when short rates are rising and long rates are flat to down. If bankers are really working to the benefit of their customers, why aren't they locking in long rates in this environment?" she asked.

Bies was also alarmed that more and more mortgages were being securitized and that the number of option ARMs was increasing. She was further troubled by the huge run-up in home equity lines of credit, or HELOCs, which were being used in combination with the first mortgage to buy a house with no money down.

The fact that more bad loans were being made at a time when consumers should be locking in low interest rates illustrated "a lack of [market] discipline relative to previous periods," Bies said. "In the ancient days, when mortgage loans stayed on the books of financial institutions, liquidity limitations forced them to choose the higher quality credits. This isn't happening today. And it isn't clear if the marketplace currently understands the structure of these loans any better than some of us do in terms of pricing the risk."

Fed Governor Mark Olson said the securitization market's "avaricious" appetite for risk made no sense to him, given that house prices had stopped rising and were falling in some markets. The advent of flat house prices "is clearly likely to produce unrecognized risk somewhere in the financial system," he warned.

Following these comments, Fed Governor Ed Gramlich argued strongly against the Fed trying to prick any kind of bubble that might arise in the markets, including the current "slight" housing bubble. Even if the Fed decided to intervene, he argued, what should it do?

Should it raise rates to bring down home prices or lower rates because the Fed expects home prices to crash?

Gramlich did not entirely rule out intervention, however. When asked when to intervene, he replied—borrowing a few lines from Captain Corcoran in Gilbert & Sullivan's *HMS Pinafore*—"Well, never. Or hardly ever." That retort provoked a round of laughter.

After the meeting and its debate on the housing bubble, the Fed continued on its measured policy of steadily increasing short-term interest rates.

Two years later in August 2007, some members of the FOMC "believed that a collapse of the housing market was imminent," according to Bernanke. At least one member was not particularly worried. "If the more optimistic scenarios proved to be accurate, we might look back and be surprised that the financial events did not have a stronger impact on the real economy," the member suggested.

Other participants were pessimistic. "One participant, in a paraphrase of a quote he attributed to Churchill, said that no amount of rewriting of history would exonerate us if we did not prepare for the more dire scenarios discussed in the staff presentation."[52]

WORRIES ABOUT IOs AND OPTION ARMS

By 2006, mortgage insurance companies were beginning to warn of early signs of rising delinquencies with certain mortgage products. Under their charter, Fannie and Freddie are required to insure the amounts of a mortgage that are above 80 percent of loan to value. This mortgage insurance was designed to mitigate losses at Fannie and Freddie. The mortgage insurers, by contrast, did not generally play a similar role in the private-label market, where their function was replaced by structuring deals to have larger slices of a securitized pool set up to cushion the triple A investors from losses.

United Guaranty Corporation of Greensboro, North Carolina, was one of the mortgage insurers that had become increasingly worried about declining credit quality of mortgages that Fannie and Freddie were buying from a host of mortgage originators, most prominently, of course, Countrywide.

Not surprisingly, worry focused on IOs and option ARMs originated in 2004 through 2006.

"A sizable population of mortgages will have to be reset by midyear 2007," warned Kurt Smith, senior vice president of risk management.[53]

"We're starting to see an increase in delinquency rates in our IO book of business," he said.

Smith estimated that between 5 percent and 7 percent of United Guaranty's overall population of insured borrowers at the time would experience "a payment event" during 2007. Among United's insured risks were loans from 2004 that had a fixed rate for three years and then converted to ARMs[54] (the 3/27s) and those with one-year ARMs from both 2005 and 2006. United Guaranty had decided to cut back on the amount of IOs it was willing to insure. (The company refused to insure option ARMs.)

Smith's outspoken comments led to sharp rebukes in private by Angelo Mozilo at Countrywide.[55] One might be tempted to believe that Mozilo believed his own rhetoric. In 2003, for example, Mozilo was invited to give the John T. Dunlop lecture[56] in Washington, D.C., sponsored by the Joint Center for Housing Studies of Harvard University. In his speech, Mozilo called for an elimination of down payments for all minorities and low-income households. Countrywide was prepared to make a commitment to do $600 billion in affordable lending by 2010.

Mozilo dismissed "alarms" about subprime delinquency rates hitting 20 percent. Not to worry, he admonished. "If 80 percent of the subprime borrowers are managing to make ends meet and make the mortgage payment on time, then shouldn't we, as a nation, be justifiably proud that we are dramatically increasing homeownership opportunities for those who have been traditionally left behind?" Four years later, Countrywide would be on the verge of collapse.

The sheer size of the gains in the volume of new issues of private-label subprime and Alt-A securities in 2003 to 2006, combined with the decline in the share of loans in the jumbo prime category, would seem to have suggested to even the laziest observer that the overall credit quality of outstanding mortgages had grown decidedly weaker.

Not everyone was drinking the Kool Aid—least of all Stuart Feldstein, president of the mortgage research firm SMR Research in Hackettstown, N.J. "It gets harder to believe that credit quality is consistently improving when people with troubled credit histories are a growing part of the market," he said.[57]

Feldstein found a number of troubling trends in 2004 that appeared to be creating a "perfect storm" for bad credit and warned about it in the company's annual *Mortgage Industry Outlook*. In 2005, the annual report's perfect storm warning section was expanded. The report stated with alarm that piggyback deals—home purchases with a combined first and second mortgage—had grown to such a point that they constituted 48 percent of all home purchase loan dollars.[58] In 2001, by contrast, piggybacks were 14 percent.

"If you purposely set out to ruin the secondary market—the mechanism that fuels today's mortgage banking industry—we could think of no better way to do it than to populate mortgage securities with high-risk loans that investors cannot foresee," the SMR Research report stated. "Then, the investors . . . get a nasty surprise, then demand for mortgage securities falls."[59]

Worries were beginning to surface at the credit rating agencies. Even as the volume of Alt-A was rising, Moody's found that 35 percent of private-label securitized Alt-A loans had a simultaneous second mortgage. The weighted combined loan-to-value ratio of all the 2005 Alt-A securitized pools was 79 percent—5 percentage points higher than the weighted average for all mortgages, according to Moody's.

Moody's also saw trouble brewing in subprime home equity lending and raised its estimate of expected losses to 35 percent from 30 percent, based on the early poor performance of some of those loans originated in 2005.[60]

Moody's acknowledged there was no large database of historical performance data for new mortgage products such as option ARMs and IOs. "We may have to make more assumptions," said Moody's analyst Mark DeRienz. "We may have to analyze how an IO will perform, especially in the subprime arena, based on what we've seen in higher LTV loans."

Moody's also began to require Wall Street to beef up the credit enhancement levels for various classes of securities. S&P, too, began to require more loss coverage to gain a given credit rating.[61]

Greenwich Capital's Crawford was not concerned about the increase in risk represented by IOs and option ARMs. "The risk is broadly distributed, and investors are cognizant of potential declines in housing prices," he said in 2006. "In the riskier tranches, which are often purchased by hedge funds, investors are looking at every loan in every deal," he added.[62]

True enough. But as it would turn out, many of the less sophisticated institutional investors buying the AAA tranches were not doing any due diligence. They were foolishly relying on the AAA rating to ensure they were buying a safe investment. What was that phrase they taught us in school to warn us about being skeptical about any potential purchase? Oh, yes. *Caveat emptor.* Let the buyer beware. Maybe they stopped teaching that lesson.

6

Wall Street's Subprime CDO Mania

Sometimes markets do not act rationally in the face of a new opportunity. Instead, those who seize the opportunity are overtaken by an intense and urgent greed that leads to a market mania or panic, according to the late economist Charles Kindleberger.

"Rational exuberance morphs into irrational exuberance, economic euphoria develops and investment spending and consumption spending increase. There's a pervasive sense that it is 'time to get on the train before it leaves the station, and the exceptionally profitable opportunities disappear,"[1] Kindleberger has written. "An increasingly large share of the purchases of these assets is undertaken in anticipation of short-term capital gains and an exceptionally large share of these purchases is financed with credit."

The frenzy that erupted between 2004 and 2007 around collateralized debt obligations for asset-backed securities, or CDOs of ABS, seems to fit into Kindleberger's definition of a mania. These CDOs were created mostly from the lower investment grade tranches of private-label residential mortgage-backed securities—those rated A, BBB, or BBB-minus. (See Figures 6.1 and 6.2.) The buzz around these subprime bond CDOs is at the heart of the overall subprime securitization frenzy that Wall Street drove over the cliff—taking the financial system and the economy with them.

Wall Street successfully launched subprime bond CDOs by 2003. A year later, such CDOs had already become the hottest segment of the structured finance business.

By recycling existing subprime mortgage debt to new buyers, the CDOs freed up mortgage originators and mortgage securitizers to engage in another cycle of subprime lending. Because the creators of CDOs preferred subprime mezzanine tranches, the creation of CDOs created demand for more of the weaker varieties of subprime mortgages and more subprime mortgage-backed securities. They began to influence what kind of loans would be originated and in what volume.

The rapid rise, accelerating growth, and then sudden collapse of the subprime CDO market suggest that the product itself was fundamentally flawed and that it created uniquely perverse incentives that imperiled the mortgage markets and financial system.

What exactly is this thing called a CDO? Well, for starters, it is a structured finance deal that is housed in a special-purpose vehicle, or SPV, which is set up as a trust and which holds the collateral in the deal. The SPV issues certificates, which are similar to bonds and are often called *notes*, that are offered to investors. The payments that investors in the certificates receive are funded from the loans, bonds, or structured finance products that are in the pool of collateral. The flow of cash from the collateral is prioritized to investors in the various tranches or credit classes of the CDO and is often referred to as a *waterfall*, where the available supply of water (incoming money flows) first hits the highest-rated tranche.

This basic CDO is a cash flow or cash CDO.[2] The CDO mimics the structure of mortgage-backed securities and is, in fact, another type of securitization. The term *collateralized debt obligation* covers a broad category that encompasses collateralized bond obligations (CBOs) and collateralized mortgage obligations (CMOs), among others.[3] Structured finance CDOs are the ones made up of mortgage-backed securities and other asset-backed securities. So it is, in fact, a securitization of a securitization.

The first rated CDO was assembled in 1987 by leveraged buy-out king Michael Milken at Drexel Burnham Lambert.[4] This was done by pooling a mix of mostly lesser corporate bonds, including junk bonds, and then structuring a deal so that most of the tranches were investment grade or even AAA. The AAA slices were protected from losses because the lower tranches were set up to absorb the expected losses that might occur in the collateral. The creation of a deal with equity and lower-rated tranches to protect the highest-rated tranches is called *credit enhancement*.

From its inception, the concept for the CDO sounded dubious. Yet there was some financial logic to it. The pooling of many bonds from many companies reduced investors' exposure to the failure of any one bond.

Figure 6.1

Residential Mortgage-Backed Securities

Financial institutions packaged subprime, Alt-A and other mortgages into securities. As long as the housing market continued to boom, these securities would perform. But when the economy faltered and the mortgages defaulted, lower-rated tranches were left worthless.

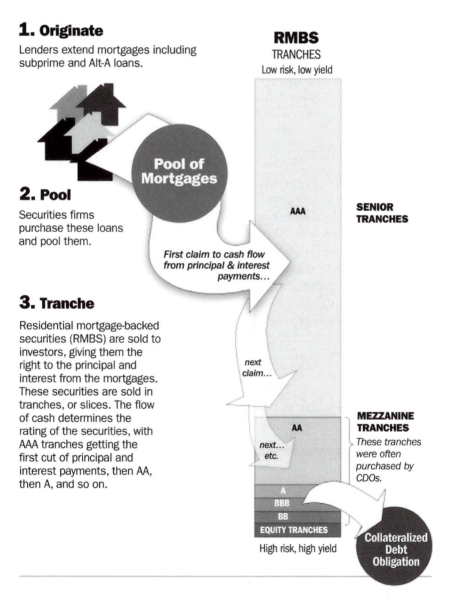

1. Originate
Lenders extend mortgages including subprime and Alt-A loans.

RMBS
TRANCHES
Low risk, low yield

2. Pool
Securities firms purchase these loans and pool them.

Pool of Mortgages

AAA

SENIOR TRANCHES

First claim to cash flow from principal & interest payments...

3. Tranche
Residential mortgage-backed securities (RMBS) are sold to investors, giving them the right to the principal and interest from the mortgages. These securities are sold in tranches, or slices. The flow of cash determines the rating of the securities, with AAA tranches getting the first cut of principal and interest payments, then AA, then A, and so on.

next claim...

AA

MEZZANINE TRANCHES
These tranches were often purchased by CDOs.

next... etc.

A
BBB
BB
EQUITY TRANCHES
High risk, high yield

Collateralized Debt Obligation

Source: Financial Crisis Inquiry Report.

Those who put the deals together liked to tout them as tailored classes of investments choices from which investors can pick their preferred level of risk and return. It helped that the corporate bonds were often of known companies where there was a good deal of public information to give investors sufficient confidence to buy. A cynic might say that the CDO was invented to create a place to dump lower credit quality or junk bonds and hide them among better credits.

The advent of CDOs also created a cottage industry of CDO managers who oversaw the SPVs housing the CDOs and received periodic payments based on the value of the assets managed. One of the reasons CDO managers were necessary is that there would periodically be changes in the collateral mix in the trust pools backing the CDOs. Some CDOs are set up with fixed collateral, and others are set up so that collateral could be bought, sold, and managed.

During the 1990s, CDO managers expanded the list of collateral from low-rated corporate bonds to emerging market bonds and bank loans. These were known as *multisector CDOs*, where the collateral can be mortgage-backed securities, asset-backed securities, corporate or government bonds, or loans. In the financial meltdown of 1998 that followed Russia's default on its bonds, the multisector CDOs were hard hit and faced an uncertain feature.

Prudential Securities, one of the firms in the CDO business at the time, began to look around for more stable and more attractive forms of collateral. Christopher Ricciardi, who headed the trading desk in securitized assets at Prudential, settled on the lower-rated tranches of asset-backed securities as the new collateral. Putting together a CDO of ABS was a new wrinkle. Prudential launched the first one in 1999.

"We thought ABS was excellent collateral for CDOs because asset-backed securities—particularly subordinate classes of, let's say, home equity loans—traded at much wider levels than corporates of the same rating," Ricciardi later told *Credit* magazine.[5] By wider levels, Ricciardi meant CDOs of ABS pay a higher coupon rate than similarly rated corporate bonds.

When Ricciardi's boss at Prudential, Joseph Donovan, left the firm in 2000 to go to work at Credit Suisse, Ricciardi followed and became the head of that bank's U.S. structured credit products.[6] Soon, Ricciardi's team pushed Credit Suisse to number one in the league tables. By 2001, they were underwriting one new CDO every month for a total of $12.7 billion that year.

Other Wall Street firms also made a similar move with their CDO capabilities. "Everyone looked at the sector and said, the CDO

Figure 6.2

Collateralized Debt Obligations

Collateralized debt obligations (CDOs) are structured financial instruments that purchase and pool financial assets such as the riskier tranches of various residential mortgage-backed securities (RMBS).

3. CDO tranches

Similar to mortgage-backed securities, the CDO issues securities in tranches that vary based on their place in the cash flow waterfall.

1. Purchase

The CDO manager and securities firm select and purchase assets, such as some of the lower-rated tranches of mortgage-backed securities.

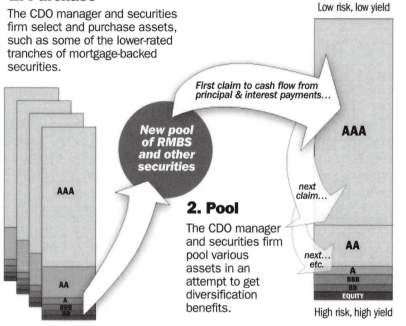

First claim to cash flow from principal & interest payments...

New pool of RMBS and other securities

Low risk, low yield

AAA

next claim...

2. Pool

The CDO manager and securities firm pool various assets in an attempt to get diversification benefits.

AAA

AA

next... etc.

AA

A
BBB
BB
EQUITY

High risk, high yield

Source: Financial Crisis Inquiry Report.

construct works, but we just need to find more stable collateral," said Wing Chau, who ran Maxim Group and Harding Advisory, managers of CDOs, mostly those underwritten by Merrill Lynch.[7] "And the industry looked at residential mortgage-backed securities, Alt-A, subprime, and non-agency mortgages, and saw the relative stability," Chau explained.

It was while at Credit Suisse that Ricciardi and his boss, Donovan, came up with the idea of boosting the share of subprime securities in the collateral pools of CDOs of ABS. The idea came as a result of declining institutional investor interest in the mezzanine tranches of subprime mortgage-backed securities deals. While one would expect financial markets to pull back from subprime bond deals when investor appetite waned, they instead embraced these deals more enthusiastically—a move that perplexed market observers such as Fed Governor Susan Bies, among others.

"We told you these [BBB-rated securities of mortgage-backed securities] were a great deal, and priced at great spreads, but nobody stepped up," Donovan told structure finance bankers at a Phoenix conference in 2002. "So, we created the investor," meaning that Wall Street created CDOs to be the investor to buy the unwanted mezzanine tranches of subprime mortgage-backed securities.[8]

After being contacted by a headhunter, Ricciardi jumped ship to Merrill Lynch in 2003 with most of his team.[9] Once there, Ricciardi turned Merrill into a CDO powerhouse, pushing it to number one in the business in 2004, with $25 billion in new CDOs, according to Thomson Reuters. Ricciardi not only put together the deals but also invested in them through Merrill's proprietary trading activities.

Under Ricciardi's leadership, Merrill Lynch's CDO underwriting machine grew from $3.4 billion in 2003 to $44 billion in 2006. Ricciardi left in early 2006 to become chief executive officer at Cohen & Company, a client of Merrill's that invested in CDOs. In the first half in 2007, Merrill underwrote $28 billion in subprime CDOs.

The rest of the CDO industry followed Ricciardi's lead in placing mortgage bonds as collateral in CDOs of ABS. By 2004, creators of CDOs were the primary buyers of the lowest-rated mezzanine tranches of mortgage-backed securities.

The CDO business was generating huge fees for Wall Street, helping drive up overall profits at investment banking firms from $23 billion in 2003 to $43 billion in 2006.[10] More importantly, compensation soared for top Wall Street executives, especially those in the CDO and mortgage-backed securities business and other exotic financial products. Compensation in Wall Street firms doubled from $34 billion to $65 billion over the same period.

Aite Group, a financial industry research and advisory firm based in Boston, has estimated that underwriters at the beginning of the subprime CDO craze were paid 2 percent of the notional value of a deal.[11]

For a typical $1 billion CDO deal, that's $20 million in fees. While the $20 million fee might looked good in theory, "it may not necessarily have been more profitable" in practice, according to John Jay, a structured finance analyst at Aite. Much of the potential higher return came from increasing the overall leverage in the whole subprime securitization business, which requires creating a large buffer of credit protection, which adds cost to the deal, to get AAA ratings for senior tranches in the deal. Higher leverage usually means higher profits, if all else is equal.

A survey of CDO managers by the Financial Crisis Inquiry Commission found that the business was quite profitable for CDO managers, too. Further, many of the hedge funds that invested in CDOs also managed them.

CDOs that invested mostly in AAA and AA credits earned $600,000 to $1 million on a $1 billion CDO deal.[12] CDO managers invested mostly in lower-rated credits earned more—$750,000 to $1.5 million on a $500 million deal. It has been estimated that CDO managers earned at least $1.5 billion between 2003 and 2007.[13]

Citigroup, like Merrill Lynch, jumped on the CDO bandwagon with a vengeance in 2005. Citigroup's mortgage bond trading chief Thomas Maheras said the bank became a big player in CDOs "based in part on a careful study from outside consultants hired by our senior-most management."[14] While he did not identify anyone by name, the senior-most managers were Sandy Weill, who was chairman in 2005; and Chuck Prince, then CEO but who became chairman in 2006; and Robert Rubin, chairman of the executive committee on the board. Broadcast journalist Charlie Gasparino in *The Sellout* identifies Rubin as pressuring Prince to hire an outside consultant, which Prince did. The unnamed consultant determined that Citigroup was falling behind its competitors in the use of leverage and risk to boost its profits. Rubin used the study to successfully convince Prince to push Citi to take on more leverage and more risk—including expanding its CDO business.[15]

CDOs generated huge incomes and profits in the short term, and virtually no one at the Wall Street firms ginning up the CDO business seemed to worry much about the risks they were taking on.

WHY DID WALL STREET LOVE CDOs?

Why did Wall Street love CDOs so much? Why would CDOs flourish when the subprime mortgage-backed securities money train should have been chugging to a halt?

In his book *The Big Short*, Michael Lewis reports that hedge fund executives who wanted to short subprime were also scratching their heads over why people were buying CDOs loaded with subprime mortgages destined to fail in very large numbers. One who was especially perplexed was Vincent Daniel, the accountant for Steve Eisman's hedge fund, Front Point Partners.

Daniel recounted his experience with trying to audit Salomon Brothers for Arthur Anderson in the 1990s. That experience taught him that management often had no idea what was going in the firm's trading and holding of mortgage bonds.[16] He concluded that there was no way of telling whether money was being made or lost in mortgage bonds at Salomon. "They were giant black boxes, whose hidden gears were in constant motion," Lewis wrote, describing Daniel's view of Wall Street firms. Daniel asked questions of his fellow accountants to better audit the mortgage assets, and getting no answers, went looking for another job.

Lewis, a former Salomon bond salesman who became famous in 1989 for writing a best seller—*Liar's Poker*—described the creation of CDOs as both shady and magical in 2010 in *The Big Short*. "The CDO was, in effect, a credit laundering service for the residents of Lower Middle Class America." For Wall Street it was a machine that "turned lead into gold."[17]

From the moment Wall Street discovered CDOs of ABS, the production of private-label subprime securities zoomed ahead. A key catalyst came in 2004, when interest rates began to rise, and housing prices began to reach the point where the ability of households to afford a median-priced home was starting to decline.

Mortgage lenders, to provide products that improve affordability of the initial payments for higher-priced homes, offered mortgages with lower introductory teaser rates. Perversely, the teaser-rate mortgages led people to buy more home than they could afford, as they based their purchase decision on the initial monthly payment and not a higher payment once the rates adjusted upward, which could happen anywhere from 2 years to 10 years. In subprime, a common product was the 2/28, which adjusted after only two years.

A rise in interest rates would generally lead to a decline in the volume of mortgage originations. Indeed, in 2004, as interest rates rose, overall mortgage originations fell 30 percent, from $3.725 trillion to $2.59 trillion.[18] A closer look shows a sharp divergence within the segments of the mortgage market. While the agency (Fannie and Freddie) business fell, private-label subprime securitization lending took off, rising 84 percent to $363 billion from $195 billion the prior year.

Mortgage lenders, instead of retrenching as they had after previous mortgage refinancing waves, geared up to gain market share in a race to the bottom of the mortgage credit pool.

In 2005, private-label securitizations soared to $465 billion and remained high at $448 billion in 2006 before falling back to $202 billion in 2007. In the five-and-one-half years from 2002 to mid-2007, $1.59 trillion in subprime loans were turned into private-label securities. In the prior seven years, private-label issuers securitized only $377 billion in subprime loans.

Countrywide was the leader in agency mortgage originations in 2003 but redirected its originations into the private-label business in 2004. While Countrywide sold 61 percent of originations to Fannie and Freddie in 2003, it sold them only 20 percent of its originations in 2004. Countrywide did everything along the mortgage food chain, from originating the mortgages, to securitizing them, and, eventually even creating CDOs.

The Countrywide business model was so compelling that Lehman Brothers and Bear Stearns went into the mortgage origination business in order to reap the perceived financial rewards of the vertical integration business model, as well as to assure a sufficient supply of mortgages, mostly subprime, to feed the beast creating the mortgage-backed securities.

Fannie and Freddie fed the growing frenzy in private-label subprime by purchasing $180 billion, or 45 percent, of all private-label subprime securities issued in 2004. This was higher than the $82 billion and 40 percent share they purchased in 2003.

Wall Street's subprime CDO mania is critical in explaining the surge in risky lending that went into the creation of private-label mortgage-backed securities.

The ability of CDOs to drive demand for subprime mortgage-backed securities was remarkable, given that only a sliver of the subprime mortgage bonds, the mezzanine tranches rated A, BBB, and BBB-minus, were in great demand as raw material for CDOs. Thus, to make the CDOs work, it required more and more subprime securitizations and more and more mezzanine tranches.

In 2002, CDOs snapped up the lower-rated tranches of 20 percent of all new private subprime mortgage-backed securities issued. In 2003, CDOs were securitizing slices of 60 percent of subprime bonds. By 2004, it was 80 percent. And then afterward, until it all collapsed, there were not enough subprime securities to meet the demand of CDO arrangers and investors.

Between 2002 and 2007, 697 CDO of ABS deals were underwritten on Wall Street—each deal representing about a billion dollars. Merrill Lynch was the number-one underwriter with 107 deals, with Citigroup in second place with 80 deals.[19] Credit Suisse (64) was third and Goldman Sachs (62) fourth, followed by Bear Stearns (60) and Wachovia (52). Deutsche Bank (50), UBS (46), Lehman Brothers (35), and Bank of America (32) completed the list of top 10 underwriters.

SOPHISTICATION ARBITRAGE

The CDO engine would not have taken off quite a strongly as it did if yet another thing had not occurred—finding a new crop of insufficiently sophisticated investors to buy the AAA tranches of the CDOs. The idea that you can take the lowest-rated parts of a subprime mortgage-backed securities deal and turn it into AAA was always suspect because it defied logic and common sense.

In fact, by 2003, American institutional investors from pension funds to insurance companies were beginning to have doubts about the wisdom of snapping up the lower-rated tranches of subprime mortgage-backed securities and stopped buying them.

Wall Street bond salesmen, just like good used car salesmen, needed a new crop of credulous buyers to keep the clunkers—the A, BBB, and BBB-minus tranches—rolling off the lot in order to keep the CDO dealership in business. A goodly number of the new prey turned out to be banks and investors in Europe and Asia, according to J. Kyle Bass, who ran a couple of funds that invested in subprime mortgage-backed securities at Hayman Advisors LP in Dallas.

Bass recounted the startling story of how he learned about what he called "The Greatest 'Bait and Switch' of ALL TIME" in an investor letter to his clients July 30, 2007.

"I recently spent some time with a senior executive in the structured product marketing group (Collateralized Debt Obligations, Collateralized Loan Obligations, Etc.) of one of the largest brokerage firms in the world," Bass began his letter.[20] "I was in [the Mediterranean coastal resort of Rosas], Spain, attending a wedding for a good friend of mine who thought it would be an appropriate time to put the two of us together (given our shared interests in the structured credit markets)."

"This individual proceeded to tell me how and why the Subprime Mezzanine CDO business existed," Bass continued. "He told me that the 'real money' (US insurance companies, pension funds, etc.) accounts had stopped purchasing mezzanine tranches of US Subprime debt in late 2003 and that they needed a mechanism that could enable them to 'mark up' these loans, package them opaquely, and

EXPORT THE NEWLY PACKAGED RISK TO UNWITTING BUYERS IN ASIA AND CENTRAL EUROPE!!!!" Bass wrote using all capital letters for emphasis.

"He told me with a straight face that these CDOs were the only way to get rid of the riskiest tranches of Subprime debt. Interestingly enough, these buyers (mainland Chinese Banks, the Chinese Government, Taiwanese banks, Korean banks, German banks, French banks, UK banks) possess the 'excess' pools of liquidity around the globe. These pools are basically derived from two sources: 1) massive trade surpluses with the US in [U.S. dollars], 2) petrodollar recyclers," Bass wrote.

"These two pools of excess capital are US dollar denominated and have had a virtually insatiable demand for US dollar denominated debt . . . until now [in July 2007].They have had orders on the various desks of Wall St. to buy any US debt rated "AAA" by the rating agencies in the US," Bass told his investors.

"This will go down as one of the biggest financial illusions the world has EVER seen," Bass wrote. "These institutions have these investments marked at PAR or 100 cents on the dollar for the most part," he stated. "When they are downgraded, these foreign buyers will most likely have to sell them due to the fact that they are only permitted to own 'super senior' risk in the US. I predict that these tranches of mezzanine CDOs will fetch bids of around 10 cents on the dollar," Bass told his investors.

CDOs were extremely complex and opaque. Like too many other instruments and entities in the financial markets, they had become black boxes to regulators, to AAA investors, and to the public. Both the complexity and opaqueness should have been a red flag to any prudent investor by 2004. Yet, instead of winding down, the flow of funds into subprime CDOs was about to explode even more as demand prompted yet more innovations that turned CDOs into casinos—black box casinos where only the most astute and informed could ascertain the considerable risks and reap the bountiful rewards that lurked there.

The CDO also accelerated the growth of the shadow banking system, which is in the business of borrowing and lending money outside the traditional banking system. This shift, in turn, moved risky new assets into locations where they made the entire financial system more vulnerable to declines in home values and other shocks. Also, by moving more financial activity into the shadow banking system, the shift reduced regulatory oversight of the risks that were being created in the financial system.

Not long after penning his alarming letter to investors, Bass shared with Congress his insight into the vulnerabilities created by the CDO mania in the wake of the mortgage meltdown in 2007.[21]

"An important concept to appreciate is that each securitization is essentially an off-balance sheet bank. Like a regular bank there is a sliver of equity and 10–20 times leverage in a securitization or CDO, and 20–40 times leverage in CDO Squared and [other] instruments," he testified.

"The booming securitization market has in reality been an extraordinary growth in off-balance sheet banks" without federal or state regulators to monitor them. The only regulator for the CDOs, as far as Bass could see, were the crediting rating agencies—"bodies that are inherently biased towards their paymasters, the securitization firms."

CREDIT RATINGS ARBITRAGE

As Bass noted, the CDO mania could never have occurred without a compliant and supporting role by the credit rating agencies. So it's important to know just how those agencies came to have so vital a role. Ironically, it was handed to them by banking regulators as part of an effort to strengthen banking capital through new risk-weighted standards incorporated into the so-called *recourse rule*, which was approved in 2001 and went into effect in 2002.[22]

In the 1980s, U.S. bank supervisors, under the leadership of former New York Fed president William McDonough, had ushered in the era of risk-weighting of assets in determining how much capital banks should hold. The 2001 recourse rule, which is actually a broad new capital standard, was introduced to counter the practice by banks of gaming the risk-weightings standards then in place.

The new U.S. capital rule also came out of the conceptual framework for improved capital regulation by the Basel Committee on Banking Supervision. That committee is the one that decided that the risk-weighting for various tranches of mortgage-backed securities should be based on their credit rating.

The new risk-weightings created distorted incentives in the securitization business. Under the new rule, BBB tranches would need 8 percent capital because of their higher risk-weighting, while A tranches required 4 percent capital and AAA and AA required only 1.6 percent capital. This was a huge incentive to get rid of the BBBs and As and hold onto the AAAs and AAs.

Whether banking supervisors realized it or not—and they probably did not—they had given banks dueling incentives that in combination had a negative impact on credit quality of mortgages while boosting demand for them. There was an incentive to include as many lower-quality loans in a mortgage-backed securities transaction as possible to make it more profitable, while at the same time to construct deals to obtain the most yield in AAA-rated tranches. That is, make sure that the share of the deal represented by the AAA classes was as large a slice of the deal as possible.

A discussion paper for the Federal Reserve in 2009 suggested that the new capital standards created perverse incentives.[23] In the paper, Taylor Nadauld, then a doctoral candidate at Ohio State University, and Shane Sherlund, a Fed economist, analyzed the incentives that drove the loan purchase decisions of investment banks that underwrote the deals. The authors analyzed the structure and ratings of 1,267 subprime mortgage bond deals from 1997 to 2007 involving 6.7 million loans.

The authors concluded that the deal dynamics in the securitization process expanded the overall level of subprime lending and boosted the degree of risk in subprime residential mortgage-backed securities deals.

Nadauld and Sherlund found empirical evidence—evidence derived from an experiment or observation as opposed to theory—that changes in securitization incentives can increase the level of credit extended by mortgage lenders. The evidence comes from measuring the impact in 2005 following a 2004 change in capital requirements made by the SEC, when William Donaldson was chairman.

The SEC rule change was part of the response of the United States to a formal notice from the European Union that required that the affiliates of the five largest U.S. broker-dealers be subject to some form of consolidated supervision by a U.S. regulatory authority—or come under European supervision. The SEC supervised broker-dealers for investor protection and not for safety and soundness and had no authority over the holding companies that owned the broker-dealers.

The proposed change would allow broker-dealers "to use mathematical models to calculate net capital requirements for market and derivative-related credit risk," the SEC stated. The SEC rule affected Bear Stearns, Goldman Sachs, Lehman Brothers, Merrill Lynch, and Morgan Stanley. By the Fed's own calculations, "broker-dealers taking advantage of the alternative capital contribution would realize an average reduction in capital deductions of approximately 40%."[24]

Nadauld and Sherlund found that the five banks "did indeed increase their demand for subprime mortgages relative to competitor banks that did not experience a change in capital requirements."[25] Thus, the change in capital rules led to a greater demand for lower credit quality subprime mortgage purchases.

Thanks to the SEC capital rule change in 2004, Wall Street did not just increase the level of subprime securitized but also raised the overall leverage during the years of the mortgage bubble and CDO mania. This made the investment banking firms more vulnerable to a decline in the value of subprime and other mortgage assets.

By the Boston Fed's count, the leverage of the five investment banks rose from an average of 22 to 1 in 2003 to 31 to 1 in 2007, based on their 10-K annual report filings with the SEC.[26]

A closer look, however, reveals a wide range in leverage ratios among the investment firms and the large commercial banks with major investment banking subsidiaries. If one looks at leverage to tangible common equity, both Lehman Brothers and Morgan Stanley were leveraged 40 to 1 at the end of 2007.[27] Bear Stearns was leveraged 36.8 to 1, while Citigroup was leveraged 35 to 1.

Taking into account off-balance sheet assets, the leverage was much higher: 68 to 1 for Citigroup, 54 to 1 for Bank of America; Lehman, 52 to 1, JPMorgan Chase, 44 to 1; and Morgan Stanley, 44 to 1.

Leverage was at stratospheric heights if one goes further to add illiquid Level 3 assets, which includes mortgage-related securities and notes that were marked to model in trading accounts. Bear Stearns topped the charts with a Level 3 leverage of 262 to 1. Lehman followed at 225, Morgan Stanley at 222, Citigroup at 212, and Goldman Sachs at 200 to 1. They only bit of not-so-bad news was that JPMorgan Chase's Level 3 leverage was only 58 to 1.

Weaker assets and higher leverage were made worse by a heavy reliance on and undue respect for complex computer modeling formulas to achieve credit ratings.

The idea that one is going to take mezzanine tranches of subprime mortgage-backed securities and use them as collateral to create a CDO, thereby converting 70 percent or more of them into AAA securities, sounds implausible to the man on the street applying basic common sense.

However, computer models failed to see the perils of the obvious by assuming that there would be less correlation between the performance of the AAA tranches and their underlying subprime mezzanine assets. They also assumed less correlation between the performance of the weakest links—the equity and lower-rated tranches for the CDO—and the super senior tranches. The models also failed to adequately engage in stress testing. They assumed that the worst that could happen would be that home prices would perform as they have in regional markets that suffered downturns in the last few decades. That would include Texas, California, and New England.

Computer modeling errors were compounded by a widespread reliance on a single approach to modeling the pricing of CDOs—the Gaussian copula model[28] developed by David Li at JPMorgan Chase.[29] The model relied on the price history of credit default swaps against a given asset to determine the degree of correlation rather than rely on historical loan performance data. "People got very excited about the Gaussian copula because of its mathematical elegance, but the thing never worked," chided Nassim Nicholas Taleb, who has claimed that any attempt at measuring correlation based on past history is "charlatanism."[30]

The significant shortfalls of the computer models widely employed on Wall Street threw more logs onto the bonfire that would melt down the financial world. It turned out the original assumptions in the models were not just wide of the mark—they were wishful shots in the dark.

Fast Money and High Stakes

Winston Churchill famously said of Russia: "It is a riddle, wrapped in a mystery, inside an enigma." It was difficult enough when collateralized debt obligations of asset-backed securities (CDOs of ABS) were cash CDOs with real collateral—but they were even more of riddle when they became synthetic with virtual collateral. With synthetic CDOs, Wall Street crossed over to *The Matrix*, a world where reality is simulated by computers.[1]

The synthetic CDO is built on credit default swaps that reference tranches of mortgage-backed securities that can be from any mortgage bond deal. Those referenced bond assets are not part of the CDO and do not have to be acquired by the CDO.

With the advent of the synthetic CDOs, there also emerged hybrid CDOs with both synthetic and cash features. There were CDOs of CDOs or, as they are also called, CDO squared. Those are CDOs made up of parts of other CDOs.

The synthetic CDO tied to subprime mortgage bonds emerged in 2005 to meet the demand by various investors in tranches of the CDOs that could not be met by CDOs created from lower-rated mezzanine tranches of mortgage-backed securities.

The credit default swap is a derivative, meaning its value is derived from the value of another asset. Thus, the credit default swap is in the same category as interest rate swaps and futures, currency swaps and futures, and even commodity futures. Unlike the derivatives that can be traded on exchanges, credit default swaps are private contracts between two parties traded over-the-counter.

In a CDS contract, the buyer of protection agrees to make payments much like premiums to a seller of protection over a designated period of time. If a credit event occurs—that is, if there is some deterioration in the performance of underlying loans or the securities—then the buyer of the credit protection would be entitled to receive funds to mitigate the losses from the party that sold the credit protection. Usually the credit event—defined in the swap contract—is the failure of the issuer of an insured bond to make timely payments to the investor in the bond.

This credit default swap is a form of shadow bond insurance and is distinctly different from traditional bond insurance regulated by state insurance departments. Parties in a CDS contract that offer credit protection have to post collateral and raise the level of collateral as the performance of insured assets deteriorates. With bond insurance, a default precedes a claim and money is paid out after the claim is determined to be valid. Generally, the bond insurer does not have to post collateral preceding a default.

The creation of the first credit default swap is generally attributed to Blythe Masters, a British woman who came to work for J. P. Morgan in New York in 1994 as part of the investor derivatives market team led by her fellow countryman Peter Hancock. The story of how Masters came up with the credit default swap has been told in *Fool's Gold* by *Financial Times* reporter Gillian Tett.[2]

The idea for doing a credit default swap came from an assignment to figure out a way to unload J. P. Morgan's part of a $4.8 billion credit line extended to Exxon in the wake of the Valdez oil tanker spill. Masters contacted the European Bank for Reconstruction and Development (EBRD) in London to see if the loan could be off-loaded without selling it.[3] She proposed to EBRD that J. P. Morgan pay the bank a fee each year in exchange for the bank assuming the risk that Exxon would default on the loan. If Exxon failed to make payments, then EBRD would owe J. P. Morgan the amount of the loss. If Exxon never defaulted, then EBRD would not have to pay and would keep all the premiums it earned during the term of the contract.

Andrew Donaldson, director of the EBRD, agreed to the deal, and Masters oversaw the crafting of the first credit default swap.

The CDS market gradually gained traction over time and became a frequent way to guarantee payment on corporate and municipal bonds for institutions that held the debt. Wall Street put together CDS deals against bonds issued by Enron and WorldCom, but also bought hedges to cover their exposure as the credit provider. When Enron and WorldCom collapsed, the Wall Street firms that did the deals emerged mostly unscathed because they had hedged their exposures.[4]

It was shortly after Wall Street navigated its way through the carnage of CDS contracts against Enron and WorldCom and others that CDO arrangers decided to use credit default swaps to structure a *synthetic* CDO of ABS. The structure was even more complex that the one used for cash CDOs. It required the creation of a new super senior tranche made up of credit default swap contracts that reference specific tranches of mostly subprime mortgage-backed securities. (See Figure 7.1.)

Credit default swaps that are used to buy and sell protection on asset-backed securities are known in the industry as ABS CDS. Synthetic CDOs did not finance a single home purchase.[5]

The introduction of ABS CDS was the catalyst that allowed the already large CDO of ABS market to expand even more rapidly in 2006, according to former chief of UBS Securities' securitized products research team, Laurie S. Goodman et al. (*et al.* is Latin for "and others").[6]

There were two kinds of investors in synthetic CDOs. The "funded" long investors purchased securities issued by the CDO that came in tranches with different levels of credit, ranging from AAA to BB and even an equity tranche. The "unfunded" long investors enter into swaps with the CDO, making money if the reference securities performed. These investors own the super senior AAA tranche at the top of the synthetic CDO structure. The "short" investors take the other side of the swap contract from the CDO itself. The "shorts" make money if the reference mortgage bond securities fail.

Funded investors receive interest payments as long as the reference securities perform. The funded investors can lose all of their investment, however, if the reference securities default. Unfunded investors have highest priority to receive payments from the so-called waterfall of payments ahead of the funded investors, in the event of a shortfall in payments.

Finally, the CDO would pay out funds to the short investors from its accumulated cash, including the funds placed there by the unfunded long investors.

The credit default swap offers two distinctly different opportunities for the protection seller and the protection buyer.[7]

For the seller who has a high cost of funding, the CDS makes it possible to assume the credit risk of a low-coupon bond that might otherwise not be an attractive acquisition. That's because the cost of selling the insurance to the protection buyer is less than the cost of buying the underlying credit risk.

Figure 7.1

Synthetic CDO

Synthetic CDOs were complex paper transactions involving credit default swaps.

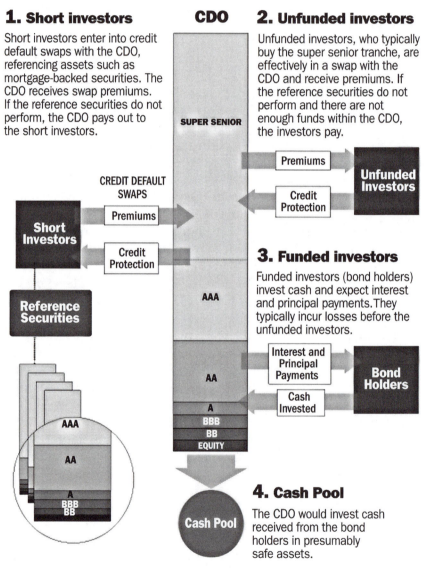

1. Short investors

Short investors enter into credit default swaps with the CDO, referencing assets such as mortgage-backed securities. The CDO receives swap premiums. If the reference securities do not perform, the CDO pays out to the short investors.

2. Unfunded investors

Unfunded investors, who typically buy the super senior tranche, are effectively in a swap with the CDO and receive premiums. If the reference securities do not perform and there are not enough funds within the CDO, the investors pay.

3. Funded investors

Funded investors (bond holders) invest cash and expect interest and principal payments. They typically incur losses before the unfunded investors.

4. Cash Pool

The CDO would invest cash received from the bond holders in presumably safe assets.

Source: Financial Crisis Inquiry Report.

Conversely, with a credit default swap, a fund that has low-cost funding can take a short position on a CDO without having to purchase it. For the short, the credit default swap is a lottery ticket with an enormous payoff, if the bet is placed at the right time on the right asset.

The potential windfall can come from a credit event that can be anything from credit downgrade to a failure of the underlying bond to make interest payments to the investor. Depending on the swap, if there is an adverse credit event on the underlying mortgage bond, the credit protection buyer could get a windfall payment for the amount of markdown on the underlying asset. In some cases, the protection buyer can get the full notional value of the mortgage bond. That makes it the mega-lottery.

There was such a frenzy in synthetic CDOs that a single tranche from a subprime mortgage-backed securities deal could be referenced several times by different CDOs. Thus, synthetic CDOs turned subprime bond assets into super fancy versions of old-fashioned performance bets, not all that different from the storied jumping frog of Calaveras County.[8] But in the case of mortgage bonds, instead of penny ante bets, billions of dollars could be wagered on a single bond's performance. And like the champion frog Daniel Webster, who suddenly could not jump very far because a load of lead shot was slipped into its mouth, the bonds were chosen because they were unlikely to perform as expected.

INSIDE THE CDO MACHINE

The synthetic CDO proliferated quickly once it was introduced because, among other reasons, it was easier and quicker to put together. Further, synthetics offered higher returns on the equity tranche than did the cash CDOs. By one estimate, the equity tranche on a synthetic would offer a 21 percent yield, while the equity tranche of a cash CDO offered 13 percent.[9] This made it even more desirable for hedge funds to acquire.

The concentration of risk created by the mania for CDOs is illustrated by the experience at Merrill Lynch. After Ricciardi left Merrill, Dow Kim, the company's co-president of global markets and investment, told the CDO team to "do whatever it takes" to keep the CDO engine going.[10] And so apparently Merrill did, if one judges by the results. In 2006, Merrill created $38.9 billion in CDOs, making it again number one in the CDO business, according to Thomson Reuters.

Increasingly, Merrill had to retain tranches of its newly minted CDOs after the number-one provider of credit protection—AIG Financial Products—got out of the business in 2006.[11] Citigroup was shipping some of them to off-balance-sheet SIVs with a liquidity put. That meant that the effective ownership of them could return to Citi, a provision that would cause enormous losses and imperil the solvency of the bank.

Merrill was also increasingly repackaging the BBB tranches of its own old CDOs, which were getting harder and harder to sell to investors, and putting them into new CDOs. This, in a sense, was repeating the 2003 miscalculation that first created the mania in CDOs—repackaging the BBB tranches of the mortgage-backed securities into CDOs because "real money" institutional investors had become increasingly unwilling to buy them.

Over time, the credit rating agencies allowed a higher and higher percentage of CDOs to be recycled parts of other CDOs and still get an AAA rating. From 2005 to 2007, the percentage of recycled CDOs rose from 5 percent to 30 percent, according to CDO manager Wing Chau.[12]

One estimate found the share of old CDOs inserted into the collateral of new CDOs rose from 7 percent in 2003 to 14 percent in 2007.[13] The number of CDO squared deals (CDOs of CDOs) grew from 36 in 2005 to 48 in 2006, and then fell back to 41 in 2007.

There were few signs that "real money" was a significant part of the CDO mania by late 2006. Merrill is a case in point. It created 44 CDO deals from the fourth quarter of 2006 until August 2007. CDO managers—as opposed to institutional investors—purchased nearly 80 percent of the mezzanine tranches from those CDO deals.[14] Chau reported that 88 percent of the mezzanine tranches sold by the CDOs he managed were sold into collateral pools in new CDOs. In one instance, CDO managers were the *only* purchasers of Merrill's Neo CDO.[15]

Apparently, there was a gentleman's agreement on Wall Street that was described as "you buy my BBB tranches and I'll buy yours."[16]

Deutsche Bank mortgage trader Greg Lippmann reported that his trading desk brokered deals for 50 to 100 hedge funds that wanted to short the mezzanine tranches in mortgage-backed securities.[17] UBS and Citigroup "were the most aggressive underwriters of [synthetic] CDOs," he recalled.

This meant that the firms that bought BBB tranches of mortgage-backed securities would still end up keeping much of the risk of those tranches because they recycled them into newly created CDOs. Hedge funds were, in fact, the real market for new CDOs but only for the lower investment grades—A, BBB, and BBB-minus—and the equity tranches. There were no longer any "real money" buyers of the investment-grade tranches.

The issuance of synthetic CDOs rose from $15 billion in 2005 to $61 billion, if you classify CDOs with 50 percent or more synthetic capital as synthetic. The Financial Crisis Inquiry Commission estimated that by 2006, 27 percent of the CDO collateral of $225 billion of CDOs was synthetic.[18] By comparison, the synthetic share was 9 percent in 2005 and 7 percent in 2004.

A STARRING ROLE FOR HEDGE FUNDS

A number of investors who took the short position in credit default swaps on mortgage-backed securities during the peak housing boom years made enormous fortunes—most famously hedge fund manager John Paulson. He devoted essentially his entire fund to shorting subprime bonds via credit default swaps. In 2007, the fund reaped a $15 billion bonanza.[19] In 2008, Paulson switched to credit default swaps on the bonds of troubled financial institutions, such as Bear Stearns, and made another $5 billion.

Even before Paulson famously shorted subprime, CDOs had generated a frenzy of buying from hedge funds. Synthetic CDOs ginned up the frenzy. Freed of the cost of acquiring assets in order to take a position on them, both sellers and buyers of credit default swaps could, in short, more easily speculate on the subprime market—as opposed to investing in the subprime market.

For the protection seller, there was a huge downside risk. For the protection buyer, there was huge upside gain. This was not investing. This was high stakes gambling, and the CDO was the casino where the bets were placed. Wall Street became bigger and chancier than Las Vegas and Atlantic City combined—and more.

In time, hedge funds came to rival banks as sponsors. Often CDOs are divided into two basic types based on the motivation of the sponsors of the CDOs. There are balance-sheet CDOs, which are sponsored by banks seeking to reduce regulatory capital requirements. And then there are the arbitrage CDOs, where the motivation "is to arbitrage the price difference between the underlying pool of debt obligations and CDO tranches."[20] Structured finance expert and consultant Janet Tavakoli insists the hedge funds were not engaging in arbitrage per se, because their gambit did not offer a risk-free payoff by simultaneous bets on the same investment—but was instead engaging in a trading strategy with multiple investments.[21]

Individual hedge funds found they could reap big payoffs with the so-called correlation trade that involved going long on the equity tranche and short on the rated tranches. With this strategy, the hedge fund would make money from the high yields on the equity tranche as long as the CDO continued to perform. The attractive returns— 21 percent—were usually made even more attractive by high leverage at the hedge fund. Then, if the CDO crashed, the hedge fund would reap a windfall because it shorted a rated tranche. So your bet paid off while the CDO performed and paid off even more when it failed.

The investment strategies of hedge funds contrast sharply with the investment strategies of insurance companies that invested in mortgage-backed securities. This more traditional approach was to purchase AAA-rated tranches of a mortgage-backed security for the high yields they offer and then buy protection from bond insurance companies in case there was a default. By contrast, the synthetic CDO created two types of investors in the same deal with opposing interests—the sellers and buyers of credit protection—which, in turn, raised potential conflicts of interest for the CDO underwriters and possibly the CDO manager.

A Financial Crisis Inquiry Commission survey of more than 170 hedge funds with $1.1 trillion in assets found half of the equity tranches from CDOs issued in the second half of 2006 were purchased by mid-sized hedge funds that also shorted other tranches in the transaction.[22] The hedge funds were also using the same correlation strategy to make dual bets on tranches of mortgage-backed securities. The survey found that by June 2007, large hedge funds held $25 billion in equity and other lower-rated tranches, while also holding $45 billion in short positions.

With the synthetic CDO, the hedge fund investors in CDOs no longer had an incentive to carefully choose collateral to contain credit risk. Indeed, there did not appear to be a party whose interests would lead them to monitor credit risk in CDO deals. Consider the case of Merrill Lynch's $1.5 billion Norma CDO Ltd., issued in 2007.[23] Magnetar Capital, the hedge fund investor in Norma's equity tranche, was engaged in a correlation trade strategy. It simultaneously shorted other tranches of Norma, as well as shorting other CDOs.

Magnetar Capital LLC is an Evanston, Illinois-based hedge fund founded in 2005 by Alec Litowitz, a former trader who headed equity strategy at Citadel Investment Group.[24] He recruited to his firm his former colleague David Snyderman, who headed credit trading at Citadel.

An inside look into the structure of Norma was provided by court documents from a civil case brought by Rabobank, a Dutch bank that had extended to Norma a secured loan of $57 million and was still owed $42 million when Norma defaulted and was liquidated in 2008.[25] When filing its complaint, Rabobank charged that Merrill misrepresented Norma as being a carefully constructed deal. Instead, the bank charged, Norma was "a dumping ground" for Merrill's worst CDO assets and was structured to benefit Magnetar, an important hedge fund client of Merrill's.[26]

Rabobank claimed that Magnetar played a role in selecting collateral in the CDO even though NIR Capital Management was the designated CDO manager and was supposed to select collateral. The Dutch bank claimed that NIR frequently abdicated its asset-selection duties to Magnetar, with Merrill's knowledge. When one Merrill employee, a risk manager, learned that Magnetar had executed $600 million in trades without NIR knowing about it, she sent an e-mail to her colleagues at Merrill. "Dumb question. Is Magnetar allowed to trade for NIR?"[27]

The Dutch bank also alleged that Merrill did not disclose to NIR that Magnetar was paid $4.5 million by Merrill Lynch. It was also claimed that Merrill did not disclose to NIR that Magnetar was selecting collateral when it also had a short position in one of Norma's tranches.[28] Even when NIR was involved in an asset selection, Magnetar had the right to veto it, the lawsuit claimed. For example, when NIR asked James Prusko, head of structured products at Magnetar, whether or not NIR could buy the TABS 2006-6A cash bond, Prusko sent an e-mail saying no, "tabs in particular I don't want the cash in there."[29]

Jonathan Pickhardt, trial attorney for Merrill Lynch, wrote to Judge Bernard Fried of the Supreme Court of New York on May 11, 2010, to inform him that Magnetar was not taking a neutral position but was much more interested in its short position with Norma that its long position. "Indeed, Magnetar's equity investment in Norma totaled less than $50 million after receiving undisclosed discounts through the loan from Rabobank. This meant that Magnetar stood to make 10 times more from its $600 million short position if Norma failed than Magnetar had invested in Norma's equity," Pickhardt wrote.[30]

Pickhardt was seeking permission from Judge Fried to engage in discovery with Magnetar to strengthen Merrill's defense against fraud charges from Rabobank. The case against Merrill, filed in April 2010, was settled later that year.

Magnetar also gained fame as the subject of an investigative report by ProPublica, an investigative journalism organization that published a story claiming the fund was involved in the creation of 30 CDOs that later crashed and burned, leaving investors with $40 billion in losses.[31]

After that story broke, Magnetar wrote to its investors to defend its investing strategy as "in essence a capital structure arbitrage," based on the relative value and pricing between differing tranches of a CDO.[32] "From early 2006 to late 2007, there was a systematic relative value mispricing between the equity tranches of mortgage CDO structures, which offered approximately 20% target yields, and mezzanine debt tranches of mortgage CDO structures, on which credit protection could be bought from between 1% and 4%," the Magnetar letter stated.

Magnetar insisted to investors the fund was market neutral on the outlook for the housing sector and subprime mortgages and that it was not using its influence to select collateral for CDOs that would make them more likely to implode. At least in the case of Norma, the relative amounts of Magnetar's bets—$50 million in long and $600 million in short—suggest otherwise.

THE WINNERS OF THE CDO LOTTERY

Hedge funds were the fast-money and high-stakes players. Their demand for equity tranches in CDOs prompted the creation of more subprime mortgage-backed securities and more subprime mortgages. It was, in fact, the riskier subprime loans that created the potential for better returns for hedge funds in CDO correlation trading strategies. This demand, in fact, drove the structure of CDOs away from conservative toward riskier designs.

This helps explain the significance of a statement by William Dallas, founder and president of Ownit Mortgage Solutions. "The market is paying me to do a no-income-verification loan more than it is paying me to do the full documentation loans."[33] By creating demand for riskier mortgages, Wall Street was handing incentives to mortgage lenders to engage in predatory lending. This also explains why an unidentified executive at Saxon Capital, another subprime lender, told investors in 2005 that deteriorating credit posed a "perfect storm" with dire consequences from new riskier mortgages that were likely to blow up.[34] Saxon was originating the bad loans Wall Street and Fannie and Freddie wanted—loans so bad Saxon was unwilling to hold them on its balance sheets.

The demand by hedge funds for equity tranches in subprime CDOs also had a multiplying effect on the mortgage industry—generating a response proportionally larger than the demand. This was the case because only a fairly small sliver of a subprime mortgage-backed security deal is made up of mezzanine tranches—the tranches needed to create a CDO.

According to Goodman et al., the volume of subprime mezzanine tranches incorporated into CDOs increased from $27 billion in 2005 to $50 billion in 2006, before receding to $33 billion in 2007.[35]

In a typical subprime mortgage-backed securities deal, 4 percent was rated A and 3 percent was rated BBB, while 2 percent was rated below investment grade or unrated, for a total of 9 percent of the deal.

So to create the $27 billion of mezzanine tranches for CDOs in 2005 required the creation of $300 billion of the $456 billion of subprime mortgage bonds issued that year. In 2006 and 2007, to create the $50 billion and $33 billion respectively in mezzanine tranches as collateral for the creation of the CDO required more than all available mezzanine and unrated tranches of subprime bonds plus mezzanine tranches from Alt-A mortgage-backed securities.

The advent of ABS CDS did not contribute to the demand for more subprime mortgage-backed securities but did magnify the impact of the disaster in the making. "While a liberating experience for [subprime CDO] managers in 2005, the single-name ABS CDS swap market magnified the size of the [subprime CDO] disaster in 2007," concluded Goodman et al.[36] While synthetic CDOs were wreaking havoc, hedge funds were able to "reap billions in profits."[37]

When the CDO market began to crater, it was the short sellers who were the big winners in a zero sum wealth transfer from all the other parties in the deal and beyond—with the taxpayers picking up a big piece of the tab.

Bass of Hayman Advisors was one who early on saw that subprime was going to crash. He was able to win over a fellow convert in Alan Fournier of Pennant Capital in Chatham, New Jersey. Finding other investors was not an easy task for the duo. "We were saying that there were going to be $1 trillion in loans in trouble," Bass said in 2007. "You had to have an imagination to believe us."[38] As part of his research to find particular subprime bonds to bet against, his hedge fund, Hayman, and Pennant Capital hired private detectives, rifled through news reports, and interviewed Wall Street mortgage bond underwriters. They were looking for mortgage originators whose loans were the most likely to default and found a likely prospect in Quick Loan Funding of Costa Mesa, California, headed by Lebanese immigrant Daniel Sadek.

Bass and Fournier soon learned that Quick Loan was so profitable that Sadek was funding a movie, *Redline*, about racing expensive cars that starred Nadia Bjorlin, a soap opera actress he was dating. Further, during the filming of the movie, stunt men catapulted and wrecked a Porsche Carrera GT from Sadek's own stash of expensive cars. "That's the guy you want to bet against," he told Fournier.[39]

Bass raised about $100 million and leveraged it to sell $1.2 billion of subprime securities short. The trades were placed in August and September of 2006. By the time Bass testified before the House Financial Services Committee a year later, he had been completely vindicated in his views and handsomely rewarded. Bass told CNBC's David Faber his investment had soared 600 percent in value in 18 months.[40]

In betting against the mezzanine tranches of mortgage bonds placed into CDOs, Bass and Fournier were betting that the credit rating agencies and Wall Street had it all wrong.

Evidence of failed credit ratings appeared dramatically in early 2007 with the sudden collapse of subprime lenders, followed by the crash of the subprime CDO machine, and finally the collapse of the entire private-label mortgage-backed enterprise by mid-year. It was not for several years, however, that it was clear just how poorly the underlying loans originated in 2006 and 2007 performed against historic trends.

It has been argued that the short sellers finally ended the madness generated by the CDO mania. While that may have been true in part, one can argue that the arrival of more and more short sellers, in turn, allowed the CDO merry-go-round to continue turning and kept the calliope playing long after evidence was mounting that a disaster was in the making.

THE SAVVY AND CLEVER PREVAIL

When the market for CDOs crashed and bank regulators began to sift through the ashes, they came to the conclusion that the hedge funds had the firmest grasp on the underlying credits that went into the CDOs.

"Our interviews," reported the Basel Committee on Banking Supervision, "suggested that only the most sophisticated market participants, including some of those who specialized in fundamental credit analysis as the holder of first-loss equity positions, said they were able to drill down to underlying assets within their [information technology] systems and analyze this information in detail."[41]

The hedge funds, for various reasons, were reluctant to share what they knew about the underlying assets, even with investors in various tranches of the CDOs, the interviewers found.[42] Further, many investors in CDOs "may not be allowed access to detailed information about the underlying portfolio," the report stated.

CDOs represented the most opaque of all transactions involving credit risk transfer, according to the Basel Committee. Documentation of underlying assets and risks is not made public because these are private placements under securities laws.

CDO managers and investors have many reasons to keep the data private, not the least of which is that making the data public would reveal "the manager's proprietary trading strategy," the Basel Committee reported.

In fact, one might be more specific and say that details on the underlying pool of loans must be kept secret if the correlation trading strategies were to work.

Therefore, buy-side sponsors of CDOs were attracted to the fact that CDOs can indeed be financial black boxes. The greater the opacity, the better the odds for the success of any trading activity. The other parties who invested in the CDO tranches may not understand that ultimately the strategy of the sponsor who helped put together the CDO and selected the collateral may not be to gather a portfolio of assets that will protect the interests of the owners of the other tranches. Indeed, it may only be to assemble the collateral needed to create speculative trading opportunities that are structured to increase the odds of huge financial rewards for the CDO sponsors.

The CDO manager is under no legal requirement to consider the suitability of an investment for any institution or person who invests in any of its tranches. The parties to the transaction, thus, actually need to do their own in-depth due diligence, which is not always possible given how carefully guarded are the details on the characteristics of the loans in the underlying portfolios. The due diligence should also be done in analyzing the structure of the CDO transaction.

The fact that CDOs are black boxes may also create more opportunities for fraud. Some risk analysts, such as Christopher Whalen, have contended that the aggressive level of innovation and aggressive limits on transparency that characterize CDOs and CDSs are "so extreme as to approximate deliberate fraud."[43] It also makes the assets so difficult to value that it is "on the verge of being deceptive by design—that is, a deliberate criminal enterprise."

As troublesome as Whalen's comments may be, the negative impact of the black box CDO casinos goes beyond these important concerns.

Recall that part of the justification for the unregulated and unrestrained spread of derivatives and structured finance is that it transfers and therefore reduces the chance that concentrations of risk could lead to a failure at a key institution that might have a systemic impact.

Indeed, credit default swaps did not just spread risk; they multiplied risk and then spread it. Just how much more risk and to how many parties is hard to calculate precisely. The risk was spread both through the CDO tranches and to those who sold insurance protection through credit default swaps for underlying tranches of mortgage-backed securities.

An accountant, Richard R. Zabel, calculated the total value of speculative bets placed with credit default swaps by the end of 2007 through a simple mathematical formula. The entire credit default swap market had a notional value of $45 trillion, while the corporate bond, municipal bond, and structured investment vehicles markets totaled $25 trillion. "Therefore, a minimum of $20 trillion were speculative 'bets' on the possibility of a credit event of a specific credit asset not owned by either party to the [credit default swap] contract," Zabel has written.[44]

Credit default swaps also concentrated risk in specific financial institutions—making a mockery of the claim that they spread the risk. Monoline insurance companies function mostly as financial guarantors for municipal bonds, but also sold protection to investors via credit default swaps in the super senior part of the capital structure of the CDOs. Because of the considerable level of credit enhancement protecting the super seniors, they were thought to be super safe. In fact, they became just one more class of toxic assets after the mortgage meltdown.

Credit risk transfer activity by monolines, in fact, rose from 10 percent of their portfolio in 2005 to 20 to 30 percent by 2007, according to the Basel Committee.[45] During the subprime meltdown of 2007, these monolines came under tremendous stress and lost their AAA ratings. One of the largest, Ambac Financial Group Inc., filed for bankruptcy in November 2010. MBIA, Inc., another monoline, was downgraded and greatly weakened as a result of its backing of tranches of subprime mortgage-backed securities in CDOs.

A THOUGHT EXPERIMENT

One way to measure the magnitude of the impact of the CDO mania on the larger financial crisis and the global financial system is to consider how much smaller the subprime mortgage market might have been without it.

One interesting way to do this is to consider an alternative history without the CDO mania that began in 2004. To do that, one needs to go back to 2003, when subprime securitization volume was only $195 billion. If CDO creation volume, and thus demand for subprime bonds, remained at the 2003 level, there would have been $795 billion less in overall subprime bond issuance from 2004 to 2007.[46]

Or take another alternative scenario. Assume that CDO issuance fell back to the $123 billion level of 2002, when private-label securities first qualified for preferential treatment under bank capital regulations. If issuance remained at the 2002 pace, there would have been $1.12 trillion less demand for subprime mortgage bonds by 2007.[47] One could add in, of course, the entire subprime CDO of ABS market of $700 billion that depended on the issuance of subprime bonds as an amount to subtract from the total cost of the crisis in this scenario. This would represent an alternative history where there would have been $1.82 trillion less in subprime bonds and CDOs. Given the calculation of the entire universe of subprime at Alt-A was $4.6 trillion in mid-2008, there would have been 40 percent less risky assets in the system, and it would have largely eliminated the contribution of private-sector mortgage-backed securities to the crisis.

In short, without the CDO mania, there would not have been so large a private-label subprime bubble to keep the housing boom going, and it would have been contained mostly to government-related subprime lending. It's hard to imagine a mortgage meltdown on the scale that occurred without the role of Wall Street's CDO frenzy. Importantly, without the CDO mania, there would have been far fewer toxic assets on the balance sheets of Wall Street firms and banks that crashed the shadow banking system.

Fannie and Freddie may still have done as much subprime and Alt-A lending without a large private sector involved—but more likely they would have scaled back, too. So there might still have been a lot of bad mortgages in the system that would fail when the housing bubble burst. Instead of so many catastrophes in the world of banking, insurance, and Wall Street, we may have only had the failure of Fannie and Freddie.

In short, the subprime bond bubble and the CDO mania that fed it would seem to be central to the origins of the entire financial crisis.

8

American International Group

The emergence of credit default swaps introduced risks and uncertainties into the financial markets in ways that few market observers—certainly not the regulators—could fully observe, even as it was happening. This was due, in part, to the fact that these are private bilateral contracts and the parties to the contracts do not have to reveal the terms of the contracts publicly.

The securities markets were creating insurance products from derivatives that were often completely unregulated or even monitored by regulators unless some of the parties happen to come under prudential regulators for other reasons. Thus, each credit default swap contract was potentially a financial black box.

In the United States, insurance products are tightly regulated by states, which overall have a fairly good track record in monitoring the ability of insurance companies to meet the obligations insurers make when they issue insurance policies. Further, states require insurance companies to disclose important information that investors and the public can see and that can be evaluated by anyone in the markets who wishes to assess whether or not a given company can honor its commitments in good or bad times.

Bond insurance is one of the products that states regulate. Typically, bond insurers are monoline companies. That means they are in a single line of business and must be adequately capitalized to pay claims during severe economic downturns and other calamities that might result in payment default by the bond issuers.

When Wall Street discovered it could issue bond insurance almost without any rules, it led to a huge run-up in business.

No casualty to credit default swaps looms larger than American International Group, Inc., or AIG, the world's largest insurance conglomerate that, before the crisis, had a pristine reputation and a rare AAA credit rating for its bonds. AIG's Financial Products Group (AIG FP) in Wilton, Connecticut, fell outside state regulation and was lightly regulated by, of all entities, the sleepy and sometimes clueless Office of Thrift Supervision.

The financial catastrophe at AIG comes close to being on par with that at Fannie Mae, which by far suffered the greatest losses in absolute terms and on a relative basis to their earnings. The key metric on the calamity scale is the accumulated net loss from the third quarter of 2007 to the third quarter of 2009 expressed in the number of years of profits those losses erased.

In those nine quarters, AIG lost $109 billion, which erased 17.5 years of its cumulative profits. In other words, it would take 17.5 years for AIG to recover those losses if it could immediately return to the level of profitability that existed prior to the mortgage meltdown. This measure was one put together from public data by Dallas hedge fund manager J. Kyle Bass of Hayman Advisors LP and presented to the Financial Crisis Inquiry Commission.[1]

Only Fannie Mae scored higher on this measure, having lost $120 billion during the same period, an amount that is equal to 20.5 years of cumulative profits. Freddie Mac was in third place, with $67.9 billion in losses, representing 11 years of cumulative profits erased.

By this measure, AIG's financial disaster is fundamentally more severe than the financial losses that hit Lehman Brothers, Bear Stearns, Merrill Lynch, Citigroup, Washington Mutual, and Wachovia—only one of which, Citigroup, survived as an independent entity.

Monoline bond insurers, all of which are state regulated, have to set aside reserves for losses when they enter into an insurance contract. Not so AIG FP on its credit defaults swaps. Nor did its counterparties. "AIG, Bear Stearns and Lehman would not have been able to take on as much leverage as they did," Bass testified, "had they been required to post initial collateral on day one for the risk positions they assumed."[2] The requirement for an "initial margin" applied then and still today only to counterparties of lesser credit quality, which excludes most hedge funds.

"Imagine if you were a 28-year-old mathematics superstar at AIG Financial Products Group and you were compensated at the end of each year based upon the profitability of your trading book, which was ultimately based upon risks you were able to take without initially posting any money. How much risk would you take?" Bass asked. "In

AIG's case, the risks taken in the company's derivatives book were more than 20 [times] the firm's shareholders equity."

This was such an enormous loophole in regulation that it meant that from a balance sheet and capital perspective, AIG could have written credit protection on tranches or slices of collateralized debt obligations or CDOs "to infinity and beyond"—to borrow a phrase from Buzz Lightyear from *Toy Story*. CDOs are securitizations of other assets, including loans and securities.

A number of financial institutions that had been in the business of being CDO underwriters took on the risk of being protection providers for the cash and synthetic mezzanine tranches in CDOs. (Mezzanine tranches are those rated A to BBB). And many of them turned around and bought protection from AIG or the monoline insurers or any other counterparty deemed to be suitably reliable and able to pay off the credit protection if and when the market turned against the subprime assets.

Goldman Sachs was one of the Wall Street firms that entered into credit default swaps with AIG to hedge its own position as a seller of credit protection in synthetic CDOs, those built on credit default swaps and not actual securities. (See Chapter 7.) This underscored another weakness in the unregulated credit default swap market. The counterparty to the original credit default swap written by Goldman Sachs could theoretically be any entity or individual on the planet, given that the responsibility for meeting collateral calls could be passed along in an infinite chain.

This weakness was lampooned by a blogger two years before the mortgage meltdown. "One thing we do know is the derivatives bubble has become too large for transparency of any kind," wrote Mike Shedlock, an investment adviser for SitkaPacific Capital in September 2005.[3] "No one fully understands exactly what the counterparty risk really is. Everybody has vast positions, most of which are 'netted out,' but it's also a chain that no one has complete control over or even knowledge about," he continued.

"What if the ultimate guarantee of a slew of contracts is Madame Merriweather's Mud Hut in Indonesia? How would anyone know?"

AIG FP was started in 1987 by Howard Sosin, a refugee from Drexel Burnham Lambert, the Wall Street firm that, before it blew up, made fortunes on leveraged buyouts in the 1980s under Michael Milken. Sosin hired Joe Cassano, a former Drexel colleague. Cassano later took over the unit as president. He was in charge of AIG FP when Blythe Masters, who originated the credit default swap concept, approached him with the idea of having AIG insure the super senior tranches of CDOs of ABS (asset-backed securities) originated by J. P. Morgan.[4]

According to Gillian Tett in *Fool's Gold*, AIG received only 0.02 cents on every dollar it insured each year. This tiny amount, however, could translate into a considerable cash flow given the size of CDO deals, typically around a billion dollars each. The modeling for the risk that AIG faced was done by Gary Gorton, a Yale University economics professor.[5]

According to a former colleague, Gorton's work "helped convince Cassano that these things were only gold, that if anybody paid you to take on these risks, it was free money" with virtually no chance AIG would ever have to pay out a single dime to the protection buyer.[6] Gorton earned an estimated million dollars a year advising AIG.[7]

CREDIT PROTECTION ON SUBPRIME BONDS

After the green light from Gorton, AIG FP started pitching seller protection first on corporate bonds and later on super senior tranches of synthetic CDOs of ABS to banks around the globe. While others entered this line of business, AIG FP led the pack in business tied to subprime CDOs. In 2005, AIG FP tripled its book of business of protection on super senior CDO tranches from a notional amount of $17.9 billion to $54.3 billion.[8] This tripling of exposure was unknown to Martin Sullivan, AIG's chief executive officer, and Stephen Bensinger, the company's chief financial officer.[9]

Even more shockingly, Sullivan, Bensinger and other former senior AIG executives told investigators at the Financial Crisis Inquiry Commission they did not know prior to 2007 that the credit default swaps required AIG to post collateral based on declines in the market value of the underlying mortgage bonds.[10] Apparently, the earliest any of the senior executives learned about the requirement to post collateral was when chief risk officer Robert Lewis received a margin call from Goldman Sachs in 2007.

Andrew Forster, an executive vice president at AIG FP, raised a red flag about the risks in the credit default swaps business in an e-mail on July 21, 2005, that was sent to, among others, Gorton at Yale and Alan Frost, AIG's marketing executive, as well as to Tom Ewings, a managing director of AIG FP in London who worked directly for Joe Cassano.[11]

The e-mail was sent out before 7 a.m. in Connecticut for a transatlantic phone conference for 9 a.m. Eastern United States and 2 p.m.

London time. The intent of the notice was to provide some points to start a discussion on the effectiveness of the modeling of AIG's risk in the business and to take a frank look at the rising level of risk. "We are taking on a huge amount of sub prime mortgage exposure here and it is clearly a fast evolving market," Forster wrote.

Forster highlighted a worrisome trend where some CDO managers "can pick up spread by buying deals more biased to low FICO scores, or with new collateral types such as option ARMs, or with heavy geographic concentration."

Forster was beginning to fret about the deals that CDO managers sponsored. "Do we know enough about each [CDO] manager to decide whether they are not just out to create the biggest [arbitrage] possible and that they know enough to select a decent pool of assets even if the deal is static?" Forster suggested that by offering to sell protection for CDO deals indiscriminately, AIG FP was "encouraging guys to remain focused on sub prime" and to exclude other asset types.

Forster was also concerned that AIG FP might be required to post collateral on the contracts it was writing and worried how far credit downgrades would have to go to trigger an event of default that required posting collateral.

Around the same time, another AIG FP executive, Gene Park, became troubled about AIG's credit default business on CDOs after an old college friend with no job told him lenders were offering him loans to buy a house.[12] By late 2005, Park, who sold the swaps, was promoted to lead trader and head of derivatives marketing.

Cassano, in his testimony before the inquiry commission, had a chance to defend himself against the claim he was the man who crashed the world, as author Michael Lewis once described him,[13] and he presented a spirited defense of his role that was sketchy on key details. The commissioners not only failed to probe his claims but also made no effort to get him to fill the gaps in his story.

Cassano did confirm some of the facts already known. "In mid-2005, AIG FP's head trader was concerned that changes in the subprime mortgage market may have meant more risk in new deals compared to existing ones,"[14] Cassano said, speaking of Gene Park as head trader but not naming him. "We discussed taking a harder look at the market, and I asked for his recommendation," he continued. Next the "head trader" asked to convene a group to do further research on the subprime CDO market. "I agreed his course was a prudent one, and we selected a team to assist in the fact-gathering and analysis," Cassano said.

"After that detailed review and analysis, the head trader believed AIG FP should stop writing [credit default swap] protection on CDOs with subprime exposure," Cassano testified. Based on the "head trader's" recommendation, AIG stopped writing deals with subprime exposure.

AIG FP decided sometime in late 2005 and early 2006 to exit the business but to go ahead with the deals in the pipeline. Unfortunately for AIG FP, the pipeline was enormous.

On February 28, 2006, Park sent an e-mail to Cassano and others outlining how he was planning to announce AIG's decision to exit the business.[15] Park proposed to tell Wall Street that AIG would no longer write protection for mezzanine layers of any nonprime mortgage securitizations, which would include both subprime and Alt-A. This, in effect, meant AIG was out of the business.

When Wall Street traders received the AIG FP notice, it should have been a wake-up call. Yet, except for a few people like Greg Lippmann at Deutsche Bank, who advocated AIG's exit from the business, its message was ignored, and banks and Wall Street firms not only continued to arrange CDO deals but also began to increase the number of new deals!

While Citigroup was the only major player without credit default swap protection up to this point, with AIG's exit, some of the other dealers were now tempted to go without hedging the protection they were offering the players who wanted to bet against subprime.

Whatever concerns Cassano had about the subprime business, he decided not to hedge AIG's own exposure to a subprime meltdown, although he briefly considered it.[16] Cassano later defended that decision as being based on his belief that the existing vintages of subprime covered by the firm's swaps had not been "tainted by any slippage in underwriting standards."[17]

In November 2007, Joseph St. Denis, an accountant hired to oversee AIG FP transactions, ran into roadblocks set up by Cassano when he was trying to determine the value of AIG's credit default swap positions.[18] Exasperated, St. Denis resigned. A few months later Cassano was fired. As collateral postings mounted, AIG was downgraded by the credit rating agencies, accelerating the decline of the once mighty giant.

Cassano argued that if the swaps had not been unwound, AIG would have suffered only temporary accounting losses, citing the subsequent performance of mortgages it covered with AIG swaps. Those toxic assets ended up in Maiden Lane III, a special-purpose vehicle set up by the New York Fed to manage the collateral backed by the

AIG swaps that were unwound in order to buy them. Maiden Lane is the name of a street in New York's financial district.

"As I look at the performance of some of these same CDOs in Maiden Lane III, I think there would have been few, if any, realized losses on the [credit default swap] contracts had they not been unwound in the bailout," Cassano claimed.[19] He further crowed that had he not been fired in early 2008, he would have fought more vigorously against the collateral calls. By the time Cassano left AIG FP, he had earned $280 million in cash and $34 million in bonuses.[20]

In 2007, when the subprime market collapsed, AIG's super senior tranche book of business was valued at $78 billion, pushing dangerously close to AIG's net worth of $95.8 billion. As counterparties, such as Goldman Sachs, began to demand and receive steadily higher collateral postings from AIG to cover serial downgrades in subprime securitizations, it began to put a squeeze on AIG, setting it on the road toward collapse.

It is hard to imagine the CDO market would have gotten so big so fast without the major role of insurer of last resort played by AIG FP. Its exit in the late middle of 2006 did little to slow down the CDO engine, which by then had become a locomotive driven by the fast-money aspirations of many hedge funds.

AIG made another colossal strategic business blunder that came back to haunt the company. It had decided to take the cash it had received for lending out its highest-rated bonds and invest that in subprime, Alt-A, and other mortgage-backed securities. Now it needed the cash. And to raise the cash to unwind the credit default swaps, AIG needed to sell the mortgage-backed securities at a huge loss.

As evidence of growing interest by federal banking regulators in credit derivatives, banks were required to disclose credit derivatives activity in their quarterly call reports beginning with the first quarter of 2006. Regulated commercial banks are required to file the call reports with the Office of the Comptroller of the Currency. Neither AIG FP nor Wall Street's investment banks had to file such call reports. In the first quarter of 2006, JPMorgan Chase held the most, $2.85 trillion in notional amount in credit derivatives, with presumably nearly all of them credit default swaps.[21] Citigroup Inc. held $1.12 trillion. Bank of America was third with $813.3 billion. HSBC North American Holdings, parent of Household Finance, a subprime lender, held $489 billion in credit derivatives, the fourth largest holding.

Since banks held both positive and negative credit protection, the actual exposures of these banks was much lower but unknown.

The surviving investment banks converted to bank holding companies and began filing a call report on derivatives in the first quarter of 2009. Not surprisingly, Goldman Sachs was near the top at number two, with $6.6 trillion, while Morgan Stanley was third with $6.3 trillion. Bank of America was now fourth at $5.6 trillion, absorbing the positions held by Merrill Lynch. JPMorgan Chase still topped the charts at $7.5 trillion.

A DETESTED BAILOUT

The bailout of AIG did not start out as a public bailout by taxpayers. It began as an effort to craft a private-sector rescue under the guiding hand of the New York Fed.

On Monday morning, September 15, 2008, after Lehman's bankruptcy had already been announced, New York Fed President Timothy Geithner convened a meeting in his office with teams from JPMorgan Chase and Goldman Sachs to work out a private-sector solution to AIG's problems.[22] He had already received a pledge from Jamie Dimon, chairman and CEO of JPMorgan Chase and Lloyd Blankfein, chairman and CEO of Goldman Sachs, to put together a private rescue package.

AIG was facing a possible credit rating downgrade that day by Moody's that would push it into bankruptcy. At this point, it was thought that a bridge loan of $50 billion in return for warrants for 79.9 percent of AIG would get the insurer over the hump until it could sell some of its assets.

Despite a half-hearted phone call from a trouble-shooter at Treasury to the credit rating agency to delay the credit downgrade, Moody's downgraded AIG's senior debt from A2 to Aa3.[23] Geithner called the bankers back to the Fed for further discussions. By now the due diligence teams were estimating the capital hole in AIG to be $60 billion.

By Tuesday, September 16, AIG's situation was so dire, the insurer needed $85 billion, according to former Treasury Secretary Hank Paulson.[24] The private-sector rescue was fizzling. The Fed would have to step in—and did, providing a 24-month credit liquidity facility from which AIG could draw up to $85 billion, only a day after Lehman filed for bankruptcy. The rescue loan was possible because there was sufficient collateral from all the assets of AIG and its subsidiaries to back it up, the Fed explained. In exchange for the credit facility, the U.S. government received warrants for a 79.9 percent equity stake in AIG, with the right to suspend the payment of dividends to AIG common and preferred shareholders.[25] The government had essentially nationalized AIG, and the company immediately drew down $28 billion the next day, September 17. By October 24, AIG had drawn down a total of $122.8 billion and needed more.

On November 10, 2008, the U.S. Treasury announced it would purchase $40 billion in newly issued AIG senior preferred stock to bolster the company under the authority of the newly authorized $700 billion Troubled Asset Relief Program, or TARP. The Fed also announced it had authorized the New York Fed to set up Maiden Lane III, funded with $24.3 billion from the New York Fed in the form of a senior loan plus a $5 billion equity investment from AIG. Maiden Lane III, in turn, would acquire the toxic CDO assets from AIG's counterparties.

Almost forgotten in the reporting of AIG's woes was the other store of toxic assets—the mortgage-backed securities it had purchased with the cash from its securities lending program. To remove these assets from AIG, the New York Fed was also authorized to set up another entity, Maiden Lane II, and lend it $22.5 billion to fund the purchase of these assets. AIG agreed to lend Maiden Lane II a billion dollars and bear the risk of the first billion dollars in losses.

A year after the AIG bailout, TARP's special investigator general Neil Barofsky released a report[26] that claimed Treasury and the New York Fed had not just rescued AIG, they had, in effect, engaged in a "backdoor bailout" of AIG's Wall Street counterparties. The Fed agreed to have Maiden Lane III pay $27.1 billion for the assets held by the counterparties. This amount, when combined with $35 billion in collateral already posted to the counterparties, totaled 100 percent of the $62.1 billion of the full value of the collateral covered by AIG's swaps. (See Table 8.1.) The government had essentially not only filled the capital hole in AIG, but unfairly enriched AIG's counterparties with funds above and beyond the value of the assets they held.

This 100 percent bailout contrasted starkly with the 1998 rescue of hedge fund Long-Term Capital Management arranged by the New York Fed. In that instance, the equity holders in the hedge fund, including Wall Street trading legend John Meriwether, lost everything they had put into the company.

In 2008, the biggest beneficiary of Washington's largesse, France's Société Generale, received $6.9 billion of the bailout money and kept $9.6 billion in collateral it had already obtained from AIG. Goldman Sachs pocketed $5.6 billion in bailout money while keeping $8.4 billion in posted collateral.

Table 8.1   Payments to AIG Counterparties

Payments to AIG Securities Lending Counterparties		Payments to AIG Credit Default Swap Counterparties		
Sept. 18 to Dec. 12, 2008	Billions of Dollars	*As of Nov. 17, 2008*	Billions of Dollars	Billions of Dollars
Barclays	$7.0		Maiden Lane III payment	Collateral payments from AIG
Deutsche Bank	6.4	Société Générale	$6.9	$9.6
BNP Paribas	4.9	Goldman Sachs	5.6	8.4
Goldman Sachs	4.8	Merrill Lynch	3.1	3.1
Bank of America	4.5	Deutsche Bank	2.8	5.7
HSBC	3.3	UBS	2.5	1.3
Citigroup	2.3	Calyon	1.2	3.1
Dresdner Kleinwort	2.2	Deutsche Zentral-Genossenschaftsbank	1.0	0.8
Merrill Lynch	1.9	Bank of Montreal	0.9	0.5
UBS	1.7	Wachovia	0.8	0.2
ING	1.5	Barclays	0.6	0.9
Morgan Stanley	1.0	Bank of America	0.5	0.3
Société Générale	0.9	Royal Bank of Scotland	0.5	0.6
AIG International	0.6	Dresdner Bank AG	0.4	0.0
Credit Suisse	0.4	Rabobank	0.3	0.3
Paloma Securities	0.2	Landesbank Baden-Wuerttemberg	0.1	0.0
Citadel	0.2	HSBC Bank USA	0.0	0.2
TOTAL	**$43.7**[a]	**TOTAL**	**$27.1**	**$35.0**

[a]Of this total, $19.5 billion came from Maiden Lane II, $17.2 billion came from the Federal Reserve Bank of New York, and $7 billion came from AIG.
Note: Amounts may not add due to rounding.
Source: Special Inspector General for TARP.

Goldman's role in AIG's swap exposures was greater than would appear at first blush. The firm had created $23 billion in toxic assets, 37 percent of the collateral in the backdoor bailout—giving Goldman a "starring role in the near collapse of the global markets," according to Janet Tavakoli, president of Tavakoli Structured Finance in Chicago.[27]

The list of banks that owned toxic CDO assets created by Goldman and bailed out by the New York Fed included Société Generale, Deutsche Bank, JPMorgan Chase, and others. As Tavakoli put it,

Goldman Sachs had "poisoned its own well by elsewhere issuing deals [that] eroded market trust in this entire asset class and drove down prices."

The extent to which Goldman had created toxic assets was revealed in a November 27, 2007 memo[28] written by AIG's Cassano. The memo detailed a number of transactions that were the basis of $4 billion in collateral calls to AIG, $3 billion from Goldman Sachs. For example, Société Generale had bought credit default swap protection from AIG on two tranches of Davis Square VI, a deal Goldman had put together. Further, the bank obtained from Goldman its 67.5 cents-on-the dollar pricing for its exposure and collateral calls.

Barofsky was highly critical of the fact the negotiators did not press the banks for a haircut on the assets. "It was not like they were asked for all that much ever. It was a dismal, halfhearted lack of effort of actually seeking a discount," he said, "especially when you compare it with what occurred just a few weeks earlier, when the president of the New York Fed, Tim Geithner, sat with Hank Paulson and Ben Bernanke and told the banks they were going to be accepting $125 billion" as part of TARPs capital purchase program.[29]

Barofsky also faulted as "a nonsensical defense" the claim that the New York Fed did not have the authority to require less than 100 percent payment.

Barofsky pointed out that "the regulators did not force any of the banks to take any of the capital" a few weeks earlier. "They were prepared to, but they didn't, because they took them in a room and they said to them [that] this is really important and we really want [you] to do this. They were fully prepared to tell them they had to take the capital. They didn't have to. They summoned them down to Washington on very short notice. They put them all in a conference room. And they said, 'This is really what we think you should do,'" he said.[30]

"Now, [what] if they had done a similar effort of gathering of AIG's counterparties in a room—with, again, not a mid-level executive at the Federal Reserve Bank of New York, but Tim Geithner himself, and maybe some of the other players and regulators—and said, 'We think it's really important you take a haircut on this because you know it's important. You've gotten this tremendous benefit from the bailout of AIG, which is helping you survive. This is taxpayer money that is going to be put at risk, and we think it's really important for you to step up and have some shared sacrifice here.'"

The failure to do so meant the government and taxpayer made whole "speculative bets" by Wall Street, Barofsky said, and in the process created "moral hazard."[31]

A GREEN LIGHT FOR CREDIT DERIVATIVES

At its hearing on derivatives, the Financial Crisis Inquiry Commission heard testimony from University of Maryland law professor Michael Greenberger.[32] Companies that underwrote credit default swaps did not have adequate capital to pay off guarantees and there was nothing risk free about accepting small premiums for huge guarantees, he testified. Because credit default swaps are private agreements with no meaningful reporting to federal regulators, the triggering of collateral obligations often comes as a surprise to regulators, Greenberger added. As house prices fell, it triggered CDO obligations unexpectedly to the markets and led to a widespread uncertainty about the viability of financial institutions that may have obligations under the agreements.

Credit tightened, Greenberger argued, because "no institution could be trusted because there was no transparency as to which institutions held toxic [positions in credit default swaps]."

The crisis was further heightened by the presence of a large volume of "naked" credit default swaps to parties who did not own any of the underlying risk. It meant that when a single subprime mortgage defaults, "there is both the real financial losses and the exponential loss derived from failed bets," Greenberger said.

Probably no one on the commission was more receptive to Greenberger's message than Brooksley Born, who had been chairman of the Commodity Futures Trading Commission during the Clinton Administration when Greenberger worked as one of her top aides.

After she became chairman in 1996, the Commodity Futures Trading Commission floated the idea of doing a concept paper to explore whether or not there should be regulation of over-the-counter (OTC) derivatives. This market was already a vast one with $25 trillion in notional value, and very little of it had to do with credit derivatives, such as credit default swaps. Most of the OTC market was in interest rate swaps, currency swaps, and futures contracts. The agency Born headed, in fact, had been created to regulate futures contracts by farmers to hedge against price fluctuations of their crops and livestock.

Born's idea for a derivatives regulation review immediately ran into fierce opposition from Treasury Secretary Robert Rubin, his deputy

Larry Summers, Securities and Exchange Commission chairman Arthur Levitt, Fed Chairman Alan Greenspan, plus a number of members of Congress.

Financial industry executives made a beeline to Born to beg her not to release the concept paper. Summers mounted a campaign against it, according to Daniel Waldman, a former top aide to Born.[33] Summers called Born and said, "I have 13 bankers in my office and they say if you go forward with this, you will cause the worst financial crisis since World War II," recalled Greenberger, who was then director of the division of trading and markets at the agency.

In May 1998, the Commodity Futures Trading Commission released its paper anyway. The financial world did not crash, as predicted.

Congress responded to Born's concept paper by passing a moratorium on any regulatory action by the Commodity Futures Trading Commission. Born, denouncing the move as "muzzling an independent agency," said she would not seek reappointment to a second term. She left office in the spring of 1999.

The moratorium was a huge victory for Wall Street and a big win for Rubin, Summers, and Greenspan. Levitt would later express his regrets that he participated in efforts to shackle the Commodity Futures Trading Commission.

The whole dust-up made Wall Street and its Washington allies all the more intent on preventing any future regulation of derivatives. In the lame duck session in late 2000, Congress enacted the Commodity Futures Modernization Act, which removed OTC derivatives transactions from the requirement of exchange trading and clearing.

With that new law, any potential that the Commodity Futures Trading Commission could regulate credit default swaps and other OTC derivatives was taken away. Under the new law, derivatives were exempt from capital adequacy requirements and from reporting and disclosure required under the Commodity Exchange Act. Incredibly, this meant swaps were exempt from an existing bar against fraud and manipulation and excessive speculation.

Tellingly, the Commodity Futures Modernization Act exempted financial swaps from anti-gambling laws and anti-bucket shop laws in effect in several states.[34] "Had those laws not been preempted, it is almost certain that at least some states would have banned these investments as unlicensed gambling or illegal bucket shops," Greenberger testified. "An action by even a single state would have disrupted the 'naked' [credit default swap] market throughout the country," he contended.[35]

The availability of naked credit default swaps "encourage[d] wide-spread betting on the subprime market," according to Greenberger. By allowing naked short selling, Congress put the taxpayer on the hook for the "bankrupt credit default swap casino."

The argument from those who favor regulation of derivatives, including credit default swaps, has been that the absence of regulation has prevented the functioning of free markets and blocked the arrival of the benefits of transparency and competition. "Had the norms of market regulation been applicable, these swaps transactions would have been adequately capitalized by traditional clearing norms," Greenberger said. "And the dangers building up in these markets would otherwise have been observable by the transparency and price discipline that accompanies exchange trading."

It was not to be. Able to hire some of the most brilliant talents to fight with an open-ended purse, Wall Street had outmaneuvered everyone else.

9

Bear Stearns

In early 2008, with the arrival of each month's set of loan performance data, the value of mortgage assets continued a steady march downward. With each decline, banks, Wall Street firms, and other financial institutions were taking hits against their earnings and capital. With each decline, the financial system was shaken again, further weakened, and pushed toward the next crisis.

In February 2008, American International Group announced it had lost $5.3 billion. In response, Meredith Whitney, an analyst with Oppenheimer who had gained fame in the fall of 2007 for her prediction of massive losses at Citigroup, forecast trouble ahead for AAA-rated Ambac and MBIA. These monolines had boosted their volume of insurance on subprime mortgage bonds when AIG bailed from the credit swaps business in early 2006.

One of the monolines, A-rated ACA, which had provided credit default swap insurance against subprime bonds, had already gone belly-up in November 2007, leaving Merrill Lynch stuck with major losses on its subprime mortgage assets. The bond insurers had tiny capital bases, mostly because they had largely been insuring the super safe municipal bond business and because the credit rating agencies continued to give them top credit ratings.

The losses at AIG and lower credit ratings for bond insurers meant that protections against declining mortgage assets were steadily being eroded, heightening the vulnerability of Wall Street firms and banks holding toxic assets. Like a series of mini-quakes, the steady diet of reports of higher delinquencies, defaults, and write-downs weakened all structures, making them more vulnerable to the next quake.

On March 10, Brad Hintz, a respected financial analyst at Sanford Bernstein, forecast an oncoming rush of write-downs from Wall Street firms with subprime holdings, such as Bear Stearns, in their next quarterly earnings reports. "This difficult credit environment is increasing the funding challenges of even the largest and highest-rated brokers," he wrote in a note to clients. Bear's stock fell 9 percent that day. Alan "Ace" Greenberg, chairman of Bear's executive committee, assured investors that Bear was not in a liquidity crisis.[1]

On March 11, the Federal Reserve moved to shore up confidence by offering a $200 billion lending facility[2] aimed at the liquidity concerns that had surfaced at Bear Stearns and elsewhere. On the same day, however, an unidentified party made a pricey bet that Bear Stearns would quickly stumble toward collapse.

The unknown party or parties bought $1.7 million in put options for Bear Stearns stock, giving them the opportunity to sell 5.7 million shares for $30 apiece and 165,000 shares for $25 apiece by March 21. Whoever sold the puts would have to supply the shares of the stock to the owner of the puts if the owner exercised the option to buy them at any time before they expired. Bear was trading at $62.97 on March 11 when the order was placed. The bet was that in only 10 days the value of Bear's shares would be cut in half.

A put is an options contract that gives the buyer the right to sell the underlying commodity or asset at the strike price at any time up to the expiration date. The potential profit on the deal, should Bear's share price crash, would be $270 million or more. "Even if I were the most bearish man on Earth, I can't imagine buying puts 50 percent below the price with just over a week to expiration," said Thomas Haugh, general partner at PTI Securities and Futures LP in Chicago. "It's not even on the page of rational behavior, unless you know something."[3]

The $1.7 million bet with a potential $270 million payoff fueled speculation. Blogger Judd Bagley of Deep Capture posted a YouTube video a year later detailing circumstantial evidence of naked short selling of Bear Stearns shares between March 12 and 20. The video recounts the daily tally of shares purchased but not delivered, an occurrence that suggests the seller never had possession of the shares.

Under securities rules, the seller of shares has to own or borrow the shares sold. On any day the number of shares bought and not sold is quite small, but between March 12 and 20, the number of Bear's shares per day that were bought but not sold ranged from a low of just below 750,000 to a high of 13.8 million. "All told, between the days those options were purchased and the day they came due, somebody caused the supply of Bear Stearns stock to artificially swell by many millions of shares," said Bagley.[4] This effort to flood the market with shares was designed to drive down the price of those shares.

Bear was not remotely prepared for what was about to happen. Alan Schwartz had just been promoted to CEO in January. Bear's non-executive chairman Jimmy Cayne was out of town in Detroit playing at the North American Bridge Tournament.[5] Cayne is an accomplished bridge player who has earned the title of Grand Life Master, the highest rank of the American Contract Bridge League.

On Monday, March 10, Bear Stearns had $18 billion in cash. Throughout the week, the firm maintained a capital ratio "well in excess" of the 10 percent level required to be well capitalized, according to Sam Molinaro, the former chief operations officer and chief financial officer. The run on the bank began with the sudden appearance Monday morning of "unsubstantiated and inaccurate rumors" that Bear was facing a liquidity crisis, which was clearly not the case, Molinaro said. Yet these rumors persisted and escalated into a panic.

Prime brokerage clients moved cash and securities from Bear to other brokers. Counterparties with Bear to derivatives contracts "moved aggressively to assign away our trades, causing market disruptions and margin calls," Molinaro recalled. Late on Thursday "a significant proportion of our repo counterparties informed us that they would no longer lend to us, even on the basis of secured collateral."

By end of day Thursday, March 13, Bear had only $2 billion in cash.

In Washington, Bob Steel, Treasury undersecretary for domestic finance, rushed into the office of Treasury Secretary Hank Paulson to tell him he had been talking with Rodgin Cohen, a banking lawyer advising Bear Stearns. "Before Bob finished [his sentence], I knew Bear Stearns was dead," Paulson wrote in his book *On the Brink*.[6]

Treasury did not have a plan ready to deal with a crisis like the one erupting at Bear Stearns. Unlike banks, which can be taken over and liquidated by the Federal Deposit Insurance Corporation (FDIC), Bear Stearns was an investment banking firm and did not fall under the regulatory umbrella of the FDIC or any regulator with similar powers. Under the law, the regulator, the Securities and Exchange Commission, and federal authorities had no authority to intervene, even if a failure posed a systemic risk.

Paulson called Timothy Geithner, head of the New York Fed, who assured him he was on the case. The Treasury Secretary next called

SEC chairman Christopher Cox, who suggested that Bear would be an attractive acquisition target.[7] Cox had already spoken to Alan Schwartz, who told him that Bear's collateral was unencumbered, which meant its collateral could back up a loan to finance its acquisition.

Facing a dwindling reserve of cash, Bear Stearns approached JPMorgan Chase for a loan against its collateral, according to Molinaro.[8] After JPMorgan Chase declined, Schwartz realized the company was in dire straits and would have to call the Fed for emergency funding.[9]

BEAR STEARNS WEEKEND

Five a.m., Friday, March 14, 2008, there was a mega phone conference of federal officials to discuss how to deal with Bear: Paulson, Geithner, Fed Chairman Bernanke, plus Kevin Warsh and Don Kohn from the Fed, Tony Ryan and Bob Steel from Treasury, and Erik Sirri from the SEC.[10] Chris Cox was not present due to a technical glitch. At one point Jamie Dimon, chairman and CEO of JPMorgan Chase, the clearing bank for Bear Stearns, joined the call and said he foresaw disaster if Bear failed.

Geithner came up with a plan to get Bear through the weekend. The Fed would lend money to JPMorgan Chase and JPMorgan Chase would lend it to Bear. Bernanke wanted Treasury to indemnify the Fed. Paulson was not sure if Treasury could do that, but decided he had no choice but to go ahead and do it in order to announce a deal before the repurchase (repo) markets opened at 7:30 a.m.

The Fed announced a 28-day loan facility to Bear (via JPMorgan Chase) ahead of the opening of repo market. "Unfortunately, the announcement, in the context of that week of panic and rumors, made matters worse by appearing to confirm the rumors that the company was insolvent," Molinaro said.[11] The run on Bear continued Friday, but Bear survived the day, with its shares as low as $30 at one point. Geithner's gambit looked like it had succeeded in giving Bear a chance to survive the weekend.

"Late Friday [March 14] Bear's credit was downgraded by the rating agencies," Molinaro said. Paulson and Geithner placed a joint call to Bear CEO Schwartz to let him know a deal had to be done over the weekend. Schwartz objected, saying he thought he had a month to work something out because the loan had been for 28 days. "[O]n Friday evening we were informed that the JPMorgan Chase facility would mature on Monday," Molinaro recalled.

Federal regulators quickly settled on JPMorgan Chase as the best potential acquirer of Bear Stearns. Dimon's firm was in better shape than other financial firms because it had pulled back from the subprime market, and did not carry a large volume of super senior CDO tranches. Importantly, its gross leverage at year-end 2007 was 17.5 to 1, less than half Bear's and the lowest of any of the Wall Street firms and on par with many large banks.

JPMorgan Chase began an intense examination of the books at the offices of Bear Stearns at 383 Madison Avenue ahead of making any offer. Assistant Treasury Secretary Neel Kashkari had been shuttling back and forth from Bear at 383 Madison and JPMorgan Chase at nearby 270 Park Avenue as the due diligence effort was under way. After Paulson completed a round on the Sunday talk shows, he learned that Dimon didn't want to go forward with the deal. Dimon did not want Bear's $35 billion in mortgage assets.

The Fed agreed to fund a special-purpose vehicle, later to be called Maiden Lane LLC, to purchase the unwanted assets from Bear. The Fed brought in BlackRock to evaluate Bear's mortgage portfolio. Sources at JPMorgan Chase said they were considering offering $8 to $15 per share.[12] Paulson, however, claimed JPMorgan Chase was considering an offer of $4 to $5 per share.[13]

Paulson thought $4 to $5 was too high, and was already looking ahead to the possibility that JPMorgan Chase might also have to be called on to acquire a failing Washington Mutual.[14] Geithner agreed the price was too high. Paulson told Dimon he should only offer $1 or $2 a share. Dimon decided to offer $2 a share.

Treasury's general counsel Bob Hoyt had been researching whether or not Treasury could indemnify the Fed against losses on its loan to Maiden Lane to purchase Bear's assets, and told Paulson that it was prohibited under the Anti-Deficiency Act without Congressional authority.[15] There was a provision in the law, however, for the Fed to lend money if it was secured to the satisfaction of the Fed. BlackRock's chief executive officer Larry Fink assured Geithner that his firm had done enough due diligence to write a letter stating the loan was adequately secured by collateral.[16]

In the absence of indemnification, Treasury would write a letter to Geithner at the New York Fed in support of the Fed's actions and acknowledge that if the Fed incurred a loss, then the Fed would be able to reduce the level of profits it could send to Treasury by an amount similar to the loss. This was a backdoor way to cover the Fed's potential losses, and, thus, they would fall on the taxpayer. If there had been losses on the Fed's loan, then the taxpayers would have, in essence, bailed out the Fed, a point Paulson acknowledged.[17] With Treasury's letter to Geithner, the Fed would, then, go ahead with a loan to Maiden Lane to purchase $30 billion of mortgage assets at Bear.

The board at JPMorgan Chase approved the offer of $2 a share at 4 p.m., Sunday, March 16. Two hours later, the board at Bear Stearns approved the sale. The $2 share price translated into a sale price of $236 million, a pittance of the firm's value before the crisis began. It was a tiny fraction of the 52-week high of $133. The headquarters building for Bear Stearns at 383 Madison Avenue was believed to be worth more than the sale price. Plus the unidentified purchaser(s) of the $1.7 million in puts on March 11 walked away with $271 million— more than the price at which Bear was sold.

The next task was to get shareholders at Bear Stearns to approve the deal. Employees, who owned one-third of the firm's shares, were understandably livid at the low price of the sale. The markets did not find it credible either, pushing shares above $4. Worried that an unhappy Schwartz might look for another buyer, Dimon decided to offer $10 a share. Paulson wanted to keep it at $8.[18] Bernanke wanted certainty and questioned Paulson's holding out for $8. Paulson relented. Ten dollars would be offered. JPMorgan Chase had also agreed to take the first $1 billion loss on the mortgage assets in Maiden Lane. On May 29, Bear's shareholders approved the deal.

WALL STREET'S BUSINESS MODEL FAILS

One thing had emerged loud and clear in the Bear Stearns experience. Given the skepticism of the investors who provide Wall Street firms their funding, "without a lender of last resort or the stability of a deposit base, neither we nor the independent investment banking model itself could survive," Molinaro explained.[19] It was painfully clear that the doubts that had engulfed and then forced the sale of Bear Stearns could also engulf other firms, particularly Lehman Brothers and Merrill Lynch. In the wake of the sudden fall of Bear, as a precautionary move, Lehman raised $4 billion in convertible preferred shares on April 1. Lehman's chairman Dick Fuld also sought but failed to get Warren Buffet to invest.[20]

Schwartz has contended that Bear was brought down by a liquidity crisis brought on by falling confidence and not because it was insolvent or lacked enough capital. "Now, if one asks, why wasn't there enough confidence? I believe that with the benefit of hindsight the whole system was relying on the fact that the senior tranches of mortgage debt securities . . . were very highly rated," he said.[21] "And, that when the market perceived that some of those very highly rated tranches were actually not high-quality securities, the lack of transparency in the instruments made it impossible to determine which ones on anybody's balance sheets were actually very risky versus less risky."

Schwartz continued, "So there was a reliance on ratings to figure out what somebody's balance sheet looked like. And then when the ratings failed, there was no other way to distinguish who was holding risky instruments, and who was holding safe instruments."

The credit rating agency ratings were, for many market observers, the only window of transparency into the CDOs and the underlying mortgage-backed securities. When confidence was lost in the credit ratings, all parties in the market were unable to judge counterparties and began to assume the worse. Or as Schwartz explained it, "I think that the rating agencies were part of the problem, but I think that the biggest part of the problem was a reliance on the rating agencies without any other measure of transparency."[22]

Bear Stearns was vulnerable to runs because, like most of Wall Street, it had been funding its operations from short-term secured and unsecured cash. When those short-term arrangements did not roll over and new arrangements could not be secured, cash was drained out of the firm.

Paul Friedman, who oversaw the fixed-income repo desk at Bear Stearns, has explained how the firm had sought to improve its liquidity. In 2006, Bear decided to reduce the amount of short-term unsecured funding it borrowed through commercial paper by other means. The move away from heavy reliance on commercial paper was because it "tended to be confidence-sensitive" and thus more subject to being withdrawn in a time of market stress, Friedman said.[23] On the other hand, "Secured borrowing based on high-quality collateral is generally less credit sensitive and therefore more stable."

By moving to secured funding, Bear reduced its short-term unsecured financing from $25.8 billion in 2006 to $11.6 billion by year-end 2007. Commercial paper borrowing was reduced from $20.7 billion to $3.9 billion. The short-term funding was replaced by longer-term secured funding, principally repo funding.

Repo is short for repurchase agreement. It is the sale of securities together with an agreement for the seller to buy back the securities at a later date. The repurchase price is greater than the original sale price, the difference effectively representing interest being charged for the funds provided—or the repo rate.

Friedman said Bear was able to obtain longer-term repo facilities of six months or more to finance the purchase of whole loans and non-agency or private-label mortgage-backed securities. Bear used its short-term funding through commercial paper to purchase only the most secure assets: Treasury or agency securities, referring to Fannie, Freddie, and Ginnie mortgage bonds.

Friedman recounted how the repo market began to undergo stress in the wake of the mortgage meltdown of 2007. Fixed-income repo lenders began to shorten the duration of their loans and started "asking all borrowers to post higher quality collateral to support those loans." This was the beginning of a process of "hair cuts" applied to the collateral, which was in, effect, driving up the cost of obtaining the funds.

While Bear was still able to line up long-term fixed-income repo facilities, lenders were showing less willingness to offer such facilities.

Friedman told the Financial Crisis Inquiry Commission that he did not think anything could have prevented the collapse of Bear Stearns. This view contradicted his view in the immediate aftermath of the firm's collapse, when he said he thought that if the firm had more equity and less leverage, it might have been able to survive.

> However, after witnessing the unprecedented and overwhelming market forces in the fall of 2008—including the bankruptcy of Lehman Brothers, the fire sales of Merrill Lynch, Washington Mutual and Wachovia, and the severe distress faced by larger financial institutions such as Citigroup, Goldman Sachs and Morgan Stanley—it became clear to me, as it is today, that those beliefs are incorrect.
>
> Bear Stearns was the smallest of the major investment banks, and I do not believe that obtaining more long-term secured financing or making any other changes in Bear Stearns's funding strategies would have enabled the firm to overcome those unprecedented market forces or withstand the liquidity crisis that the firm experienced in March 2008.[24]

In reaching his conclusion, Friedman also took back his comments from 2008 to author William Cohan in his book *House of Cards*.[25] Friedman told Cohan: "We did this to ourselves. We put ourselves in a position where this could happen. It's our fault for allowing it to get this far and for not taking steps to do anything about it. It's a classic case of mismanagement at the top. There's no question about it."

FLAWED CAPITAL RULES

New rules governing how much capital Wall Street firms were required to hold and how that capital requirement would be calculated went into effect in 2004. A successor chairman of the SEC, Christopher Cox, would later describe those rules as "fundamentally flawed from the beginning."[26]

The SEC's regulatory oversight of investment banking holding companies—including rules setting capital requirements—was a voluntary program put into place because, among other reasons, the SEC lacked statutory authority to regulate the firms as consolidated corporate entities. The SEC only had authority to regulate the broker-dealer subsidiaries of Wall Street firms.

The lack of a prudential regulator for investment banking holding companies was, in fact, the weakest link in financial institution regulatory oversight. How did this come about? It was part of the fallout from the passage of the Gramm-Leach-Bliley Act of 1999,[27] which had put the final nails in the coffin of the Glass-Steagall Act of 1933. That Depression-era law prevented banking and deposit-taking institutions from also being in the securities business.

Gramm-Leach-Bliley knocked down the whole wall separating commercial banking from investment banking. It allowed commercial banks, investment banks, securities firms, and insurance companies to consolidate. Indeed, the most important consolidation it blessed had already occurred in 1998, the merger of Travelers, an insurance company, and Citigroup, a commercial bank. The Gramm-Leach-Bliley Act specifically barred the SEC from regulating investment banking holding companies, leaving in place a gaping hole in prudential oversight of investment banking that had existed since 1933.

The European Commission in 2002 threatened to put European subsidiaries of American investment bank holding companies under its laws if the United States did not implement its own consolidated oversight of the holding companies. In response, the SEC, under chairman William Donaldson, put together a regulatory framework for the holding companies.

There were only five "entities" in the SEC's consolidated supervised entities program: Goldman Sachs, Morgan Stanley, Merrill Lynch, Lehman Brothers, and Bear Stearns.

This program imported wholesale the capital standards recommended by the international Basel II agreement from the Basel Committee for Banking Supervision without considering whether or not they would be appropriate to investment banking. This meant that investment banks, just like commercial banks, had to have 10 percent in capital to be considered well capitalized.

Taking another leaf from the pages of Basel II, the investment banks were subject to risk-weighted capital rules that heavily favored mortgages. U.S. commercial banks had been under risk-weighted rules since just after the Basel Capital Accord of 1988. U.S. banking regulators had revised and expanded the scope of its risk-weighting capital rules in 2001 to come more in line with the thinking that was eventually reflected in the 2004 Basel II capital accord.

For investment banks, beginning in 2004, mortgage loans held on the books would require only 4 percent of capital instead of 8 percent. Further, mortgage-backed securities—Fannie, Freddie, Ginnie, and private label—all could be held with only 1.6 percent capital backing them.

While risk-weighted standards were supposed to push banks (and investment banks) away from risky assets, they actually did the opposite. By making the assets with low capital requirements more attractive to hold, companies were tempted to load up on them. Bear Stearns was the ultimate example of a company overly concentrated in mortgages.

Basel II standards also encouraged banks to move assets to off-balance sheet entities. That's because the way Basel computed leverage ratios and capital requirements, it did not count off-balance sheet exposure. This was an incentive to move more assets "into what eventually became the shadow banking system," according to Cox.[28] It also "created incentives to hide risky assets off the banks' balance sheets."

The fact that assets were out of sight and no one knew what risks were harbored there fueled the liquidity crisis that brought down Bear and threatened to bring down other investment banks, Cox contended. "Bear Stearns demonstrated that this reliance on the internationally-accepted Basel Standards was a fundamental flaw" in the Basel II-based American regulatory regime, he said.[29]

"The [SEC capital] rules required an early warning, a notice if the firms were even coming close to the 10 percent capital ratio that the Fed uses to determine a well capitalized bank," Cox said. "And yet at all times, even during the weekend of its sale to JPMorgan Chase, Bear Stearns had a Basel capital cushion well above that," he noted.

BEHIND WALL STREET'S LEVERAGE

While Bear Stearns was occupying center stage, another drama was also unfolding at Carlyle Capital Corporation, a firm based on the English Channel island of Guernsey, off the Normandy coast. Although invested almost entirely in super safe government agency securities, the firm declared bankruptcy on March 16. It was, in fact, the forced liquidation of mortgage-backed assets by Carlyle Capital that prompted the Federal Reserve on March 11 to give Wall Street's primary dealers the right to post mortgage-backed securities as collateral for loans of up to $200 billion. Carlyle's big mistake was to become leveraged 30 to 1; that is, to hold assets worth 30 times its capital base.

The plight of Carlyle and Bear Stearns—especially the high leverage—prompted short seller David Einhorn of the hedge fund Greenlight Capital to deliver a memorable jeremiad at Grant's Spring Investment Conference in April 2008.[30] Referring to the fate of Carlyle Capital, Einhorn observed that the world "has learned that investment companies with thirty times leverage are not safe."

Einhorn proceeded to explain how high leverage had come to define and ultimately put Wall Street on the road to ruin. High leverage, he charged, was the result of concerted efforts at Wall Street firms to maximize employee compensation by outmaneuvering the watchdogs—the credit rating agencies and federal regulators. The simple truth for Wall Street is that the higher the leverage, the higher the payout to employees. With 50 percent of revenues paid out as compensation, that's a powerful motivator, Einhorn said.

Wall Street firms, enamored of the compensation rewards, justified the leverage through "flawed risk models," most especially Value at Risk or VaR, according to Einhorn. Such models only tell a firm that most of the time the risk is manageable.

"A risk manager's job is to worry about whether the bank is putting itself at risk in the unusual times." Because VaR does not do this, it is "useless as a risk management tool and potentially catastrophic when it creates a false sense of security among senior managers and watchdogs." Ignoring tail risk by relying on VaR encourages investment banks to "take excessive but remote risks."

This explains, he said, why investment banks loaded up on some AAA-rated assets, such as the super senior tranches of subprime CDOs. Risk models suggested these assets had tiny risks because the likelihood of such risks was outside the predictive power of VaR models. Thus, institutions would only have to hold a small amount of capital.

"Value-at-Risk-driven risk management encouraged accepting a lot of bets that amount to accepting the risk that heads wouldn't come up seven times in a row" in a coin toss, Einhorn said. "In the current crisis, it has turned out that the unlucky outcome was far more likely than the back-tested models predict." What is worse, he said, is that the remote risks backed by little capital are highly correlated. "You don't just lose on one bad bet in this environment, you lose on many of them for the same reason." This is why so many investment banks had write-downs that were many times higher than the VaR models for the entire firm showed, he said.

The second watchdog that did not bark is the SEC, Einhorn said. The SEC's adoption of a new rule[31] on alternative net capital requirements in 2004 allowed broker-dealers to use their internal risk management practices to determine their capital needs. This was the carrot to get investment banks to voluntarily accept additional supervision, Einhorn explained. The rule, in effect, allowed broker-dealers to use VaR to calculate their regulatory capital. The rule was amended to allow illiquid securities, those "with no ready market," to be valued for capital purposes using VaR.

Without that change in the rule, such securities would have to be counted as a 100 percent deduction against capital ratios.

The SEC also allowed subordinated debt to count as capital. "For everyone else except the broker-dealers, subordinated debt is leverage," Einhorn said. Reading through the comment letters to the proposed rule, it appears that the SEC "made concession after concession to the large broker-dealers."

Einhorn, who wrote the initial version of his speech before the collapse of Bear Stearns, was going to warn that the regulators were going to bail out highly leveraged and undercapitalized financial institutions because they were too big to fail, and the taxpayers would pick up the tab. "This is called private profits and socialized risk. Heads, I win. Tails, you lose. It is a reverse-Robin Hood system."

For Einhorn, the rescue of Bear Stearns by JPMorgan Chase was not a rescue but a bailout. The fact the shareholders were punished does not make a convincing case that Bear was not bailed out because there is no bubble in equity, he said. The government was, in fact, bailing out Bear's counterparties. "The government appears to have determined that the collapse of a single significant player in the derivatives market would cause so much risk to the entire system that it could not be permitted to happen. In effect, the government appears to have guaranteed virtually the entire counter-party system."

In sum, Einhorn was saying that Wall Street had imperiled the financial system in order to maximize its compensation, and Washington regulators had arrived at the conclusion that the system was so fragile, Wall Street firms were too big to fail and would have to be bailed out no matter what the cost.

A deadly cocktail had been created for the global financial system, and it was about to poison us all.

10

Fannie and Freddie

While Bear Stearns grabbed the headlines in the spring of 2008, a bigger crisis was brewing at Fannie Mae and Freddie Mac, the two government-sponsored enterprises or GSEs. Investor confidence in the two was continuing to fall as delinquencies and defaults rose on the underlying mortgages pooled to back the securities they guaranteed. Plus, both were heavily invested in private-label securities, and those securities were losing value on their balance sheets. With $5.87 trillion in assets and $83.3 billion in core equity at the end of 2007, rising losses and reserves were eating away at their capital and driving up their leverage dramatically, pushing them toward insolvency.

Fannie had a leverage ratio of 76 to 1 with $45.4 billion in core capital and $3.36 trillion in loans, securities. and guarantees. Freddie had a leverage ratio of 64 to 1 with $37.9 billion in core capital and $2.41 trillion in assets.

Just as falling house prices and rising defaults put Wall Street firms in the crosshairs of short sellers, they were doing the same to Fannie and Freddie. These two institutions were far larger and their failure would have far more disastrous consequences. Yet the GSE reform legislation needed to take over the two enterprises should they fail had stalled in the Senate for years after twice winning passage in the House.

Washington's fumbling of the reform ball was reflected in the share prices for the two firms. Fannie Mae's share price, which stood at 66.95 on October 6, 2007, fell to 35.10 by February 1, 2008, and was down to 19.81 by March 10, the week Bear Stearns collapsed.

No one was more frustrated with the lack of reform than reform's strongest advocate in Congress—Richard Baker, Louisiana Republican.

Throughout his time in Congress—1987 to 2008—he was fearless and relentless in pushing first restraints and then reform on Fannie and Freddie. The forces arrayed against him consisted of politically connected senior executives at Fannie and Freddie; an almost unlimited bank account for lobbying and campaign contributions; a swarm of Gucci-shod, glad-handing, K Street lobbyists; a couple of pliable non-profit Fannie and Freddie charitable affiliates; and passionate defenders in Congress who stood poised to descend abusively on anyone who dared raise questions about the GSEs—most prominently Representative Barney Frank, Massachusetts Democrat.

At first blush, Baker would seem an unlikely candidate to lead the GSE reform effort. He represented the blue-collar Sixth Congressional District in Louisiana that includes the state capital Baton Rouge. He began his political career as a Democrat in the Louisiana House of Representatives. He switched to the Republican Party in 1986 just before making his first run for Congress for a vacant seat.

Baker brought to Washington business know-how from his experience as a realtor and homebuilder in the 1970s and 1980s. He launched and led the Central Area Home Builders Association. The Pelican State native, born in New Orleans in 1948, also saw firsthand how housing policies crafted in Washington wasted money and imperiled local economies.

Many savings and loans had failed in Louisiana, victim to a deep regional recession caused by a sharp downturn in the oil and gas industry. As a result, a lot of Louisiana properties ended up in the inventory of the Resolution Trust Corporation (RTC), set up by Congress to dispose of the assets of failed thrifts.

Baker found the rules Washington imposed for handling these assets baffling and misguided. "Without regard to the underlying asset value, products were being pushed to auction without logical or business sense being applied at all," Baker recalled.[1] "There was an idiotic prohibition that if I owned them, the RTC couldn't negotiate with me, the owner" to buy the property at a higher price than it would sell at auction. Owners were motivated to offer a high price to clear their credit history. "They might be willing to pay 80 cents on the dollar in order to get their name cleared from an adverse credit report," he explained.

On the other hand, the RTC was allowed to sell to brokers. "So what happened was that brokers would come in and buy the notes and securities for 20 cents [on the dollar] and turn around and make a deal with me for 50 cents," Baker explained. "So, the government was giving up significant value by not negotiating directly with the maker of the note—and this was by statute," he said, meaning that's how Congress wrote that policy into law.

"So all of these things struck me as not making a lot of common sense," Baker said.

Meanwhile, the more Baker learned about Fannie and Freddie, the more flaws he found in the policies that governed them.

"When we moved into the world of mortgage-backed securities, there was a hearing in 1989[2] where Leland Brendsel, CEO of Freddie Mac, was describing the value of the new mortgage-backed securities," Baker recalled. Brendsel said that Freddie Mac would "never buy the mortgage-backed securities and put them back on their books [in any great quantity] because the whole idea was to move this risk off the books." Over time, however, because of the attractive yield of the securities, compared to traditional lending, a huge amount of those securities were "moved back onto their books," Baker said.

Baker was further distressed by the fact that Fannie and Freddie were able to take on this new risk without adding any new capital. Also, Fannie and Freddie were "the only entities in the world of finance who had a regulator that was hobbled by Congress." He was referring to the Office of Federal Housing Enterprise Oversight.[3]

Everywhere else in the United States and around the world, the funding of regulators is taken from a fee assessed on the financial institutions being regulated. "OFHEO had to go to Congress every year to get funding." The regulator was perpetually underfunded as a result and subject to retaliation if they took too aggressive an approach to overseeing Fannie and Freddie, according to Baker.

Fannie and Freddie were major campaign contributors and spent huge sums on lobbying. Fannie Mae seeded the Fannie Mae Foundation with $350 million of its shares in 1996, and it served as a conduit to give away $500 million to a wide range of organizations.[4] Fannie also had a grassroots effort coordinated through regional Partnership Offices beginning in 1994. These were frequently staffed by former political operatives. The offices provided photo opportunities for politicians when grants were announced, or Fannie enabled local housing development by purchasing the mortgage. Fannie had lots of carrots and even more sticks with which to keep politicians in line. "There was no upside to taking them on," Baker recalled, and an enormous downside in retribution from the GSEs.

"There was an absolute calculus—and you could put a dollar amount or a vote number on it—to being perceived as opposed to

Fannie and Freddie in a political context," Baker said. "Everybody [in Congress] said these guys are what they say they are. They are models of corporate governance. They are well run. They provide a service that is absolutely needed."

Fannie and Freddie also had important allies in two business constituencies—realtors and homebuilders—that could usually be counted on to show up in Congress and defend Fannie and Freddie. "The realtors and homebuilders were front line guys" for the GSEs, "the shock troops in every Congressional district," Baker said.

Because of Baker's background in real estate and homebuilding and his continuing good relationship with those business interests in his district, Fannie and Freddie could not call on these traditional allies to wage political war against their Congressman. This gave Baker a degree of political immunity to the GSE political juggernaut that practically no other member of Congress could muster.

Baker was also not intimidated by the powerful Congressional Black Caucus, the staunchest of all GSE allies on Capitol Hill. Baker tried to make the case to the caucus that the GSEs were "not doing what they are telling you they're doing for you," that is, they were not doing very much to target the populations they claimed to target.

One member of the Congressional Black Caucus, Lacy Clay, Missouri Democrat, accused Baker of being a shill for the business group FM Watch, an alliance of private-sector competitors of Fannie and Freddie who were concerned about its encroachment on their turf, Baker recalled. The concern of private-sector players was legitimate, Baker agreed, because any market Fannie and Freddie entered, they dominated, given their lower cost of funding from the implicit government guarantee of their debt and securities. Even so, Baker said he was motivated by concerns about the safety and soundness of the two giants.

Baker was paradoxically invigorated by the constant struggle with his adversaries. "And it got down to almost a silly level of political assault, where I knew they were up to anything they could do to subvert my direction. And, at the same, I was willing to do just about anything to put them in the worst possible light to bring attention to their circumstance," he said.

Baker wanted to reform the GSEs by raising their capital standards, creating a new independent regulator with more authority, giving the regulator discretion to direct Fannie and Freddie to reduce their portfolios, moving the affordable housing goal from the Department of Housing and Urban Development to the new agency, and enabling the new regulator to place Fannie and Freddie into receivership and not just conservatorship (to show they can go bankrupt).

For years, Baker would introduce his reform, the Federal Housing Finance Reform Act of year x, hold hearings, and be completely ignored.

In March 1999, Baker got the first traction ever in his cause. That occurred when Gary Gensler, assistant secretary for financial markets at Treasury, testified in favor of Baker's latest iteration of GSE reform.[5] Gensler was the first public official to come out in support of most of the elements in Baker's proposed reform, including the repeal of the line of credit to Treasury. Gensler "took a lot of grief" over his testimony, "although I'm told the testimony was vetted all the way to the White House," meaning it was cleared by Treasury Secretary Robert Rubin and President Clinton, Baker said.

When Gensler went public with his support, it increased the odds for GSE reform and also raised Baker's political profile. He had been mostly regarded as a nuisance prior to this point. "I moved from just being an abrasive force to being a little bit more obnoxious," he joked.

The exit of Franklin Raines and the arrival of Daniel Mudd as chairman and chief executive officer of Fannie Mae in late 2004 paved the way for the first serious run at getting GSE reform through Congress. It ushered in a new era in better relations between the agency and the Congressman. "Dan Mudd brought a different demeanor to the discussion from any of his predecessors," Baker said. "He was willing to address directly any deficiencies or at least discuss why my view wasn't something to have a concern about."

Baker said that the one and only time he ever made a visit to Fannie Mae was when Mudd invited him to come over and speak to a group of board members. Mudd's introduction was memorable. "It was something to the effect that few people thought that Gorbachev would embrace *perestroika*. Even fewer thought Nixon would go to China. But even fewer thought Richard Baker would come to Fannie Mae," Baker said. It was a pleasant meeting and exchange of ideas.

Mudd later told Baker that the agency had developed a Richard Baker test. "I heard that before they rolled out a press statement on something new, they asked, 'What would Richard Baker think about it?'" Baker believed that after Mudd arrived, Fannie Mae "wanted to get the regulatory risk behind them. They just wanted to get the bill done. They wanted to have a voice, but not dictate."

Given that the Republicans controlled both Houses of Congress and the Bush Administration was firmly behind GSE reform, the odds were moving in the favor of a successful outcome in Congress. Baker introduced the Federal Housing Finance Reform Act of 2005 on April 5. The bill had 19 Republican cosponsors and no Democratic sponsors.

Most of the provisions Baker had sought were in the bill. It placed Fannie and Freddie, as well as the Federal Home Loan Bank System, under a new regulator, the Federal Housing Finance Agency, or FHFA. There were also some provisions Baker had not sought. One would allow Fannie and Freddie to raise conforming loan limits in areas with high home prices. Such a provision would potentially give the GSEs more reach into states like California and New York where the median price of houses in some markets had been consistently above the GSE loan limit. There was also a provision to set up what was basically an Affordable Housing Fund by having Fannie and Freddie contribute an amount equal to 1.2 basis points of all outstanding loans and securities. This would have increased the political clout of the GSEs even more, as it would have made available $450 million to $650 million annually to fund nonprofits, most of them reliable allies of the Democratic Party.[6] Republicans labeled it a "slush fund" to elect Democrats and reward party allies.

With victory in the House, it appeared that the Senate would move toward passage of a bill in early 2005. Yet there was a burning issuing lurking in the background that was about to undo all Baker had accomplished. Fed Chairman Alan Greenspan opposed the House bill because it did not call for shrinking significantly the investment portfolios of Fannie and Freddie. He said the enormous portfolios posed a systemic risk in the event one or both of the GSEs were to fail. He argued in Senate testimony in April 2005 that the investment portfolios added nothing of value to the economy, and their only purpose seemed to be to rev up return on investment at the two GSEs to a torrid 25 percent pace, far above the 15 percent target for most large financial institutions. Congress should reduce the size of the portfolios "while we can," he said, because if a crisis emerged, it would then be impossible to do so.[7]

Baker was worried Republicans were about to snatch defeat from the jaws of victory. He sought to assure Greenspan in private about the issue of the investment portfolios. "I said look, I hear you. I agree with you, and I want to incorporate your suggestion into the legislation. I have several questions. If the portfolio is $1.5 trillion today, to what level should it go? And secondly, if we have a target, tell me the methodology we should require the regulators to follow for systemic risk concerns," Baker told Greenspan. "I never got an answer from Greenspan" on any specific ways to reach the goals he desired, Baker recalled.

When asked about Baker's request, Greenspan responded, "I do recall many conversations with Representative Baker, but not a specific request to offer legislative recommendations."[8] He pointed out that he outlined principles of such legislation in his April 6, 2005, testimony in the Senate.

Lacking a reply to his request to Greenspan, Baker set out to add a provision he thought would enable the regulator to reduce the investment portfolio. Under this provision the regulators could reduce the size of the portfolio to any level, including zero, and at any pace that seemed appropriate. "We didn't say how. We didn't say when. But we didn't prohibit. We authorized." Greenspan said this was not enough because "it didn't require any action and that political pushback would be so strong that it would never be implemented anyhow," according to Baker.

Baker conceded that the provision's vulnerability to political pressure was a legitimate concern, but he felt that Greenspan then had an obligation to say how a regulator could achieve a specific mandated reduction by a date certain. "I was asking the chairman of the Federal Reserve to give us the cover of a professional response, so we could include it [in the bill], so we could say, you're not arguing with me, you're arguing with Alan Greenspan. Go take it up with him." But there was no answer. Baker felt that if he made a proposal with specific target dates and amounts, he would be quickly dismissed without someone of Greenspan's stature weighing in to say it would work.

By October 26, 2005, the House voted out the Federal Housing Finance Reform Act by a lopsided 331 to 90 vote.[9] On Halloween 2005, the House bill was received in the Senate and referred to the Senate Banking Committee.

When the Senate took up the House bill, Treasury Secretary John Snow objected to the fact that the bill did not specify a reduction target for the investment portfolio and how to achieve it. "I was just flabbergasted," Baker said. "It was the one moment when Republicans had both houses [of Congress], and the Treasury Secretary threw himself in front of the whole thing."

This opposition stalled action in the Senate. Given the urgency with which Administration officials and Greenspan had talked about the need to act, the decision to throw cold water on the reform effort defied common sense.

All the political capital for reform created by the accounting scandals at Freddie Mac and Fannie Mae was squandered. "It was almost illogical from a political view that something didn't get passed. The public had every right to be enraged," Baker said. "You had multi-million dollar restatements of income over multiple years by public corporations where the executives of both had been dismissed and brought under a legal cloud. There was clear and convincing evidence of manipulative conduct for personal gain and you couldn't pass a reform bill in that environment?" he asked rhetorically. "The irony was it was coming from our own team because the bill wasn't strong enough."

Was there a more compelling reason for the opposition of the Bush Administration? Perhaps. "Trying to assign the most legitimate reason to the [Bush Administration's] view, there wasn't a willingness to pass something that Alan Greenspan was going to be critical of," Baker offered as the most plausible explanation. Greenspan apparently "had a political veto" over what the Administration was willing to support, Baker said. And he apparently voted no.

This unhappy outcome, Baker contended in hindsight, appears to make Greenspan's failure to provide a specific regulatory framework for legislation the single element that killed a timely reform that could have substantially mitigated the severity of the ensuing financial crisis. If there had been reform in 2005, it may have held back Fannie and Freddie from another $230 billion in private-label purchases in 2006 and 2007. And if the GSEs were also selling securities from their portfolios, it would have diminished overall demand by an even greater amount, taking a substantial amount of air out of the mortgage and housing bubbles. Increasing affordable lending goals may also have led the GSEs to acquire somewhat more than a trillion dollars in risky mortgages in those same two years. (See Table 4.1 in Chapter 4.)

Even without the Administration's opposition, GSE reform faced a combination of apathy and opposition in the Senate. Among Republicans, there was considerable opposition to the affordable housing fund provision, a long sought-after goal of housing advocates. "The conservative Republicans were worried the passage of the bill [with the Affordable Housing Fund provision] would open an avenue to taxpayer funding of political activities by ACORN and other housing groups," Baker said. In addition, the Senate did not have an advocate for reform as passionate as Baker was in the House. The Congressman said he had met with Chuck Hagel, Nebraska Republican, a couple of times and the two talked about reform issues. Hagel introduced bills in the Senate similar to Baker's.

A NEW SHERIFF IN TOWN

In May 2006, the mantle for reform was also taken up by the new OFHEO director, James Lockhart, who replaced Armando Falcon, who had presided over successful investigations that uncovered accounting fraud aimed at gaming executive compensation at both GSEs. Falcon had been mercilessly vilified for it by Congressional allies of Fannie and Freddie.

Born in White Plains, New York, in 1946, Lockhart grew up in Riegel Ridge and Summit, New Jersey. He had served as executive director of the Pension Benefit Guaranty Corporation during the administration of the elder George Bush. He came back to work under the younger George Bush, first as deputy commissioner and chief operating officer in the Social Security Administration and then as director of OFHEO. In the private sector, Lockhart was managing director in Smith Barney's investment banking group for financial institutions and co-head of its private equity group in the early 1990s. He co-founded and served as managing director of NetRisk Inc. When he left government in September 2009, he became vice chairman of WL Ross and Company.

"From day one I was pushing for regulatory reform," recalled Lockhart.[10] "From day one I didn't have powers anywhere near what was needed" to do the job, he added. The 1992 legislation[11] setting up OFHEO did not give the agency power to set capital requirements, which were set by statute. The minimum capital standard in the law was a tiny 2.5 percent against whole loan mortgage assets. Even that standard was further weakened by the low risk-weighting for mortgage-backed securities. Guarantees of mortgage-backed securities by Fannie and Freddie only required 45 basis points or 0.45 percent of capital. Fannie and Freddie could leverage themselves 222 to 1 on the guarantees.

OFHEO was also further weakened by the fact that HUD was the mission regulator and could raise the affordable housing goals, "which were much too high." The goals "could be raised without consideration to how they affected the safety and soundness of Fannie and Freddie," the former director said.

Lockhart, like his predecessor, struggled against Fannie's and Freddie's opposition to reform—even as the need for reform was becoming more apparent to everyone. "In many ways it was an unfortunate thing they had so much political power. They were fighting [reform], even though they were telling me they were not fighting," Lockhart said.

Even without new legislation, the accounting scandals gave OFHEO some leeway to get the GSEs to agree to raise their very low capital by an extra 30 percent. Fannie and Freddie set out to raise capital in several ways. In late 2007 Freddie issued $6 billion in preferred stock while Fannie issued $7 billion in preferred. Both reduced their dividends.

Lockhart got Fannie to agree to 80 requirements in a consent agreement, including paying a fine of $400 million and putting a temporary cap on its investment portfolio of $727 billion.[12] Falcon had already obtained a consent agreement with Freddie, making it more difficult for Lockhart to get them to agree to a portfolio cap. "I went to the board and basically told them it would be in their interest to voluntarily agree to limits," said Lockhart. In August 2005, "with a little arm twisting," he said, Freddie agreed to voluntarily cap the rate of growth for its $722 billion portfolio to 2 percent a year until the firm was able to make timely filings of quarterly earnings with the SEC.[13]

The Senate could not seem to move the ball forward on reform in 2006 due to a strong partisan divide. "Banking chairman Senator Shelby and company really wanted a much tougher bill," he said. "And, so they went back and forth and never could come to an agreement. The Democrats argued that the Republicans were being too tough," he recalled. "In retrospect, they weren't. We did have a little bit of a problem there," he joked. There was "a big fight" over giving the new regulator systemic risk powers. "People like Barney Frank felt like [the GSEs] were not a systemic risk and that it was inappropriate to give the regulator that power," he said.

The failure of Washington to enact GSE reform in a timely manner—especially after the accounting scandals gave a political opening early in the decade—altered the course of financial history, according to Lockhart. "If they had done something in 2003 or 2004, we might be living in a totally different world today," he said.

Indeed, if GSE reform legislation of the type that passed in 2008 "had maybe passed three years before [in 2005], we would probably have had time to implement it," Lockhart said. "If legislation had passed even when I arrived in May of '06, I don't think we would have prevented the crisis, but I think it would have been certainly less" severe, he argued.

Lockhart stepped up OFHEO's monitoring of growing credit risk at the GSEs. We "were trying to use the powers of moral suasion and throttle them back some. With only a one percent capitalization, there's just no way they were going to survive this housing market," he said.

"Fannie and Freddie were very adamant that there was not a lot of credit risk in their book for a very long time. I remember a board meeting [at Freddie Mac where I talked to them] about putting caps on their portfolios. I mentioned some of the credit risk and you wouldn't believe the pushback I got from the board in May of '06," Lockhart said. "We understand credit risk. We don't have credit risk," board members said to him, he recalled.

"Historically [the GSEs] had only about 10 basis points of credit losses and they thought that would go on forever," he said. "But what happened is the bubble burst, they had taken more credit risk to get those affordable class goals which kept escalating over time," he said. "HUD had allowed them to get goals credit not only from the mortgages they guaranteed and purchased but also on the underlying mortgages in the mortgage-backed securities they bought. Fannie and Freddie were buying those [private-label] triple A mortgage-backed securities, which subsequently have turned very toxic," he said.

Freddie, in fact, was relying more on purchasing private-label mortgage-backed securities than Fannie, according to Lockhart. Virtually all of the subprime and Alt-A mortgage-backed securities Freddie snapped up have been downgraded.

Fannie and Freddie also drove demand for the private-label mortgage bonds because "they were the biggest buyer in the market," Lockhart said. "And so they helped the market prosper. If they had smaller portfolios, that market probably would not have ballooned the way it did," he added. "When you look at it, Freddie and Fannie were the biggest buyers of those triple As, which then allowed the other lower-rated tranches to be created for people looking for yield to buy," Lockhart said.

By the time elections rolled around in 2006, Barney Frank, the ranking member of the House Financial Services Committee, surprised the world by changing his mind about the need for GSE reform—as long as it included provisions he supported, such as the affordable housing fund. When the Democrats took the reins of power in the House the next year, Frank sponsored reform.[14] Frank's bill had five co-sponsors: three Republicans, Richard Baker, Gary Miller of California, and Lee Terry of Nebraska; and two Democrats, Carolyn Maloney of New York and Melvin Watt of North Carolina and a member of the Congressional Black Caucus. A Prague spring had come to housing policy.

The bill sped through the House Financial Services Committee and onto the floor of the House, where it passed May 23 by a lopsided 313 to 104 vote. Frank, who was appalled at the rising delinquencies from 2/28 and 3/27 adjustable-rate mortgages that were offered by Fannie and Freddie, inserted a provision that required all new products to be approved by the regulator. These loans targeted subprime borrowers and had a low introductory teaser rate for two or three years, after which the payment jumps up significantly.

As with the Baker bill in 2005, Frank's legislation advanced the reach of Fannie and Freddie even as it strengthened regulation. It provided for the creation of an affordable housing fund that would be administered by the new regulator, rather than having two separate funds, each administered by Fannie and Freddie. The bill prohibited use of the funds for political activities, advocacy, and lobbying. Even so, Republicans felt this was a fig leaf, since potential recipients of the funds are engaged in all those activities and could segregate the monies from this fund from those activities, but since money is fungible, it would free up other funds to pay for the prohibited activities. One-fourth of the funds would be transferred to Treasury.

Some saw the sums that would be generated by an affordable housing fund a huge potential pork barrel. Lockhart, for one, saw it as potentially a better way to meet affordable housing needs without engaging in risky lending and was encouraged because it was to be administered by the regulator.

"I give Barney a little credit. He got his legislation through in the spring of '07. It wasn't as strong as we'd like. But it was a good building block. And so that was helpful," said Lockhart. Frank worked with Treasury Secretary Hank Paulson in crafting the legislation. The House bill "was not as strong as the Senate Republicans would like, but it was a good foundation," Lockhart said.

Once again, after the GSE reform bill hit the Senate, it sat there and went nowhere. With the Democrats now in control of the Senate, the chief obstacle to getting reform through was Banking Chairman Chris Dodd from Connecticut. He was a staunch Fannie and Freddie ally and a major recipient of campaign donations from them. He also became notorious as a "Friend of Angelo," referring to Angelo Mozilo, head of the nation's largest mortgage lender, Countrywide, whose company arranged discounted mortgages for Dodd and others. Mozilo, in turn, was a staunch ally of Fannie and Freddie. The relationship was so tight that Mozilo famously quipped, "If Fannie and Freddie catch a cold, I catch the ... flu."[15] More than that, when

Mozilo became politically radioactive, it brought an early end to Dodd's career when he decided not to run again for Senate in 2010.

Not even the mortgage meltdown of 2007 moved Senator Dodd to try to advance the bill. "It was hard to get the Senate Banking Committee to focus for a variety of reasons—primarily, one of the original ones was Senator Dodd was running for President." Thus, he did not really focus on the GSE reform legislation until the spring of 2008, after the primaries ended, "when we were almost in crisis," said Lockhart.

BUILDING TOWARD A COLLAPSE

In March 2008, as Bear Stearns was sliding to collapse, Fannie and Freddie were negotiating with Lockhart to remove the caps on their investment portfolio. The idea was to allow the GSEs to use a significant portion of the additional 30 percent in capital they had achieved at OFHEO's request, to be used to back the purchase of mortgage-backed securities. In return for being allowed to expand their portfolios, Lockhart got the GSEs to agree to "a promise to raise significantly more capital, and also a promise to keep big [capital] cushions above the minimum statutory requirements."

"And the third part of the deal was to finally support reform legislation," Lockhart said. This meant Fannie and Freddie would have to call off the legions of lobbyists fighting reform at every turn in the Senate. The two GSEs agreed to Lockhart's terms, including a cessation of their campaign against reform. "I'm not sure we would have ever gotten [reform] legislation if we had not made them do that, because they were still resistant to legislation," Lockhart recalled. OFHEO released the terms of the agreement March 17.[16] This move was expected to add $200 billion of liquidity to the mortgage-backed securities market.

Part of the pressure building to remove caps came from the fact that the private-label mortgage market had collapsed the prior summer. Fannie and Freddie "were the only thing in the housing market at that point. The housing market was falling apart and we were trying to get them to be able to lend their part of the market, to keep that going," said Lockhart. "And actually that market did keep going during that whole period," he explained.

OFHEO was working with Treasury to simultaneously announce late Sunday March 16, 2008, the Bear Stearns rescue by JPMorgan Chase and a removal of the portfolio caps at Fannie and Freddie.

"But it took a little more arm twisting" before Fannie and Freddie agreed to all the terms, and the announcement was not made until Wednesday, March 19, Lockhart said.

"That was a good thing in retrospect. If you hadn't had that deal for them to support the legislation and you couldn't get the legislation through in July," then "you were in September" without it, said Lockhart.

As shares prices for Fannie and Freddie fell into single digits, Hank Paulson conferred with members of Congress in an effort to gain broad new authority to intervene and inject capital into the GSEs in return for preferred shares from each of them. Indymac, a Pasadena, California-based thrift heavily involved in Alt-A mortgage lending, was seized July 13 by the Office of Thrift Supervision following a run on the bank that had begun June 26. That was the date Democratic Senator Chuck Schumer of New York made public a letter he had sent to the regulator of the thrift stating he was concerned that IndyMac's "financial deterioration poses significant risks to both taxpayers and borrowers." When the regulator seized the bank, Office of Thrift Supervision Director John Reich pointedly blamed Schumer's careless public comments for creating a liquidity crisis that brought down the bank.

Paulson, looking around for funding sources for the ailing GSEs, said he had asked Fed Chairman Bernanke if the Fed could provide discount window funding for Fannie and Freddie in an emergency. Bernanke told Paulson the Fed could not do that. Further, such funding was more properly a "fiscal" issue and should be provided by Congress to Treasury, not the Fed.[17] The deteriorating conditions at the GSEs prompted the Bush Administration to propose to Congress July 14 to temporarily give Treasury authority to buy debt and securities of Fannie and Freddie, as well as the Federal Home Loan Banks.

In response to the proposal, Congressional Budget Office Director Peter Orszag said it would be unlikely that Treasury would use the authority to prop up the two GSEs. If the housing market were to deteriorate further and Treasury had to intervene, he added, it would only require a $25 billion commitment to Fannie and Freddie over a two year period.[18] Those views softened the opposition a bit.

Paulson then set about convincing Congress that it should grant Treasury the right to inject capital in exchange for preferred shares from Fannie and Freddie. He decided the best way to sell the idea to Congress was to make it a temporary program. Paulson also wanted the Fed to be a consulting regulator for the GSEs. Senator Dodd called a hearing on GSE reform for July 15. During that hearing, Paulson pleaded for the new authority to provide unlimited funding to the GSEs with colorful language he would later regret. "If you've got a squirt gun in your pocket, you may have to take it out. If you've got a bazooka, and people know you've got it, you may not have to take it out," he said, referring to the authority to take over Fannie and Freddie and provide unlimited funds.

House Republicans were telling Paulson they were concerned that the affordable housing fund created in the legislation would funnel money to Democratic Party activist groups like ACORN.[19] Senator Shelby was worried the legislation would give Treasury authority to put in unlimited amounts of funding. Despite these concerns, the House passed the Housing and Economic Recovery Act on July 23 and the Senate, July 26. The President signed the bill into law July 30.

The provision that allowed Treasury to fund the GSEs in exchange for senior preferred shares was critical, according to Lockhart. "If we had tried to put them into conservatorship without that, we wouldn't have been able to do it."

"There was no FDIC [for Fannie and Freddie.] There was no backup. There was no way to prop them up," he said. "The legislation did help for that reason but no other reason because it was too late for everything else." By that he meant that all the other provisions in the new law were of no immediate value when the two GSEs were on the verge of collapse.

During the summer of 2008, OFHEO began to see that the book of business at Fannie and Freddie "was starting to deteriorate badly," Lockhart said. As the share prices fell, it also meant the GSEs had to pull back on efforts to maintain their capital levels. Fannie had managed to raise $7.4 billion in new capital in May. "Freddie was not able to raise capital. I actually met with some of their board members and the bankers that they were trying to [pitch]—I think it was early August at that point—and it was very clear that it could not be done," Lockhart said. "They were hoping maybe Treasury would give them the capital."

Treasury, however, was not willing to provide Fannie and Freddie a capital infusion unless they were placed into conservatorship. "It became pretty obvious their book was deteriorating faster than anybody expected. And it was spreading not only into subprime and Alt-A but into some prime stuff as the economy was getting worse," Lockhart said. "And so, we had done a letter, sort of semiannual review of the two institutions and [we had] told them we were downgrading them from a risk perspective" sometime in July, Lockhart recalled.

"And then they put out their [quarterly earnings] numbers in early August. That was the first time Freddie [reported its earnings] as a timely filer with the SEC," Lockhart said. "And the numbers were bad—but not as bad necessarily as we thought they were," he said.

The regulator—now with its new name, the Federal Housing Finance Agency—was concerned that the GSEs were not being completely forthcoming in their earnings reports. "Certainly the roll rates on the delinquencies were accelerating pretty rapidly and there was concern about whether the reserving was conservative enough," Lockhart said.

By this point, Lockhart estimated the two GSEs combined were leveraged 100 to 1, even though their SEC filings reported a lower leverage ratio of 76 to 1. Based on their filings, by mid-year 2008, the GSEs had $6.4 trillion in assets and $84 billion in core equity.

Officially, Fannie's leverage ratio on June 30 was 81 to 1, up from 76 to 1 six months earlier. Freddie's leverage ratio had risen to 69 to 1, up from 64 to 1 six months earlier.

"There's a whole series of issues that came up," Lockhart said. "So we went into a full scale activity in August" with the Fed, in particular, but also the Office of the Comptroller of the Currency (OCC) "to figure out how big the [capital] hole was" in each of the GSEs.

"Ben Bernanke had a view, and his troops had a view, that the hole was quite large. So did Treasury," Lockhart recalled. "So, we went in there to really see if that was right or not. And we came to the same conclusion," he said. "It was obvious they had no capital left. Or, they would have no capital left in three to six months," Lockhart said.

Next the regulators had to decide whether Fannie and Freddie should be put into receivership and wound down—or put into conservatorship and propped up. "We considered the alternatives and made the decision that conservatorship was the right way to go, not only from the legal standpoint, but from the market standpoint," Lockhart said. If they had gone into receivership, they would not have been able to underwrite any more mortgage activity. That would leave the mortgage markets without origination capacity at a point when they were 70 percent of mortgage origination activity. The rest of origination was supported by guarantees from the Federal Housing Administration and portfolio lending by banks and thrifts.

"The final decision [to go for conservatorship] was made by FHFA itself, in consultation with others," Lockhart said. The agency had a board of directors made up of the director, Lockhart, and the Treasury secretary, the HUD secretary, and the chairman of the SEC, and the decision had to be approved by the board.

FANNIE AND FREDDIE WEEKEND

In his book *On the Brink*, Hank Paulson suggested that Lockhart was reluctant at first to place Fannie and Freddie into conservatorship.[20] Does Lockhart agree? "What I will say is that there is a natural concern that we wanted to get it right," he said.

"Emotionally it wasn't easy for some of the troops. And professionally either for that matter," he said. "It was a tough thing to do—to admit that we had not been able to keep them out of conservatorship," Lockhart said. "We all know it's mainly because of the legislation and the economy and all sorts of other things; but, it was tough."

FHFA "also wanted to build an extremely strong case because in theory the two organizations could have refused" to be placed into conservatorship, Lockhart said.

"It was the weekend before Lehman," Lockhart recalled. The same teams at Treasury and the Fed were working on both Fannie and Freddie, as well as Lehman. "One of things that happened was they were so tired because we had been working flat out probably three weeks at Freddie and Fannie, they never got a chance to catch their breath," he recalled.

The Federal Deposit Insurance Corporation had also looked into how many banks would fail if Fannie and Freddie failed, according to FDIC Chairman Sheila Bair.[21] The failures would come as a result of holding Fannie and Freddie preferred stock. The FDIC identified 35 financial institutions that "were at heightened risk of capital depletion" in September 2008, Bair stated. Of these 35, 10 of them, representing $13.3 billion in assets, did eventually fail.

As the teams from the regulators investigated Fannie and Freddie, they began to discover that some of the accounting methodologies being used by the two GSEs appeared to overstate their capital base in the second quarter of 2008.

For one thing, both Fannie and Freddie relied on deferred tax assets as part of their capital. With a string of quarterly losses and the outlook for more of the same, the value of deferred tax assets should have been marked down or even not claimed, since there were no profits against which they could be used and none expected in the near future.

In the second quarter of 2008, Fannie had reported $36 billion in deferred tax assets, while Freddie claimed $28 billion—enormous sums compared to the core capital they reported at the time: $47 billion and $37 billion respectively.

The authority to claim the full value of the deferred tax assets was written into the GSE Act of 1992, which governs Fannie and Freddie. Under that law, Fannie and Freddie are required to use Generally Accepted Accounting Principles (GAAP), which allows companies to claim deferred tax assets as capital. "There was no flexibility for the regulator not to give credit" for deferred tax assets, Lockhart said.[22] By way of contrast, banks are not allowed to claim full credit for deferred tax assets when calculating their capital.

When asked why Fannie and Freddie would take credit for deferred tax assets in the second quarter of 2008, given the outlook for earnings and rising delinquencies and defaults, Lockhart replied, "Obviously, if they had not taken a deferred tax asset credit, they would have violated the capital requirements, minimal as they were, [so] I think they looked to the bright side." Even so, he added, "I don't want to accuse them of manipulating their accounting or anything like that, especially given the lawsuit [against Freddie Mac].[23] I don't think it would appropriate for me to say something" that might suggest accounting wrongdoing.

The regulators also found that the GSEs had failed to mark down securities backed by subprime and Alt-A loans, as most other financial firms had done, beginning in the fourth quarter of 2007, according to Lockhart.

The mark to market rule, as written by the Financial Accounting Standards Board, is "kind of weird" in that it allows companies "to select which assets you wanted to mark to market and which you didn't," Lockhart said. "I actually think they applied it properly; but they took advantage of it in not designating those assets that needed to be marked to market," he said.

Finally, the regulators found that the GSEs had not set aside sufficient reserves to cover losses on defaulted loans, according to Lockhart. Fannie had reserved $8.9 billion, while Freddie had reserved $5.8 billion.

After completing the investigation on accounting methodologies at the GSEs, "We made it very clear to them that they were too aggressive," recalled Lockhart.

More than two years later, the SEC found Freddie Mac's and Fannie Mae's disclosure sufficiently questionable to launch an investigation of the two GSEs. Wells Notices from the SEC were sent in March 2011 to Freddie Mac's former chairman and CEO Richard Syron and its former executive vice president Don Bisenius, as well as to Fannie's former chairman and CEO Daniel Mudd and its former chief financial officer Anthony Piszel. A Wells Notice is a letter the SEC sends to firms or people to notify them they are under investigation for unethical behavior and indicates that the commission may be planning to bring an enforcement action against them.

Lockhart finds "a little irony" in the SEC's actions against Freddie Mac, as the commission had been working with the GSE on its accounting methodology for six months prior to the release of the second quarter results.[24] "They probably cleared that in advance," Lockhart said, referring to Freddie's 10-Q quarterly earnings report filed with the SEC in August 2008.

The last weekend of August 2008, Lockhart flew to join his family on Nantucket, off the coast of Massachusetts, for a vacation. "I spent the whole time on the telephone. It obviously wasn't going to work," he recalled. He had to fly back to Washington the next day after he arrived.

Lockhart had lunch with Paulson. "He made it clear it probably wasn't a good idea to go back on vacation. We were working flat out," Lockhart recalled. He did go back to Nantucket one more time. All his children were there, "so I just flew in Saturday afternoon and flew out Sunday," he said. On the flight back from Nantucket, he saw Dan Mudd and his family flying back to Washington. "I knew at that point what we were up to," meaning the decision to go for conservatorship. He was "trying to be friendly" with Mudd on the plane. "It was a little awkward," he recalled. He did not tell Mudd about plans to put Fannie and Freddie into conservatorship in a matter of days.

"We didn't really know how the two companies were going to act," he said. If they had decided to lawyer up and fight, "that would have been a terrible event" for the U.S. and world economies. Foreign investors were applying a lot of pressure on Treasury and the Fed to reassure them about their holdings in Fannie and Freddie securities and debt.

Paulson recounted that he conferred with President Bush in the Oval Office about the decision to place the two GSEs into conservatorship on Thursday, September 4. When the President asked if the CEOs—Daniel Mudd at Fannie Mae and Richard Syron at Freddie Mac—were aware of what was being planned, Paulson replied bluntly, "Mr. President, we're going to move quickly and take them by surprise. The first sound they'll hear is their heads hitting the floor," meaning each CEO was to be fired on the spot.[25]

Paulson told the President immediate action was needed in order to avoid giving Fannie and Freddie a chance to muster political opposition to thwart the takeover and executive firings. The President backed conservatorship but wanted to make sure that it did not appear to be the nationalization of Fannie and Freddie but an intervention that was "transitory" and that a new mortgage model would eventually emerge after that transition.[26]

Following the Oval Office meeting, Paulson phoned Lockhart to try to persuade him to place the GSEs into conservatorship immediately. Lockhart was still trying to document the problem of deteriorating loans and lack of capital so that there would be no legal challenge to the decision, according to Paulson. Bair sent Paulson one of her top people to help write the case supporting conservatorship. With a little extra help, Lockhart was able to get his examiners to sign off on the case.

Lockhart does not agree that FHFA had to be pressured to agree to the conservatorship. "Frankly, what was going on, nothing like this had ever been done, to put two multi-trillion dollar [institutions] into conservatorship the same day. We wanted to get it right. So we spent a reasonable amount of time working with Treasury, the Fed, FDIC and OCC," Lockhart said.

Thursday evening, Lockhart called Mudd and Syron and summoned them to a meeting late Friday afternoon, September 5. Paulson and Bernanke also attended the meeting. The meeting began after the New York markets closed. The officials met separately with teams from Fannie first, then Freddie. Lockhart made the case to Fannie that the company was being operated in an unsafe and unsound way and told Mudd and his team that he wanted them to voluntarily put themselves into conservatorship or FHFA would seize them.

Mudd and his team were stunned and became angry on hearing Lockhart's request. Paulson and Bernanke followed in support of Lockhart's decision.[27] Bernanke said Fannie's plight threatened the stability of the financial system. Mudd appeared to want to fight and said he would take the matter to the board the next day, according to Paulson. He was told that Lockhart, Paulson, and Bernanke would be at that meeting. Richard Alexander, the attorney for the FHFA, told Mudd that he wanted them to understand that when Lockhart, Bernanke, and Paulson meet with the board the next day, they would not be there to have a dialogue. Rodgin Cohen, outside counsel for Fannie, indicated he understood.[28]

The presentation was repeated for Freddie Mac. Syron remained calm when told the news. After the meeting, Paulson called Barney Frank and Chris Dodd with the news and reported he did not encounter any obvious opposition. Paulson, who praised Frank as someone who would reliably stand by an agreement once one was reached, found Dodd more troubling and worried he might oppose the effort once it was announced.[29]

On Saturday, September 5, talks by federal officials began at noon with the board of Freddie Mac. A meeting of Fannie's board followed at 3 p.m. Both boards agreed to conservatorship.

On Sunday, September 6, Lockhart announced he had put Fannie and Freddie under the conservatorship of FHFA. In making the announcement, he pointed out that the two enterprises had $5.4 trillion in debt and securities, an amount equal to the entire outstanding debt of the U.S. government. It was also announced the two chief executives—Mudd and Syron—were fired, as were the entire boards at both companies. Share prices for Fannie and Freddie fell to under a dollar. Once mighty financial giants, the two GSEs had been reduced to penny stocks and wards of the state.

Paulson announced Treasury would provide up to $100 billion in capital through preferred shares for each of the two GSEs to make sure they had sufficient capital to keep operating and assure investors in both company debt and securities that their investments remained safe. The government would receive warrants for 79.9 percent of common shares of the GSEs. Treasury agreed to set up a secured lending facility to buy mortgage-backed securities guaranteed by Fannie and Freddie to make sure there was enough funding to support the mortgage market.

Frank pinned the blame on irrational markets and not risky lending by Fannie and Freddie. "It's a case where market psychology became more important than the fundamentals, and that's why they had to act," he told the *Washington Post*.[30] "It's not like they're going to run out of money tomorrow or Monday," he scoffed.

Dodd, who first supported the conservatorship, apparently had doubts and wanted to call a hearing after Fannie and Freddie had been placed into conservatorship. The government takeover was, quite obviously, a federal bailout of Fannie and Freddie, and now that it was happening, it was potentially embarrassing to members of

Congress who had given Treasury the authority to put taxpayer funds into the GSEs.

"We accepted him at his word that all he needed was the authority and that he wasn't going to exercise it. Then he used his authority very aggressively," Dodd said.[31] The senator suggested that he now suspected that Paulson had "fooled" Congress in July and was planning from the beginning to use the funds, and therefore it was not a last-minute decision to take over the GSEs.

The mortgage meltdown, which first felled a few subprime outliers in early 2007, then knocked out all private-label securitizations in August 2007, had now taken down the two mortgage giants that were the very foundation of the industry. It was a financial calamity of historic proportions. "Everything that could go wrong did go wrong," Lockhart summed it up.

And yet Lockhart felt there was some consolation in knowing that regulators and government officials, while late to the crisis, mitigated its consequences. "If we hadn't had the legislation, I don't know what we would have done," Lockhart said.

"As I said before, without the credit and that Treasury funding, conservatorship would not have worked and we would have had to put them in receivership, which would have basically meant that they stopped writing" new mortgages, he said.

"Lehman was bad. But if Fannie and Freddie had stopped writing business in September [2008], we probably would have had a depression."

11

Lehman Brothers

After the fall of Bear Stearns, the clamoring hordes of short sellers turned their sights to Lehman Brothers, the next most vulnerable of the five major investment banks that were under the oversight of the Securities and Exchange Commission.

Their new battle cry was that Wall Street's investment banking business model was no longer viable because in a liquidity crisis such firms lacked access to deposits and funding that commercial banks have. Even the temporary credit facility offered by the Fed the day Bear began its slide in March did not deflate the new conventional wisdom.

Those who jumped on the Lehman shorting bandwagon after Bear Stearns, however, were way behind the curve. David Einhorn, president of Greenlight Capital LLC, had been shorting Lehman since the prior year. The mild-mannered Einhorn gained fame, fortune, and respect shorting Allied Capital in 2002. His hedge fund had earned outsized 22 percent returns since it was founded in 1996 with original capital of only $1 million.

In a presentation at the New York Value Investing Congress in November 2007, Einhorn blasted Lehman's lack of transparency regarding its modest write-downs in the aftermath of the mortgage meltdown. His hunch was that the firm was following its playbook from the 1998 global liquidity crisis, when it survived that crisis by taking no write-downs in spite of its considerable bond exposure.[1]

After Bear Stearns's collapse in March 2008, federal officials and regulators were ever more vigilant to prevent another crisis prompted by the steadily declining values in mortgage assets and home prices. Lehman, which had loaded up on mortgage assets, was, of course, on the radar of Treasury Secretary Hank Paulson and Fed Chairman Ben

Bernanke, as well as SEC Chairman Chris Cox. Repeating a call he first made in the fall of 2007, Paulson was once again calling for financial institutions to raise more capital. Lehman, realizing its vulnerability, was unloading mortgage assets where it could, mindful of the fact that selling some assets into a weak market would force write-downs in similar assets.

Lehman's chief executive officer Dick Fuld was belligerent in the face of a growing gaggle of skeptics that had amassed in the wake of the collapse of Bear Stearns. With $4 billion in new capital freshly injected into the firm on April 1, he taunted Einhorn, but not by name. "I will hurt the shorts, and that is my goal," he boasted to shareholders at the firm's annual meeting April 15.

In May, the SEC announced it would require Wall Street firms to report their capital and liquidity levels in their filings. Einhorn pounced on the disclosures in Lehman's filing for first quarter 2008 that revealed the firm held $6.5 billion in CDOs. Lehman shot back that the portion of the CDOs tied to subprime was less than $1 billion. The markets, however, paid more heed to Einhorn than Fuld, as Lehman's shares continued to tumble.

By May 28, Lehman's share price was less than $37, down from $60 in February.

Lehman stepped up its counterattack on its chief critic. "Mr. Einhorn cherry-picks certain specific items from our 10-Q and takes them out of context and distorts them to relay a false impression of the firm's financial condition, which suits him because of his short position in our stock," Lehman stated in an e-mail on May 28. "He also makes allegations that have no basis in fact with the same hope of achieving personal gain."[2]

Lehman was reacting to Einhorn's most recent salvo in a speech at Grant's Spring Investment Conference.[3] In that speech, Einhorn contended that Lehman needed $55 billion to $89 billion in tangible equity,[4] three to eight times the $16.9 billion average tangible equity reported in its balance sheet in November 2007.[5]

Lehman had total assets at a very high 40 times its tangible common equity—a leverage ratio of 40 to 1—in November, Einhorn had pointed out. Banks, by comparison, are expected to operate with prudent leverage ratios of 12 to 1. In the six months since November, Einhorn observed, Lehman bought back $750 million of its own shares and grew its assets by another $90 billion, pushing its leverage to 44 to 1, with the real leverage probably higher because of rosy assessments of the fair value of the firm's assets.

"Lehman does not provide enough transparency for us to even hazard a guess as to how they have accounted for these items," Einhorn said. The short seller suggested that Lehman was postponing recognizing losses to better enable it to raise capital, while regulators turned a "blind eye." With a leverage ratio of 44 to 1, Lehman only had to have its assets decline in value by a single percent and it would lose half its equity. "Suddenly, 44 times leverage becomes 80 times leverage and confidence is lost," Einhorn said.

Lehman's arch-critic was troubled by the fact that while everyone else on Wall Street was reporting losses, Lehman reported a small profit in each of the last three quarters, accompanied by modest write-downs in the value of its assets. Each quarter Lehman modestly exceeded analyst estimates of earnings. "That Lehman has not reported a loss smells of performance smoothing," Einhorn said.

COOKING THE BOOKS

In time, it would become clear that Lehman was employing accounting gimmicks to smooth its earnings in ways even Einhorn may not have imagined. The bankruptcy court examiner Anton Valukas found that Lehman engaged in the extensive accounting misuse of repo 105s to artificially and temporarily lower its assets and thus its reported leverage ratio. From 2007 to 2008, Lehman engaged in a voluminous number of these gimmicks—300,000—to mislead regulators and the public about the company's true financial condition.[6]

Repos are typically done to access cash from another firm, usually on a short-term basis. In a standard repo agreement, a firm, such as Lehman, sells securities, such as Treasury bills, and agrees to buy them back at a specified time at a price that incorporates a small amount of interest. In essence, the firm that does a repo obtains cash against the collateral it has sold and will reclaim later—for a price.

Repo 105s take their shorthand name from the fact that the transactions require a minimum of $105 worth of securities to be exchanged for $100 in cash. The extra amount in securities is there to protect the cash lender against losses. When a repo transaction was initially done, Lehman made the entries one would normally make for a repurchase contract if one were keeping a proper set of books. However, additional entries were then made to recharacterize the repo 105 from being a secured financing (a repo) to being an outright sale of a security from Lehman's inventory.[7]

The accounting gimmick was doubly useful. Not only did Lehman move assets it held out of sight from regulators, shareholders, and the public, it also used the cash to pay down debts. This reduced total liabilities by about double the amount of the transaction. These transactions were typically done just before the end of the quarter to reduce leverage. Shortly after a new quarter began, Lehman would repay the cash it borrowed, plus interest, then buy back the securities and place the assets back on its balance sheet.[8]

The examination by Valukas found that senior managers were concerned about Lehman's misuse of repo 105s. Global financial controller Martin Kelly claimed that the firm was hiding the transactions from the SEC. He warned chief financial officer Erin Callan and later her successor Ian Lowitt that the fact that the transactions lacked substance posed "reputational risk" for Lehman if they were to become publicly known.

Lehman's decision to engage in repo 105 gimmickry came in the wake of the mortgage meltdown in mid-2007. Financial market observers were calling for Lehman and other firms to reduce their leverage. There was fear that the credit rating agencies might lower Lehman's credit rating and thereby further inflict financial pain on the firm.

Rating downgrades could prove very costly. For example, Lowitt wrote in an e-mail to Lehman's head of equities Herbert "Bart" McDade on June 30, 2008: "One notch downgrade requires 1.7bn; and 2 notch requires 3.4 bn of additional margin posting."[9] By this, he meant that a single-notch downgrade in the credit rating would lead counterparties to Lehman transactions to demand Lehman advance $1.7 billion against Lehman's obligations. A two-notch downgrade would double that to $3.4 billion.

In January 2008, Lehman ordered a firm-wide strategy of cutting by half the level of leverage in commercial and residential mortgage-backed securities. But the company faced a problem. Any sales of mortgage inventory would come at a substantial loss. And such sales might lead to a loss of confidence in Lehman's valuations of remaining inventory on the balance sheet. That's because the fire-sale pricing of any assets sold would apply to the remaining loans and securities.

Lehman's dilemma was described in an internal document from early 2007, ahead of the mortgage meltdown. "Existing large [commercial mortgage-backed securities] positions in Real Estate and sub prime loans in Mortgages before quarter end would incur large losses due to the steep discounts that they would have to be offered at and carry substantial reputation risk in the market," the document said.[10] "A Repo 105 increase would help avoid this without negatively impacting our leverage ratios."

Lehman wanted to move its less liquid inventory into the repo 105 program; however, the firm was unable to find willing counterparties who would offer cash for the risky mortgage assets.[11] In lieu of being able to repo the sticky assets, Lehman instead did repo 105s of other more liquid assets and achieved the same goal of reducing its overall leverage.

Bankruptcy examiner Valukas explained the method to the accounting madness. "In this way, unbeknownst to the investing public, rating agencies, Government regulators, and Lehman's Board of Directors, Lehman reverse engineered the firm's net leverage ratio for public consumption," he wrote.[12] During earnings conference calls in 2008 with analysts, senior managers touted the reduced leverage as a sign of the firm's health. When analysts asked how Lehman was accomplishing its leverage reduction, Callan said Lehman was seeking to provide analysts "a great amount of transparency on the balance sheet." She told them Lehman was selling its less liquid assets, but did not make a peep about the repo 105 program.

By Valukas's calculation, Lehman's use of the repo 105 program reduced the balance sheet by $39 billion in the fourth quarter of 2007, $49 billion in the first quarter of 2008, and $50 billion in the second quarter of 2008. These clearly were material misrepresentations.

Lehman first introduced its repo 105 program in 2001, according to Valukas. The firm was unable to conduct the transactions in the United States because it could not find a U.S. law firm that would write an opinion letter permitting the use of repo 105s for a true sale. Lehman turned to the London law firm of Linklaters, where it obtained an opinion letter stating the practice was legal under English law for Lehman's European broker-dealer.[13] That was enough to get the program going. It did not matter that the transactions were being done in the British subsidiary. The balance sheet benefit of the repo 105s would achieve the desired effect on the entire consolidated Lehman balance sheet no matter which entity transferred the securities.

THE FIGHT TO SAVE LEHMAN

As the cavalcade of short sellers rolled on, Fuld was determined to outmaneuver them and save Lehman. On July 13, 2008, he placed a call to New York Fed President Timothy Geithner to propose to him that Lehman become a bank holding company. This course of action had been suggested by outside lawyer Rodgin Cohen,[14] and was believed to address the growing market perception that investment banking had evolved into a failed business model because of the lack of access to deposits and the Fed discount window, as well as the lack of adequate prudential regulation.

Geithner was cool to the idea and said that it was "gimmicky" and could not solve Lehman's "liquidity/capital problem."[15] Geithner was also worried that Fuld was acting in "desperation," and that the move might backfire.[16] Fuld's proposal was also rejected by the FDIC.[17]

Apparently the call from Fuld prompted an intense phone discussion among regulators the next day, July 14, on how they would deal with a faltering Lehman. The call was set up between people at the New York Fed and the Federal Reserve Board in Washington and included Fed Vice Chair Donald Kohn. A proposal to divide Lehman into a good bank/bad bank emerged from the phone conference discussion. The broad outline of the proposal was described in a July 15 e-mail from William Dudley, executive vice president for markets of the New York Fed, to the participants in the meeting and others.[18]

Dudley's idea was to set up a Maiden Lane-type vehicle, as had been done with Bear Stearns, and transfer $60 billion of Lehman's bad assets into the vehicle. The Fed would guarantee $55 billion financing to acquire the assets. Lehman would provide $5 billion in equity. This would leave a good bank with $600 billion in assets and $23 billion of equity. It would have less risk and more liquidity, Dudley wrote. This approach was seen as better than a fire sale of assets that might make Lehman insolvent or even the distressed sale of the entire company.

"If Lehman is solvent now, this preserves solvency," Dudley wrote. "If Lehman is, in fact, insolvent now—even in the absence of forced assets sales—this limits degree of insolvency due to forced asset sales," he continued. "Risk of not intervening early, Lehman is solvent now, becomes insolvent due to forced asset sales." Dudley advised that the good bank/bad bank proposal could be presented as an option to Lehman, one that might become more attractive "if the slide were to continue."

The Fed's associate general counsel Kieran Fallon, who had participated in the conference call where the idea was hatched, forwarded the gist of the proposal to his boss, Fed general counsel Scott Alvarez. He was not sure of the legality of the proposal. In a note sent from his

Blackberry, Fallon wrote, "Kohn did not push back very hard on this proposal on call last night." Fallon promised to raise "significant concerns" about the idea in a phone conference slated shortly after the e-mail was sent. Apparently, "significant concerns" about its legality led officials at the Fed to hold back on presenting the proposal to Lehman.

The Fed was also beginning to explore the potential aftermath of a Lehman bankruptcy. Patrick Parkinson, the Fed's deputy director of research and statistics, described a "game plan" in a confidential e-mail on August 8 to Steven Shafran at Treasury and others at the Fed and Treasury.[19] Shafran was a former Goldman Sachs executive in the private equity business who came out of retirement to be a senior adviser to Paulson.[20] The Parkinson plan identified two areas of investment banking activity that posed systemic risk. One was Lehman's tri-party repo borrowings, and the other was its counterparty exposures in over-the-counter derivatives activities. (In a tri-party repo, a third-party custodian assumes responsibility for safeguarding the interests of both counterparties to the repo transaction and handles the transfer of funds and securities between the two parties.)

"We have given considerable thought to what might be done to avoid a fire sale of tri-party collateral," Parkinson wrote in an e-mail to Shafran. "We still are at the early stages of assessing the potential systemic risk from close-out of OTC derivatives transactions by an investment bank's counterparties and identifying potential mitigants."

In a follow-up to Shafran the same day, Parkinson raised the possibility of forming a default management group as a front for coordinating an effort to document Lehman's derivatives counterparty exposures. Former New York Fed President Gerald Corrigan had earlier suggested such an idea outside the context of a crisis, and now might be a good time to "accelerate formation" of such a group, Parkinson wrote.

On August 15, Shafran wrote Parkinson that while the idea for an industry group "would make sense in a less stressed market, that the timing right now is problematic." If officials asked for such an industry group, "will we see anything in time to deal with some of the immediate issues that concern us?"

Shafran asked for a more focused game plan. Parkinson forwarded Shafran's comment to several others, including William Brodows, bank supervision officer at the New York Fed. Brodows said that asking for an industry group would be "less provocative than gathering info from a single firm," Lehman. Parkinson forwarded Brodows's response to Shafran, noting the "quandary" of deciding to do an industry versus Lehman approach to getting more information on Lehman's derivatives contracts.

"One potential problem is that defaults by affiliates [of Lehman] would allow counterparties to terminate trades with the legal entity that we seek to stabilize," wrote Parkinson August 19 to Shafran, Brodows, and others. "If so, how readily could the legal entity re-establish its hedges, even if the government recapitalized it or guaranteed its obligations?" Parkinson asked. The whole conversation had come back to square one. "I think the place to start is with an understanding of the legal entities' positions, hedges and counterparty exposures," Parkinson wrote. Time was running out for any pre-emptive moves, and late summer vacations promised to slow down even an accelerated effort.

Parkinson's persistence in devising a way to gather information on Lehman's derivatives positions paid off. Paulson had signed on to the idea. "Can confirm that his preference is to do this in a way that minimizes disruption or concerns," Shafran wrote Parkinson August 28.[21] "Indicating that we are working in spirit of Corrigan recommendations and with more than one institution seems a good idea."

Parkinson wrote back to Shafran on September 4 that Geithner was on board and the New York Fed was moving "forward promptly on several fronts."[22] It was decided to expand an existing industry group project rather than set up a new group.

The market's perception of Lehman steadily declined with each bit of news. On May 5, its share price was $28.30. On May 15, the firm announced it was slashing its work force by 5 percent, or 1,400 jobs. By June 2, its share price sank to $21.09. On June 9, Lehman said it expected a loss of $3 billion for the second quarter and planned to raise $6 billion in new capital. Its share price declined to $8.74 on July 7 and then rose and hovered just above $10 over the rest of the summer.

On August 29, the *New York Times* reported that Lehman planned to cut another 1,500 jobs. On September 1, Lehman's share price was $11.12 amid reports that the Korea Development Bank was buying a 25 percent stake in the firm.

Treasury's Ken Wilson was on the phone daily with Dick Fuld at Lehman. Wilson had temporarily left Goldman to advise Paulson on the rapidly escalating banking crisis.[23]

Just before 7 p.m., Monday, September 8, more than 20 Fed officials in New York and Washington were notified of a meeting the next morning to continue discussions on dealing with "a failing nonbank." Attached to the notice was a list of key metrics of liquidity, credit, and leverage at Lehman. The firm held $1.3 trillion in over-the-counter derivatives as of May 30. Of these, $361 billion were in credit default swaps. There were $200 billion in tri-party repos, far more than the $50 billion to $80 billion at Bear Stearns.

Early the next day, Tuesday, September 9, news broke that the Korean bank deal for Lehman was dead, sending the markets and Lehman's share price plummeting. Lehman lost more than half its value and closed at $7.79. Paulson said it was then that he realized another investment bank was going down and there was no plan in place to salvage it.[24]

Geithner suggested reassuring the markets with news that Treasury was looking for a buyer. Paulson talked to Fuld, who was panicky, and told him he would call on Bank of America's chairman Ken Lewis to see if they wanted to buy Lehman. Bank of America had already taken a look at Lehman twice over the summer and decided against the acquisition.[25]

Bank of America was in the catbird's seat in terms of acquiring an investment bank. Both Merrill Lynch and Morgan Stanley, in that order, were deemed next in line for a possible run by shorts and thus an opportunity to acquire at a bargain basement price. Paulson called Lewis to ask if Bank of America would buy Lehman. Lewis said he would be interested only if the commercial real estate assets could be spun off.

Bank of America had already acquired the nation's largest mortgage lender, Countrywide, in January 2008, after forestalling the company's collapse the prior year with emergency funding. Bank of America agreed to begin its due diligence at Lehman Brothers. Fuld was elated, according to Paulson, even though Paulson said he was not sure Lewis would go ahead with the deal.[26] Paulson began to prepare for the worst—no deal and bankruptcy for Lehman.

A conference call was set for 5 p.m. with Ben Bernanke, Chris Cox at the SEC, and Geithner. The issue: how to stop a Lehman bankruptcy. Geithner suggested a joint bailout by Wall Street along the lines of the rescue of Long-Term Capital Management in 1998, where Wall Street firms all pitched in $3.6 billion to prevent the hedge fund's failure in a deal overseen by the New York Fed. It was agreed to give this a try.

The same day, Fuld agreed to post another $3.6 billion of collateral to JPMorgan Chase. The bankruptcy estate later claimed that Lehman agreed to post the collateral because JPMorgan Chase had improperly threatened to withhold repo funding. JPMorgan Chase denied making the threat.[27]

Wednesday morning, September 10, Bank of America's people had still not shown up at Lehman Brothers to begin their due diligence. Before the markets opened, Lehman announced a $3.9 billion quarterly loss, including a $5.6 billion write-down. It also announced plans to sell off its asset management subsidiary, Neuberger Berman, and spin off $25 billion to $30 billion of its commercial real estate portfolio. It was too little, too late. Spreads on credit default swaps on Lehman's bonds jumped to a staggering 577 basis points.

Several large money funds immediately reduced their exposure to Lehman. At first, the efforts fell short of a "wholesale pullback."[28] Fidelity, after first hesitating to pull back on repo agreements, slashed its exposure from $12 billion to less than $2 billion.[29] A repo run was under way. In the week prior to Bear's collapse, Fidelity had pulled its entire $9.6 billion repo line to Bear.

While Bank of America dallied, Paulson learned there might be a possible new suitor. The news came from Bob Steel, former Treasury undersecretary for domestic finance who had become the chief executive officer at Wachovia. Steel had been talking with Bob Diamond, president of Barclays PLC of London. Barclays was interested in Lehman. Steel had served on Barclays's board.[30]

Paulson felt it was clear that Treasury had no legal authority to bail out Lehman by injecting money from Treasury. There was no formal mechanism in place to handle the resolution of an investment bank, a curious artifact of regulation that can be traced to the Glass-Steagall Act of 1933. The FDIC has authority to resolve failed banks and sell off the pieces—but not investment banks like Lehman. Given the political climate and the difficulty faced in getting GSE reform passed, apparently neither Paulson, Bernanke, nor Geithner considered seeking legislation in the early months after the failure of Bear Stearns to give the FDIC or another regulator the authority to take over and resolve a failed investment bank to avoid the harsh impact of going through a bankruptcy.

On Thursday morning, September 11, at Wilson's suggestion, Paulson called Diamond at Barclays to probe for further interest in acquiring Lehman. Diamond told him that he believed the CEO, John Varley, and the board would go along with a possible acquisition if the terms were right. Barclays wanted an exclusive and wanted to keep its interest in Lehman confidential until a deal could be sealed.

On Wednesday night, Parkinson at the Fed circulated a game plan for a liquidation consortium to explore a joint funding mechanism to minimize fallout from Lehman's tri-party repos, credit default swaps, and over-the-counter derivatives.[31] Participants were told they had to develop a credible plan before the opening of business Monday, September 15 (Sunday night for Asian markets). On Thursday afternoon, Fed officials circulated a broad outline of the proposed Lehman Default Management Group, made up of counterparties and creditors who were to figure out how to cope with a bankruptcy.[32] The list included Bank of America, Barclays, Citigroup, Credit Suisse, Deutsche Bank, Goldman Sachs, JPMorgan Chase, Merrill Lynch, Morgan Stanley, and RBS. The parties were expected to agree they would not close out their trades immediately. Instead, they would work out a process to "net down," to rescue exposures based on a common valuation method.

Late on Thursday, Lewis called Paulson to say Bank of America was not prepared to go through with an acquisition because of worries about bad assets on Lehman's books. Paulson said Bank of America could go ahead with a deal to buy the parts it wanted, and he and the Fed would try to bring together a group of bankers to buy the rest. Lewis said he would put together an offer.

Paulson said he needed a deal by Sunday and needed to hear from Lewis no later than Friday about the outlines of a proposal. Paulson told Lewis to put on his "imagination hat" and figure out a deal.[33] Lehman's shares fell 42 percent to close at $4.22.

On Thursday night, officials at Treasury, the Fed in Washington, the New York Fed, and the SEC conferred by conference call to figure out how to get Lehman through the weekend.[34] Geithner reported that Lehman had borrowed $230 billion in the repo market overnight, a sign that a liquidity squeeze was going into play against Lehman, as it had with Bear Stearns.

Cox said the SEC had developed plans to deal with a Lehman bankruptcy. At the market close, shares were down sharply for Lehman, AIG, and Washington Mutual. Paulson had the press officer at Treasury inform key reporters off the record that there would be no government money involved in any deal. When the *New York Times* and the *Wall Street Journal* reported the next day that there was still a possibility that government funding would be involved, Paulson had the press officer call CNBC. Afterwards, CNBC's Steve Liesman reported that a source familiar with Paulson's thinking said that there would be no government money involved in any resolution of Lehman.

As Paulson and other officials juggled meetings, people, and options, Lehman came under attack by naked short sellers. The number of shares that were sold and not delivered to buyers reached

32.8 million by Thursday, September 11.[35] This naked short selling frenzy was even more intense than the one that brought down Bear.

Prior lack of significant enforcement activity was surely a factor in the sudden surge of failed trades. Such activity constitutes fraud. Yet investigations by the SEC have yielded little in the way of punishment against market participants who engaged in significant levels of failed trades. Complaints of naked short selling have been legion. The inspector general for the SEC, David Kotz, reported[36] that the SEC's enforcement complaint center fielded about 5,000 complaints of naked short selling from January 2007 through May 2008. Only 123 of these complaints were forwarded for further investigation. All of the 123 were related to ongoing investigations. None of the complaints led to any enforcement actions by the SEC.

Two minutes before midnight on Thursday, September 11, an official at the New York Fed, Hayley Boesky, sent out an e-mail to colleagues reporting an onslaught of panicked calls from hedge funds. "On a scale of 1 to 10, where 10 is Bear-Stearns-week-panic, I would put sentiment today at a 12," she wrote.[37] "People are expecting a full-blown recession. There is a full expectation that leh [Lehman] goes, WAMU [Washington Mutual] and then ML [Merrill Lynch]. Worries about GS [Goldman Sachs] and reports of losses in their PB [private banking] business. Apparently GS had a lot of commodity HFs [hedge funds] who took big losses," she said.

LEHMAN WEEKEND

On Friday, September 12, Paulson had a breakfast meeting with Bernanke in a conference room near the secretary's office. Paulson was hopeful one of the potential buyers would come through, but Bernanke was doubtful. The two ran through their list of options should there be no offer. No reports from Paulson or Bernanke or anyone else have emerged on the list of options on or off the table in that discussion except Paulson's report that the options they considered were few in number.

"As I knew all too well, and as Ben reminded me, if Lehman filed for bankruptcy, we would lose control of the process, and we wouldn't have much flexibility to minimize market stress," Paulson recalled.[38] Bernanke's hope was that markets had prepared for the bankruptcy sufficiently to avoid major market stresses, while both acknowledged the potential for severe disruptions. That afternoon Britain's Chancellor of the Exchequer, Alistair Darling, called to say that he had concerns about any British bank buying Lehman.

Friday afternoon, Paulson flew to New York for a weekend marathon effort to rescue Lehman. He reached Lewis by phone after his arrival, and Lewis gave him the outline of a potential proposal. Bank of America had determined that Lehman had a $20 billion capital hole. Lewis wanted $40 billion in bad assets removed from Lehman. Bank of America would agree to take half of the first $2 billion in losses on the assets left behind.

Paulson was beginning to think that Bank of America did not really want to buy Lehman.[39] Yet Lewis had not yet said no. Fuld was growing anxious. He began calling Lewis at home repeatedly. Finally, Lewis's wife told him her husband was not going to come to the phone and to stop calling.[40]

Geithner, meanwhile, had been working with Barclays. The British bank said they were not getting all the information they required as quickly as needed to put together an offer. Barclays was going to need some help with disposing of the bad assets and with funding the acquisition. Varley told Paulson that he believed the Barclays board would approve an offer and that it would clear hurdles at the regulator, the Financial Services Authority.[41]

On Friday evening, Paulson and Geithner met with Wall Street's top bankers at the New York Fed: Jamie Dimon from JPMorgan Chase, John Mack from Morgan Stanley, Lloyd Blankfein from Goldman Sachs, Vikram Pandit from Citigroup, John Thain from Merrill Lynch, Brady Dougan from Credit Suisse, and Robert Kelly from Bank of New York Mellon.

Geithner told the bankers that a Lehman failure would be catastrophic and that it was imperative to forge a rescue. Paulson followed, telling them that without their help, on Monday, Lehman would not be able to open for business. He told them there were two potential buyers. Cox then explained how the SEC would manage the bankruptcy. Finally, Geithner told the bankers the Fed was assembling options to make liquidity available to the markets.

Geithner went over plans for how Lehman might be resolved. One group of financial institutions represented in the room would look at Lehman's derivatives, secured funding, and tri-party repo transactions. Another set of firms would work on how the industry could buy Lehman with the intention of liquidating it over time. The third group would look at finding ways to finance the purchase of the bad assets that a potential buyer of Lehman would not want.[42] The bankers expressed concern about risking their capital to rescue Lehman but indicated they wanted to find a solution and agreed to return the next morning.

Early Saturday, September 13, Paulson called Lewis, who told him Lehman's assets were so bad that leaving behind $40 billion would not be enough to seal a deal. Next, Paulson and Geithner placed a conference call with Barclays, including CEO Varley, chairman Marcus Agius in London, and Bob Diamond in New York. Varley said that Barclays would need to leave $52 billion in bad assets behind. When the meeting of the financial industry leaders resumed, Paulson told them Barclays was the best prospect.

Geithner said that the Fed could not lend against Lehman's assets because they would not provide sufficient collateral to cover the loan. Bernanke would later reiterate this point in testimony. "The Federal Reserve fully understood that the failure of Lehman would shake the financial system and the economy," he told Congress.[43] "However, the only tool available to the Federal Reserve to address the situation was its ability to provide short-term liquidity against adequate collateral; and, as I noted, Lehman already had access to our emergency credit facilities," he said.

Dougan from Credit Suisse reported that his team and a team from Goldman Sachs had found a $21 billion to $24 billion hole in Lehman's real estate assets and another billion-dollar hole in its private equity assets.

Paulson next met with Bank of America chief financial officer Joe Price, financial adviser Chris Flowers, and strategy adviser Greg Curl. Price said that Bank of America's new view was that Lehman had $65 billion to $70 billion in problem assets, sharply higher than the $40 billion figure the day before. The losses on these loans could wipe out all of Lehman's equity, he indicated. Bank of America was not willing to finance any of the losses they wanted to leave behind.

One of the thorny issues facing the bankers was that they would be making a loan against assets at a price less than the stated value. Further, this would require them to take a mark-to-market loss on similar assets they each held. The bankers were squabbling over the fact that commercial banks would have to put up as much money as the investment banks, when it was the investment banks that were in trouble. Geithner and Paulson had a third call with the Bank of America team. They were out of the bidding.

Paulson, looking ahead to the next crisis after Lehman, met with Thain to discuss Merrill's plight in the aftermath of Lehman. Paulson told him the government did not have the powers to save Merrill, and Thain needed to begin actively finding someone to acquire the firm. Thain said he was in talks with Bank of America, Goldman Sachs, and Morgan Stanley. Paulson saw no logic to a merger with Morgan Stanley. He said he thought Bank of America was the only buyer with the capacity to purchase Merrill.[44]

Thain met with Ken Lewis later that day at Bank of America's New York corporate office.[45] By the next day, the two had agreed that Bank of America would acquire Merrill for $50 billion. The price was at a 70 percent premium, or $29 per share, payable in Bank of America stock. Paulson was elated, as he did not believe Merrill would have otherwise survived the week.[46] The respected brokerage name Merrill Lynch would be retained. (After the merger, it was also decided to keep the bull logo.) This was an important victory and the first time in the crisis the regulators and the banking industry were ahead of the curve.

On Saturday afternoon, Lehman's internal counsel provided the Fed with a document describing how the firm's defaults on its obligation would "trigger a cascade of defaults" through its subsidiaries with a large over-the-counter derivatives exposure.[47] In a conference call between Bernanke, Kohn, Geithner, and other senior Fed officials, there was talk of having Geithner "pitch" Congress for additional "authorities" for the Fed, according to the *Financial Crisis Inquiry Report*.[48]

Two September 13 e-mails from Fed general counsel Scott Alvarez, which might spell out what new Congressional authorities the Fed might have sought, cannot be found on the website of the Financial Crisis Inquiry Commission. The emails are identified in endnotes 91 and 92 for Chapter 18 of the final report.[49]

The FCIC website, which was touted by the commission as offering the source documents it cites in its final report, does not provide the e-mails for endnotes 91 and 92. When one submits a request for the source document for either 91 or 92, the website instead returns the e-mail identified in endnote 90.

Several requests to the commission to obtain the correct cited e-mails from Alvarez were submitted to the commission before it ceased its operations, but were ignored. Thus, it is not clear what authorities the Fed might have sought. Identifying those potential authorities would have provided insight into the options that the Fed had under consideration at the time of the Lehman crisis. In any case, the idea came too late as time had run out to get new Congressional authority.

The same group of chief executive officers and their teams who had met Friday reconvened on Saturday, September 13, to continue to try to hammer out a deal.[50] A key goal was to determine the value of the troubled assets on Lehman's books. For the deal to work, the Wall Street consortium would have to lend up to $37 billion to a special-purpose vehicle, like Maiden Lane for Bear Stearns. The funds would purchase the assets that Lehman had on its books for $52 billion, and thus provide the surviving Lehman acquisition with capital.

By Saturday evening, the bankers had determined Lehman's troubled assets were worth only $27 billion, not $37 billion. That meant that the firms that lent money to buy the assets would lose up to $10 billion. Barclays agreed to contribute some of its shares to the new bad bank entity to reduce its potential losses. It would be costly for Wall Street firms, but it would save Lehman.

After agreement was reached, Michael Klein, an adviser to Barclays, told Lehman president McDade that Barclays would be willing to buy Lehman, provided a private consortium agreed to purchase $40 billion to $50 billion of troubled assets.[51] Many people kept working through much of the night working on more details on the term sheet for the deal. Paulson went back to the hotel hopeful. He said a prayer for a good night's sleep.[52]

Bad news came with the dawn of a new week on Sunday, September 14. Just after 7 a.m., ahead of a Barclays's board meeting, Diamond told Geithner that Barclays was encountering resistance from the Financial Services Authority. Geithner and Cox then each spoke to the FSA's chairman Collum McCarthy. McCarthy had not rejected the deal outright, but he was wary that Barclays had to guarantee Lehman's trading book from the time the deal was done until the time it was approved by Barclays's shareholders, which could be from 30 to 60 days.[53]

McCarthy did not want Barclays to assume liability for Lehman trades during the time a deal was reached and the time shareholders approved it. He suggested the Fed guarantee the trades instead. This was not an option. As Bernanke later explained, "At that time, neither the Federal Reserve nor any other agency had the authority to provide capital or an unsecured guarantee, and thus no means of preventing Lehman's failure existed."[54]

Even if the Fed could have lent the money to the special-purpose vehicle to buy the assets, Paulson expected that the run on Lehman would continue without a bank with a big balance sheet guaranteeing the trades. Geithner asked McCarthy for a waiver on the shareholder vote, and McCarthy said only Chancellor of the Exchequer Alistair Darling could grant it. Paulson believed the attempted rescue had reached a point where Washington was out of options. Treasury could not inject capital. The Fed could not guarantee Lehman's trades. There was no regulator who had the authority to seize Lehman and wind it down.

At 10 a.m., Sunday, Paulson met with the bankers and told them of the difficulties faced by the British regulator. The consortium had managed to agree to lend $30 billion to buy Lehman's bad assets. Paulson then called Darling, who made it clear that Barclays could not buy Lehman because it would be asking the British government to take on too big a risk.[55] A Lehman failure could be devastating for Britain, Darling said. That veto by the Chancellor of the Exchequer sounded the death knell for Lehman.

After a meeting between Paulson, Geithner, and Cox, Paulson emerged to tell Lehman's outside counsel, Rodgin Cohen, "We have the consortium—the British government won't do it. Darling said he did not want the U.S. cancer to spread to the U.K."[56]

On hearing the news, Fuld was frantic. He reached John Mack, CEO of Morgan Stanley, who was at the New York Fed, on his cell phone. Fuld wanted to make a deal for Morgan Stanley to buy Lehman. Mack said he was sorry, but no.[57]

The Fed announced Sunday it would provide more flexible terms for lending to primary dealers, the big Wall Street firms. It would allow for additional assets to serve as collateral. A team from Lehman, led by the firm's president, McDade, went to the New York Fed to discuss the program. The government officials, including Dudley and general counsel Thomas Baxter, told them the program would not be available for Lehman.[58] Lehman's broker-dealer, however, could borrow in the expanded program—but not if the broker-dealer declared bankruptcy.

The Fed preferred that the holding company declare bankruptcy. A letter dated September 14[59] to Lehman notifying them that the broker-dealer could use expanded collateral in the lending facility was not sent by the New York Fed until Monday, September 15 at 2:24 a.m.[60] The broker-dealer borrowed $20 to $28 billion from the facility each of the following three days.

Paulson joined a conference call with Geithner, Fed governor Kevin Warsh in New York, Bernanke, vice chairman Kohn, and others in Washington to review events. All of their efforts were designed to "spread foam on the runway to cushion the coming crash of Lehman,"

Paulson said.[61] No one on the call was confident that what had been done would be sufficient. The idea of putting cash into Lehman was brought up again. Geithner reminded everyone there was no authority to do that. Paulson said it was time to go to Congress for fiscal authority to deal with the unfolding crisis. It was agreed Lehman should announce its bankruptcy at 4 p.m., three hours ahead of the opening of markets in Asia for Monday trading.[62]

On the conference call, it had been decided that the SEC was to take the lead in convincing Lehman to have the holding company voluntarily file for bankruptcy. Hours ticked by. Cox, who was also in New York, had apparently assumed that Lehman, once told it should file, would have voluntarily filed. He had spent hours since the phone conference preparing a press release assuring customers of Lehman's broker-dealer they were protected.

Worried that Lehman had not filed, Paulson, Geithner, and others finally went to Cox's office shortly after 7 p.m. Cox told them he felt it was unusual for a regulator to call and press the company to file. After being urged to make the call, Cox, along with Tom Baxter, general counsel for the New York Fed, called Fuld shortly after 8 p.m., and Fuld connected Cox to the board. Cox urged Lehman's board to have the holding company file for bankruptcy but said he could not order them to file. The only alternative would be to let Lehman fail.

Earlier in the day, Baxter had already told the Lehman team gathered at the New York Fed that Lehman should file for bankruptcy that night, Sunday, September 14, according to Harvey Miller, Lehman's outside bankruptcy counsel.[63] If they did not declare bankruptcy, then Lehman would simply fail. Next, Baxter asked the Lehman delegation to leave the New York Fed building. "We went back to the headquarters, and it was pandemonium up there—it was like a scene from *It's a Wonderful Life* with the run on the savings and loan crisis," Miller recalled.[64] Unlike the situation in the fictional town of Bedford Falls in the 1946 Frank Capra film classic, there was no wily rich man like Mr. Potter to guarantee the deposits in the Bedford Falls Trust and Savings Bank—in return for controlling interest. Also, there was no idealistic young George Bailey to plead with depositors at the Bailey Building and Loan to remain calm and convince them to reject Potter's offer of 50 cents on the dollar and thus prevent them from losing half their savings while ensuring the independence of the building and loan. This was not going to have a happy ending.

There were "paparazzi running around" and a protestor dressed "in a sort of a Norse god uniform with a helmet and a picket sign saying 'Down with Wall Street,' " Miller recalled. "There were hundreds of employees going in and out" of Lehman's office building at 745 Seventh Avenue at 49th Street.[65] CNBC covered live the onslaught of employees milling around, some rushing in, others with frantic faces walking out, carrying cardboard boxes of personal items from their offices.

For most employees at Lehman, their world was crumbling. Little did the rest of us know that a measure of our own fates was hanging in the balance late that Sunday night in the glare of the dazzling lights of Times Square.

Cox from the SEC had also weighed in with a call to Lehman to file for bankruptcy. A meeting of the board was called. When Miller arrived at the board meeting, McDade was reporting the bad news. "Most of the board members were stunned," Miller said. "Henry Kaufman, in particular, was asking, 'How could this happen in America?' "[66] McDade told the board Lehman would not be eligible for funding for its broker-dealer arm unless the holding company filed for bankruptcy. The board voted to file for bankruptcy. Lehman filed at 1:46 a.m., Monday, September 15.

A firm that could trace its roots back to cotton trading in Alabama in the 1850s, and that survived the Civil War and the Great Depression and many other natural and manmade disasters, was gone.

Filing for bankruptcy, as predicted, cascaded through many of the 8,000 subsidiaries and affiliates of Lehman. Default clauses in derivatives contracts were triggered, and counterparties were able to seize collateral and terminate contracts. The main bankruptcy of Lehman Brothers Holding Company led to 66,000 claims totaling more than $873 billion. It was, Miller said, "the largest, most complex, multifaceted, and far-reaching bankruptcy ever filed in the United States."[67] Shareholders were wiped out. Most of the firm's 26,000 employees lost their jobs.

On Monday, the headlines blared Lehman's bankruptcy, AIG on the brink, and Merrill bought by Bank of America. The Dow fell more than 500 points. The fallout was far more devastating than federal officials had anticipated. The foam on the runway was not enough to contain the damage as a crashing Lehman produced far more damage than expected. A week later, Bernanke was still hopeful for containment of the aftermath. "The troubles at Lehman had been well known for some time, and investors clearly recognized ... that the failure of the firm was a significant possibility."[68] The evidence the markets foresaw bankruptcy, he said, was captured in the high cost of insuring

Lehman's debt with credit default swaps. "Thus, we judged that investors and counterparties had had time to take precautionary measures," he said.

THE MISSING OPTION

In the aftermath, doubts arose about whether or not the Fed had taken a too restrictive view of the law that required that its lending be secured by collateral. The *Federal Crisis Inquiry Commission Report* argued that the law does not require loans be "fully secured." Instead, they noted, section 13(3) of the Federal Reserve Act—the part of the law that governs secured lending by the Fed, requires the loans be "secured to the satisfaction of the Federal reserve bank."[69] The report cited the March 2009 statement of Fed's general counsel Scott Alvarez to back up its points. Alvarez "concluded that requiring loans under section 13(3) to be fully secured would 'undermine the very purpose of section 13(3), which was to make credit available in unusual and exigent circumstances to help restore economic activity.' "[70]

Yet the report was debating a moot point in terms of the fate of Lehman. The rescue did not fail for lack of a loan from the Fed. A consortium of banks had put together a rescue plan and was ready to go forward. The rescue failed because the Financial Services Authority would not allow Barclays to guarantee Lehman's trades and contracts from the moment a deal was announced until the board at Barclays could vote on the acquisition. The discrete issue here is whether or not the Fed could have and should have provided unsecured guarantees against Lehman's contracts temporarily. As noted above, Bernanke has stated the Fed lacked authority to provide unsecured guarantees. Given that Lehman's assets were not sufficient to cover lending, they were also insufficient to allow for a guarantee.

Allan Meltzer, a professor of economics at Carnegie-Mellon University who has written an acclaimed history of the Federal Reserve System, faulted the Fed a year after the Lehman bankruptcy. "After 30 years of bailing out almost all large financial firms, the Fed made the horrendous mistake of changing its policy in the midst of a recession," Meltzer wrote in an op-ed column in the *Wall Street Journal*.[71] "Allowing Lehman to fail without warning is one of the worst blunders in Federal Reserve history."

Other players were also in a position to prevent Lehman's collapse. For example, the White House could have invoked a rare law—the

International Emergency Economic Powers Act (IEEPA) of 1977. Under that law, President Bush could have ordered whatever was required—whether it be the unsecured guaranteeing of Lehman's trades or financing the acquisition of the toxic assets or some other effort—to prevent Lehman from failing. That's the view of James Rickards, the former general counsel for Long-Term Capital Management who in 1998 negotiated on behalf of the hedge fund the terms of its $3.6 billion rescue overseen by the New York Fed.

"What I'm saying is that you can think of a hundred different ways of solving the problem," once an emergency is declared by the President, said Rickards, who is senior managing director for Tangent Capital Partners, a merchant bank based in New York.[72] "Therefore, this Washington handwringing that, well Lehman went down, it's too bad, we had no choice, is one of the greatest myths perpetrated in the whole crisis."

Under IEEPA, the President has vast authority to do whatever is needed to deal with an international economic emergency. Two conditions have to be met to invoke the law. It must be international in scope, and it must represent a threat to national security. The effort to sell Lehman to Barclays met the international test, Rickards claimed, because it involved authorities in the United Kingdom and the United States. Further, it represented a threat to national security. "There's absolutely no doubt those conditions were satisfied," he added.

During the Great Depression, President Franklin Roosevelt invoked authority under a predecessor law—the Trading with the Enemy Act of 1917—"to shut down every bank in the country and confiscate all the gold," Rickards noted.

White House counsel should have been very aware of IEEPA because it is still frequently invoked, Rickards contended, but it is not often cited. The decision of President Barack Obama, for example, to freeze Libya's American assets in March 2011 was based on the law.

Normally, White House counsel might be expected to bring such an option forward. However, since Treasury had taken charge of the crisis in 2008, one might expect that Treasury's general counsel Robert Hoyt would bring the option to the attention of Secretary Hank Paulson. We do not know if, in fact, it was ever mentioned. "Either the Treasury lawyers were unaware of the law," Rickards said, "or they didn't want to go there."

Rickards further believed that if Paulson had gone to President Bush and told him that he felt it was necessary to issue an executive order, the President would have done so. "President Bush was doing what Paulson told him needed to be done," Rickards says, referring to the actions taken during the 2008 financial crisis. "Bush is big on loyalty and there's no doubt in my mind that if Treasury told him it should be done, that the President would have issued an executive order."

While Rickards admits that although it is one thing to point out the availability of this option in hindsight, it is quite another for people in Washington handling the crisis to say there was no choice available at the time other than to let Lehman fail.

Assuming they were fully informed of the IEEPA option, the failure to offer it or employ it suggests that Paulson and others may not have fully gauged the potential severity of the impact of Lehman's failure. Paulson does not mention the option in his book *On the Brink*, nor is it mentioned in the *Financial Crisis Inquiry Report*.

"They were linear thinkers in a nonlinear world," Rickards said, speaking of Paulson and Bernanke, among others. They should have foreseen that a new shock would have been geometric, that is, an order of magnitude larger than the crisis of 1998. A decade had passed, and the financial system had become ever more complex, capital standards had created ever more perverse incentives, financial players relied more and more on derivatives with no regulatory oversight, and more activity was occurring in the shadows. These factors increased the fragility of the system and made it more vulnerable to any given crisis, according to Rickards.

The odds that each financial crisis could lead to ever-larger economic calamities parallels how each successive increase in the degree of severity of an earthquake carries proportionally larger devastation, Rickards explained.

The failure to rescue Lehman was the culmination of a number of failures to ascertain the significance of the risks posed to the financial system and to try to get ahead of the unfolding crisis. With the failure of Bear Stearns in March 2008, the vulnerability of the system was clear to any observer paying close attention. Lehman was obviously the next domino to fall. Yet "Lehman learned nothing and the government learning nothing" from the collapse of Bear Stearns, Rickards said. Lehman's response was especially tragic. "They kept sending an ambulance and Dick Fuld refused to get in it."

The failure of Lehman turned an already significant crisis into an epic one. So the decision not to rescue Lehman is central to understanding why the scale of the crisis was so monumental. The decision will likely forever remain a point of controversy.

FINANCIAL SABOTAGE

There's also another decision by regulators to factor into Lehman's demise. That would be the decision by the Securities and Exchange Commission on July 6, 2007, to abandon the uptick rule.[73] This 1938 rule disallowed short selling of securities except after an uptick, meaning an increase, however fractional, in the price of the security. For decades, the rule made it difficult for naked short sellers to mount massive bear raids. In the case of both Bear Stearns and Lehman Brothers, there is overwhelming evidence of naked short selling. Without the onslaught of naked short sales—as evidenced by tens of millions of sales with a failure to deliver the sold shares—one can make the case that Lehman would not have been pushed into bankruptcy.

A study done for the Pentagon goes even further to identify naked short selling as one of a number of tools that can be used for economic or financial warfare for organized criminals or enemies of the United States to inflict maximum damage on the financial system and economy of the West. The unclassified study *Economic Warfare: Risks and Responses* was written by financial analyst Kevin Freeman in June 2009 for the Department of Defense's Irregular Warfare Support Program.[74] The study did not surface publicly until February 2011.

The study concludes that while there is clear evidence of a massive naked short selling associated with the demise of Lehman, the potential that it was an act of financial warfare by anyone from the Taliban to the Russian mafia is only theoretical at this point.[75]

The growing size of dark pools of money flowing through the global economy makes it harder and harder to trace the identity of those who sell shares of stock, or who engage in a whole range of criminal financial activities, especially money laundering gains from criminal activities. What are dark pools? They are "private interbank or intrabank platforms that are widely used to trade stocks away from exchanges," according to Anuj Gangahar in the *Financial Times*.[76] "They are used by clients such as hedge funds to buy and sell large blocks of shares in anonymity." The idea is to avoid revealing the trades and thus move the price of the stock—or avoid public scrutiny of hedge fund trading strategies. Gangahar cited a study[77] by the TABB Group that found that dark pools account for 12 percent of a daily stock trading volume in the United States. In conducting its survey, the TABB Group, based in Westborough, Massachusetts, spoke with 66 head traders who managed $12.1 trillion in assets. That would mean that just from this group, there was at least $1.45 trillion in daily trading from dark pools in 2009.

If there were an act of financial sabotage, it could not have worked unless the financial system had presented the attackers with significant weak spots to target. In that sense, it should be viewed as a secondary cause even on a theoretical level. "You don't take a shot at a buck out of range," Freeman said.[78] "This type of attack would require events leading up to it in order to have the vulnerabilities for it to succeed."

Rickards is skeptical that the nation's enemies were behind the demise of Lehman. "I like to say that we shouldn't worry about our enemies destroying our financial system because we're doing a fine job of it ourselves."[79]

12

The Panic of 2008

The world was greeted Monday morning, September 15, with alarming news. "Crisis on Wall Street as Lehman Totters, Merrill is Sold, AIG Seeks to Raise Cash," was the two-line banner headline across the full width of the top of page one of the *Wall Street Journal*. It was an inauspicious beginning to a scary day for the financial markets and what would turn out to be a terrifying week.

As the markets opened in New York, AIG's shares were in free fall. Morgan Stanley waited in the wings to move front and center on the financial stage, with Goldman Sachs right behind them. Shares for Morgan and Goldman Sachs were plummeting. Spreads on credit default swaps against corporate bonds of Morgan and Goldman were soaring. The markets were on the cusp of a panic.

The unfolding of a financial panic is a dreadful sight to behold and frightening to live through. Most Americans alive in 2008 had not seen a panic or a run on the banks or anything like it. They were unprepared for what was about to unfold. The banking world as they knew it had been safe and sound for the most part, except for an occasional bank failure and rescue. Few even remembered the savings and loan crisis two decades earlier.

The Dow Jones fell 504 points, its biggest single-day slide since September 11, 2001. The Dow, however, did not really capture the full extent of the panic under way. That could be seen in another, more obscure indicator, the spread between the three-month London Interbank Offered Rate and the interest rate on overnight indexed swaps or OIS.[1]

The LIBOR/OIS spread captures the degree of liquidity that is available to be lent by banks to one another overnight. Normally, there is not much difference between the nightly OIS and the three-month

LIBOR. In calm times, the spreads are in the single basis points. (It takes 100 basis points to make a percentage point.) This would indicate the banks were flush with cash to lend to one another overnight. However, the wider the spread, the less cash banks have available for overnight lending. Very high spreads indicate banks are hoarding their cash because they are worried about running out of it, and they do not want to lose it by lending to a counterparty that might not pay it back.

On September 15, the LIBOR/OIS spread jumped to 105, higher than during the Bear Stearns crisis, when it peaked at 82. Bankruptcy proceedings were adding to the steadily spreading freeze-up in credit. The administrator for Lehman's bankruptcy, Pricewaterhouse-Coopers, froze all of Goldman's assets in London.[2]

On Tuesday, September 16, prices were plunging for shares of Washington Mutual, Wachovia, and Morgan Stanley. Credit default swaps on corporate bonds for Morgan soared to 728, higher than Lehman before its failure.[3]

As bank credit dried up, counterparties were demanding more collateral to cover repos, credit default swaps, and other over-the-counter derivatives exposures. The run on the banks was under way but it was occurring, as Gary Gorton would later explain it, out of sight.[4] It was occurring on trading desks on big financial firms. Traders who had provided overnight cash in return for collateral were demanding higher and higher haircuts. A reverse run was also under way in U.S. Treasuries securities lending programs. Those who had lent out Treasuries were demanding them back as panicked institutions and funds staged a flight to quality.

As the liquidity freeze-up spread, it posed the danger that commercial banks would stop lending against securities as collateral entirely— that is, the haircuts would go to 100 percent. Commercial banks and others that had advanced funds to Morgan or Goldman—the two remaining independent investment banks—would simply call in their deposits or lending facilities. This did, in fact, happen for repos and lending facilities backed by non-prime mortgage collateral.[5]

Hedge funds began to take steps to withdraw their deposits from Morgan and Goldman, on the assumption the government was unable to bail them out, with Lehman as the example.

More alarmingly, Treasury Secretary Hank Paulson learned the Treasury repo market was beginning to shut down. Reserve managers at some of the central banks of other nations, which had lent on U.S. Treasuries, started to exit the repo market even before Lehman failed.

By September 15, more central banks were racing to the repo exit door. The number of "failures to deliver" on Treasury securities surged. On Friday, September 12, before Lehman's failure, there were $20 billion in Treasury delivery failures in a market where $7 trillion in securities lending rolls over every day.[6] A week later, September 19, the amount of fails jumped to $285 billion. They skyrocketed to $1.7 trillion on September 24 and then peaked at $5.3 trillion on October 22, just short of having the entire market shut down.[7]

On Monday, September 15, a run began on the $63 billion Reserve Primary Fund, the nation's oldest money market fund. It had invested $785 million in commercial paper and medium-term notes from Lehman Brothers.[8] Shareholders (depositors) had flooded the fund with requests for redemption, and by 1 p.m., demands for cash-outs had hit $18 billion.[9]

The liquidity crisis was spreading to commercial paper. On Tuesday, September 16, at 1 p.m., Bill Osborn, the chairman of Northern Trust, called Paulson to express concern that the frozen commercial paper market was going to impair the bank's money market mutual funds.[10] Runs on the funds were threatening to break the buck. At 5:45 p.m., Paulson met with General Electric Co. chairman and CEO Jeff Immelt and learned GE was having trouble rolling over its commercial paper.

By the end of the day Tuesday, Reserve Primary Fund's assets were down by nearly $40 billion, or 60 percent, to $23 billion. The fund marked down its Lehman holdings to zero, and the fund's share value "broke the buck" falling to 97 cents per share. It was the first money market fund since 1994 to break the buck and fail. Suddenly, money market funds, which were assumed to be super safe, were not safe anymore.

The failure of the Reserve Primary Fund prompted runs on money market funds across the board. Major sponsors of money market funds, from Bank of America to Legg Mason, injected cash into their funds.[11] The urgency for action became evident the next day when the pace of money market withdrawals accelerated and Putnam Investments announced Thursday it was liquidating its $12.3 billion Putnam Prime Money Market Fund.

On Wednesday September 17, the panic spread. In the early hours, banks were hit with billions of dollars in redemption requests. The yield on the three-month Treasuries went negative, an event that meant the financial world had been turned upside down. The wheels were coming off the financial system, as a Paulson aide put it. Morgan

Stanley's shares were in free fall, and insurance on its bonds was higher than Lehman's before its failure. The SEC, considering a temporary ban on short selling, was agonizing over whether or not announcing such a temporary ban might have unintended consequences.

On Thursday morning, September 18, the Fed announced a $180 billion expansion of its swap lines to other central banks so they could provide dollars to banks in foreign countries. Yet the markets continued in their downward spiral. Morgan Stanley's vice chairman, Bob Scully, got on the phone to complain to Paulson about short sellers driving down shares and confidence in the bank. He said he did not think Morgan would make it. Paulson called SEC Chairman Chris Cox to urge him to go ahead with the ban on short selling.[12]

To stop the run on money market funds, Treasury decided to back money market funds with a guarantee funded from the $50 billion Exchange Stabilization Fund, created in 1934 to give Treasury funds to intervene in markets to stabilize the dollar. The money market funds were also finding it hard to sell the asset-backed commercial paper. The Fed was looking into how it could purchase the commercial paper from the money market funds, as well as from corporations that needed short-term funding.

Thursday afternoon, September 18, at 1 p.m., White House officials huddled with Treasury and Fed officials at Paulson's office to discuss what new authorities they needed to request from Congress to deal with the spreading financial panic. This was followed at 3:30 p.m., with a meeting with the President at the White House. Bernanke, Cox, Paulson, Fed Governor Kevin Warsh, and others gathered in the Roosevelt Room. Bernanke told the President the nation was in a financial panic. Paulson told the President the root cause of the problem was all the bad mortgage assets on the books of banks and other financial institutions and that, in order to address that, it would be necessary to buy up those assets from the financial institutions to put the financial world back on its feet. The President agreed to support whatever actions Paulson and Bernanke deemed necessary to avoid a complete financial meltdown and to back their requests to Congress.

CNBC reported Treasury was considering buying illiquid assets held by banks. The news buoyed the markets.

That evening at 7 p.m., Paulson, Bernanke, joined by Cox and others, met with leaders on Capitol Hill to press for funds to buy toxic assets off the balance sheets of financial institutions.[13] Bernanke warned that in a matter days there would be a global financial meltdown. Congressional leaders emerged from the meeting with ashen faces and shocked and bewildered expressions to face television cameras. The next day, Senator Richard Shelby, Alabama Republican, let the cat out of the bag—saying the proposal could cost up to a trillion dollars.[14] The Administration settled on a request for a less alarming $700 billion for bailout funds, making it the biggest potential bailout in financial history.

Friday morning, September 19, Treasury announced its new temporary one-year guarantee program for money market mutual funds. Funds would pay a premium, and if the net asset value of a share fell below $1, the fund could tap the Exchange Stabilization Fund to keep the value at $1. The announcement ended the run on money market funds.

In only a week, shareholders had pulled out $196 billion[15] in assets from the $2.152 trillion non-government money market fund market.[16] The rush to pull money out of money market funds marked a turnaround. From July 2007 to August 2008, $800 billion in funds flowed into money market mutual funds,[17] as other short-term markets failed, including asset-backed commercial paper and auction rate securities.[18]

Also Friday morning, the SEC ended its hand wringing and issued a temporary ban on short selling of 799 financial stocks for 10 days—later extended to 30 days. Shares of Morgan Stanley jumped higher. At 8:30 a.m., the Fed unveiled its asset-backed commercial paper money market mutual fund liquidity facility.[19] This program would lend money to banks to buy high-quality asset-backed commercial paper, giving money market funds an opportunity to unload the assets.

On Sunday night, September 21, the Fed agreed to allow the two surviving independent investment banks—Morgan Stanley and Goldman Sachs—to convert to bank holding companies. "The Fed wanted to send a strong statement that they would not allow Goldman and Morgan Stanley to be 'Lehmanized,' " a person familiar with the discussions told the *Wall Street Journal*. It was the end of the era for freewheeling, lightly regulated independent investment banking firms.[20] All of Wall Street was under prudential bank supervision, with stricter rules for capital requirements. In taking these steps, the surviving Wall Street firms closed the gap in prudential regulation of investment banks left by Congress when it passed Glass-Steagall in 1933.

On September 25, the Office of Thrift Supervision seized the nation's largest thrift, Washington Mutual, in the largest bank failure in U.S. history. The agency was forced to act after depositors began a run on the bank, removing $16.7 billion in the 10 days following Lehman's bankruptcy. The Federal Deposit Insurance Company (FDIC), the receiver of the failed thrift, immediately sold the bulk of the company to JPMorgan Chase for $1.9 billion.

No sooner was WaMu rescued than a run began on Wachovia. It began to look like a new set of dominoes was in play. By the end of the day, $5 billion in deposits had been withdrawn. Accounts above the $100,000 limit, mostly transaction accounts for short-term cash needs by businesses, such as meeting payroll, were the primary driver of the withdrawals from Wachovia.

Wachovia was facing the prospect of a run on deposits on Monday, September 29, that would lead to its collapse. Late Sunday evening, the FDIC decided to invoke a little-known systemic risk exemption in the law[21] to provide financial assistance to bail out Wachovia. The decision required approval by Treasury, the Fed, and the White House, but FDIC Chairman Sheila Bair faced no resistance from those quarters. "The Fed and the White House had already made pretty clear they were willing to support a systemic risk determination,"[22] Bair said. "It was the fog of war," and the FDIC could not "take the chance" that there would be a deposit run on Wachovia on Monday morning.[23]

Early Monday, the FDIC announced Citigroup would buy Wachovia, and FDIC agreed to absorb up to $42 billion of losses from Wachovia's $312 billion pool of loans, many of them option ARMs and interest-only mortgages. Three days later on October 2, however, Wells Fargo made a bid for Wachovia of $15.4 billion, which Wachovia accepted. Wells was willing to go forward without government assistance.

While Congress debated whether or not to support the Bush Administration's giant bailout request, Bernanke had already decided the better course would be to inject equity capital into financial institutions.[24] The proposed language for the bailout authority Treasury submitted to Congress contained a provision that allowed capital injections. On Friday, October 3, Congress passed the Emergency Economic Stabilization Act of 2008 authorizing $700 billion in funds to create a Troubled Asset Relief Program, or TARP.

The liquidity crisis grew worse. On October 7, the LIBOR/OIS spread hit 294 basis points, an all-time high.[25] At this point, Paulson said he realized it would take too long to buy up the toxic assets, so the government would have to quickly put in place its capital injection program.[26] Capital injections were also justified on the grounds that they gave more bang for the buck; that is, because banks are leveraged 10 to 1, every billion invested in capital would have as much impact as buying $10 billion in assets.

The LIBOR/OIS spread rose to 325 basis points on October 8. Two days later, the spread hit 364 basis points. Meanwhile Treasury, the Fed and the FDIC were hammering out even more sweeping and coordinated initiatives to unfreeze the markets. On October 13, Europe announced its plan to inject capital into banks through equity shares and to guarantee new bank debt. The United Kingdom announced it was injecting 39 billion pounds in Royal Bank of Scotland and HBOS PLC to purchase controlling interest with voting rights in both banks— in effect, nationalizing them.[27] The LIBOR/OIS spread pulled back to 354, from 365.

The next day, October 14, Paulson, Bernanke, and Bair unveiled sweeping new interventions in the United States to "deploy all our tools in a strategic and collaborative manner" to unfreeze the financial system.[28] Treasury said it would inject up to $250 billion into banks by purchasing non-voting preferred shares. The FDIC announced a temporary liquidity guarantee program on new unsecured senior debt of financial institutions where deposits are FDIC insured. This would include guarantees on commercial paper, interbank funding, promissory notes, and any unsecured portion of secured debt.

In addition, the FDIC stated it would temporarily guarantee non-interest-bearing deposit transaction accounts, such as those used for payroll, for amounts above $250,000, the new higher deposit insurance limit enacted in the bailout legislation.

Finally, the Fed set up a special-purpose vehicle to buy commercial paper, including asset-backed commercial paper, from issuers with top credit ratings, unfreezing the commercial paper market. This program was called the commercial paper funding facility.[29] Issuers who relied on the facility would pay a fee to the special-purpose vehicle.

The era of big bailouts of big banks had arrived in force and was on track to become wildly unpopular with the American public. In terms of effectiveness, however, the programs launched October 14 may have been the best part of it. These programs "helped bring us back from the brink of a deeper financial crisis," according to the TARP's special investigator, Neil Barofsky.[30]

"When you look at the impact [of] putting hundreds of billions of dollars in a small handful of large financial institutions, we believe that unquestionably that had a positive impact in bringing confidence back to the market, so the banks would begin lending money to one another, bringing some liquidity back into the market," stated Barofsky, who strongly faulted many of the other TARP programs, especially the back-door bailout of AIG's counterparties.

SAVING CITIGROUP

Meanwhile, the toxic assets that prompted the bailout continued to weigh down Citigroup more than any other bank. This leading money center bank, at Paulson's urging, had raised $32.3 billion before the Lehman bankruptcy in September. Even so, with the collapse in the value of mortgage assets, that meant that in the early weeks after Lehman's bankruptcy and before any capital infusions from the feds, Citigroup's Tier 1 capital unofficially stood at only $26 billion, and Citi's tangible common equity was a negative number—minus $15.8 billion. In other words, Citi was insolvent.

A quick back-of-the envelope calculation would suggest Citigroup's capital was leveraged 74 to 1 against its $1.938 trillion in assets. Under banking regulations, to be well capitalized, a bank should have Tier 1 capital equal to 6 percent. For Citigroup that would mean $116 billion capital backing its $1.938 trillion. With only $26 billion, Citi was $90 billion short of that requirement.

On October 14, Treasury injected $45 billion into Citi from TARP funds. To further boost confidence in Citigroup, which still seemed to be teetering on the edge of failure, federal authorities negotiated a loss-sharing deal with Citi to ring-fence $306 billion in mostly mortgage assets.[31] Ring fencing is a strategy of legally walling off certain assets or liabilities within a corporation—in this case to limit losses to Citigroup from the ring-fenced troubled assets. While the troubled mortgage securities would remain on Citigroup's balance sheet, the feds and Citi agreed that Citi would absorb the first $29 billion in losses from this pool of assets (above reserves for losses). After that, the remaining losses were to be split between Citigroup and the federal government, with Treasury taking up to $5 billion from TARP and FDIC taking the next $10 billion. Any additional losses were to be guaranteed by the Federal Reserve.

The Fed's exposure, which was potentially as high as $262 billion, to a single bank has to rank as the single most extraordinary action in the entire bailout and a signal that problems at Citi were at the center of concerns about capital adequacy in the financial system.

Altogether, during 2008, Citigroup had received private and public capital infusions of $77.3 billion, and the feds were on the hook for another potential additional $281 billion. At the end of 2008, Citigroup's Tier 1 capital stood at $71 billion—after its net quarterly loss of $27.7 billion, even with all the public and private capital infusions. Taking out goodwill and intangible assets, Citigroup's tangible common equity was $29.7 billion—half the $85.1 billion of a year earlier. Citi had become a zombie bank.

Citigroup also emerged as the exemplar of how banks cooked their books to conceal exposures to subprime assets. The facts emerged in a July 2010 Citigroup settlement with the SEC over a complaint[32] that the bank concealed losses and potential exposure in subprime assets in its quarterly reports going back to the first quarter of 2007—long before huge losses emerged with such damaging effect in the fourth quarter of 2008. Citi paid only a $75 million fine for failure to disclose because the SEC did not consider the deception intentional, despite evidence to the contrary in its complaint.

Two former Citi executives paid individual fines. Former chief financial officer Gary Crittenden paid $100,000 and former investor relations chief Arthur Tildesley, Jr. paid $80,000. The original SEC complaint alleged that Crittenden and Tildesley learned in April 2007 of $37.8 billion in previously unreported exposure to subprime. The exposure consisted of $14.6 billion of super senior tranches of CDOs and $23.2 billion in liquidity puts. The "puts" were against commercial paper financing of the acquisition of CDO tranches by off-balance-sheet SIVs. If the SIVs were unable to issue commercial paper, Citigroup would have to buy the commercial paper. If the put were exercised, it would, in effect, make Citi the owner of the assets.

Instead of revealing this exposure in the first-quarter 2007 earnings report in April, Citigroup put forth essentially a fairy tale at odds with its weakened financial condition, saying it had reduced its subprime exposure from $24 billion at the end of 2006 to $13 billion, according to the SEC complaint. The truth, however, was that in addition to the $13 billion disclosed, the bank also had another $39 billion of super senior tranches of subprime collateralized debt obligations and liquidity puts, pushing the bank's exposure to $52 billion.

At the end of the *second* quarter of 2007, Citi spun yet another fairy tale when senior managers told investors on a conference call the bank had reduced subprime exposure from $24 billion at the end of 2006 to $20 billion at the end of the first quarter to $13 billion at the end of the second quarter.[33]

"Citigroup materially understated the investment bank's subprime exposure during the July 20 earnings call," the SEC charged. The SEC pointed out that Citigroup had "taken unsold lower-rated tranches of previously underwritten CDOs, as well as warehoused subprime residential mortgage-related assets, [and] used those assets in the creation of new CDOs, and then had retained the super senior tranches of these CDOs." The reduced exposure Citi announced was simply "moving warehouse and unsold lower tranche inventory into new super senior tranches," the complaint said.[34] These super seniors, in turn, were undisclosed because they were considered so safe that losses were highly unlikely. Citigroup was playing a shell game of hide the toxic assets.

By mid-September 2007, cracks were starting to appear in Citigroup's fabrications. The bank had been forced to purchase $25 billion of the commercial paper to back its SIVs, as the liquidity puts were exercised. With the toll on subprime now pushing down the value of super senior tranches, Citi pre-announced a $1.3 billion loss October 1 on it subprime exposure from CDOs. The bank did not disclose, however, that this included $100 million on super senior tranches. The SEC pointed out that Citigroup still had not mentioned to investors that it now had $43 billion in subprime exposure from super senior tranches ($18 billion) and liquidity puts ($25 billion).[35] When Citigroup made public its earnings on October 15, reported losses on subprime were higher at $1.56 billion. Senior management knew at this point that the losses came from super senior tranches of subprime CDOs, the SEC stated, and yet continued to claim its subprime exposure was $13 billion when in fact it was $55 billion.[36] "In doing so, Citigroup materially understated the investment bank's subprime exposure," according to the SEC complaint.[37]

SEC's director of enforcement Robert Khuzami faulted Citi for being disingenuous. "Even as late as fall 2007, as the mortgage market was rapidly deteriorating, Citigroup boasted of superior risk management skills in reducing its subprime exposure," he said of the settlement with Citigroup. Scott Friestand, SEC's associate director of enforcement, was also highly critical. "Citigroup's improper disclosure came at a critical time when investors were clamoring for details about Wall Street firms' exposure to subprime securities," he said. "Instead of providing clear and accurate information to the market, Citigroup dropped the ball and made a bad situation worse."

The terms of the SEC settlement were disappointing, to say the least. The fine seemed pitiful, given the scope and duration of the deception that went on. For starters, the amount in dispute was not just "material," as the SEC put it, it was big enough to potentially wipe out nearly all the capital of the bank. Further, the SEC seems to have become a regulatory mouse by determining that the fraud was "unintentional," a determination that allowed the agency to impose a much lower fine.

It was not until November 4, 2007, that Citigroup revealed that it had $55 billion in subprime exposure and estimated that losses in these subprime assets would reduce net income by $5 billion to $7 billion.

Citigroup also stifled at least one internal risk monitor who warned that the bank was approving too many bad mortgages. Richard Bowen, who oversaw loan quality for over $90 billion a year of mortgages underwritten and purchased by CitiFinancial, a consumer lending subsidiary, warned in mid-2006 that as much as 60 percent of the loans CitiMortgage was acquiring did not meet loan guidelines.[38] Bowen tried to alert top managers at the firm by "email, weekly reports, committee presentations, and discussions." Nothing came from his warnings.[39] Instead, he said, "there was a considerable push to build [mortgage origination] volumes, to increase market share," he said.

Bowen took his complaints up the ladder to Robert Rubin, chairman of the executive committee of the board, in a memo titled "URGENT—READ IMMEDIATELY." The memo warned Citi could face billions in losses if investors demanded Citi repurchase defective loans. Rubin told the Financial Crisis Inquiry Commission he did recall receiving the memo. "[E]ither I or somebody else, and I truly do not remember who, but either I or somebody else sent it to the appropriate people, and I do know factually that that was acted on promptly and actions were taken in response to it," Rubin said.[40] After the complaint, Bowen's supervisory responsibilities were curtailed from 220 to 2 people, his bonus was cut, and he received a downgraded performance review.

Citibank's sudden stumble toward collapse would not come as a surprise to the federal regulators or the public at large if it had not hidden away so much of its potential problems off balance sheet in those pesky black box SIVs and refused to disclose exposures in holdings of super senior tranches of subprime CDOs, along with subprime holdings in its trading accounts.

The Citi experience is also troubling in that while misstatements and misrepresentations were found by the SEC, there was no effort to hold senior management accountable, as required under Sarbanes-Oxley. That is the law that Congress enacted in 2002 in response to corporate scandals and accounting fraud that destroyed Enron, Tyco International, WorldCom, and other companies. Under the law, senior managers take individual responsibility for the accuracy and completeness of financial reports in publicly traded companies.

At Citigroup, the senior-most executives during the time Citi was misstating its earnings were chairman and CEO Chuck Prince, ousted in November 2007, as well as Rubin. In addition, there were Michael Klein and Thomas Maheras, who jointly headed Citi's investment bank.

"In a post Sarbanes-Oxley world, these are the people who are supposed to be signing audit reports, who are supposed to be signing off on the financials," said Janet Tavakoli, president of Tavakoli Structured Finance of Chicago.[41] "And we're supposed to be held accountable for those signatures. That didn't happen. So, Sarbanes-Oxley did nothing. It didn't work. It was a total waste. It's inexplicable how people weren't held accountable," she said.

ASSESSING THE TOLL

Citi was only the tip of the bailout iceberg, albeit the largest piece. Through a variety programs, the federal government would face an exposure for TARP, FDIC guarantees, and Federal Reserve purchase and lending facilities of $2.4 trillion at its peak in July 2010.[42] By January 2011, that exposure had declined to $1.45 trillion. Citigroup was the chief beneficiary at $476 billion, with Bank of America runner-up at $336 billion.

The full financial toll for the crisis is difficult to tally. The International Monetary Fund estimated global losses from bad loans and securities at $4.1 trillion in April 2010,[43] but lowered the estimate to $2.8 trillion the following year as asset values recovered.[44] The toll in lost economic output, lost jobs, depressed housing values, and an American government sinking ever deeper into debt is far greater than the lost value of mortgage assets. At year-end 2010, 11 million households, 23 percent of all mortgage homes, were underwater, with mortgages worth more than the homes.[45] Both Greenspan and Bernanke have called it was the worst financial crisis in history.

The people on Main Street America paid a heavy toll. Yet the people in Washington and on Wall Street who took excessive risks that put the financial system into jeopardy have, for the most part, kept their enormous gains and have not been held accountable. Few have been disgraced, and fewer still have shown any sign they have been chastened by the events. Practically no one has been banned from the securities industry. And no one has gone to jail except for Lee Farkas, former chairman of Taylor, Bean and Whitaker Mortgage Company, Ocala, Florida, who ran a scam generating $500 million in fake residential mortgages and who tried to scam $553 million from TARP. In the single high-profile case that went to trial—the fraud case against Ralph Cioffi and Matthew Tannin, formerly of Bear Stearns—the accused were found not guilty.

The vast majority of investigations have led to settlements where usually no one admits wrongdoing and a fine is paid that does not seem commensurate with the alleged wrongdoing. Some of the settlements, like the one at Citigroup, are nothing more than a slap on the wrist. Wall Street firms can afford the highest-priced attorneys and can afford to hire them by the dozen and array them against understaffed investigators and prosecutors. Hundreds of civil cases have been brought by investors in mortgage-backed securities and collateralized debt obligations, with most ending in settlements where no one admits guilt.

A financial system that cannot correct and rebalance itself to re-engage as a fully productive partner in the economy is one that is not stable in the long term. As the major financial institutions grow larger and larger, their relationship with the government is coming more and more to resemble the corrupt relationship that existed between Fannie Mae and Freddie Mac, on the one hand, and Washington's political establishment.

This point was underscored in the aftermath to the passage of the Dodd-Frank Act of 2010. That new law—touted as reform to ensure there would never be a repeat of the financial crisis of 2008—provided federal regulators with the authority to rescue any systemically important financial institutions. Because of this authority, the markets have rewarded the largest financial institutions with a lower cost of funding over their peers, giving them a competitive advantage. In the fourth quarter of 2010, the average cost of funding of earning assets for banks over $100 billion was 0.67 percent, according to the FDIC. For community banks, it was 1.24 percent. By their willingness to accept lower returns for debt issued by the largest banking organizations, investors in the market have recognized an implicit guarantee the government will bail out large banks.

As much as the story line of the crisis lends itself to demagoguery, this response is counterproductive. It is likely to lead to quick fixes that are emotionally satisfying or phony solutions that do not address the underlying issues.

We need a way forward to a safer, sounder financial system where the power of sunlight on financial institutions and markets helps enable free market discipline to work its invisible hand for the good of all. Conversely, the more the financial system expands into the shadows, relies on dark pools of money, and funnels activity into black boxes and complex high-risk activities for fast-money results, the more the financial system becomes subject to the sinister hand of market manipulation. When activity moves in this direction, financial institutions and players can potentially become parasites transferring wealth from the broader economy to the financial sector and to the masters of manipulation.

It is clear that we need to move toward fuller transparency in all major financial markets. The daunting task before us will be to carefully and thoughtfully determine how to get there, and then make a concerted and sustained effort to do so.

Glossary

ABX.HE indices   A series of indices of derivatives from the prices of 20 credit default swaps that each reference individual subprime mortgage-backed securities, including securities backed by home equity loans.

Alternative A, or Alt-A   A category of mortgages that have reduced documentation of income and assets for borrowers with A credits, many of whom are self-employed.

Asset-backed securities   Securities issued against a pool of loans in a trust. The loans can be anything from auto loans to credit card receivables, student loans, small business loans, and second mortgages.

Basis point   A basis point is 1/100th of a percentage point.

CDO squared, or CDO^2   Collateralized debt obligations created from tranches or pieces of other collateralized debt obligations.

CDOs of ABS   Collateralized debt obligations where the collateral backing the securities is made up of asset-backed securities, which can be securities issued against a pool of auto loans, credit card receivables, student loans, or mortgages.

Collateralized debt obligations   Securities issued against a pool of collateral that can include debt instruments from corporate loans to asset-backed securities, including mortgage-backed securities.

Credit default swap   A credit derivative contract is an agreement between a protection provider and a protection buyer whereby the provider agrees to pay the buyer if a default event occurs and the protection buyer agrees to pay a monthly premium to the protection provider.

Government-sponsored enterprise, or GSE   A private corporation, such as Fannie Mae and Freddie, that is chartered by the federal government to pursue public policy goals but that is privately owned by its shareholders.

Hedge fund   A private partnership of investors who take large equity stakes in the fund, which typically makes highly-leveraged investments and pursues complex, often secretive investing and trading strategies.

Jumbo prime mortgages   Mortgages with principal balances above the conforming loan limit for mortgages acquired by Fannie Mae and Freddie Mac.

Liquidity put   A contract between two parties whereby one party can compel the other to buy an asset under certain circumstances, thereby ensuring a buyer for otherwise illiquid assets.

Mark to market   The accounting principle of marking to market requires firms to raise or lower the value of an asset on their books to conform to prices of similar assets recently sold.

Office of Federal Housing Enterprise Oversight, or OFHEO   The government regulator created in 1992 to oversee the safety and soundness of Fannie Mae and Freddie Mac. Its successor since 2008 is the Federal Housing Finance Agency.

Private-label mortgage-backed securities   Mortgage-backed securities sponsored by private companies rather than either Fannie Mae, Freddie Mac, or Ginnie Mae, which provide guarantees for agency-backed securities.

Repurchase agreement, or repo   A method of secured lending whereby the borrower sells securities to the lender as collateral for short-term cash and agrees to repurchase them at a higher price within a short period. In a tri-party repo, a third-party custodian assumes responsibility for safeguarding the interests of both counterparties to the repo and handles the transfer of funds and securities between the two parties.

Securitization   The process by which loans and other debt instruments are acquired and placed into a pool of assets, against which securities are issued.

Special investment vehicle, or SIV   See special-purpose vehicle.

Special-purpose vehicle, or SPV   An entity created to fulfill a narrow and sometimes temporary objective. It typically holds a portfolio of assets such as mortgage-backed securities or other debt obligations. It can also be called a **special-purpose entity, or SPE** or a **special investment vehicle, or SIV**.

Subprime mortgages   Mortgages made to borrowers with credit scores that are below 660.

Synthetic CDO   A collateralized debt obligation that holds credit default swaps against reference assets rather than hold cash assets as collateral.

Tier 1 capital   The measure of the core capital of banks, thrifts, and other regulated banking organizations. The minimum Tier 1 capital requirement is 4 percent. To be considered well capitalized, a bank needs to have 6 percent Tier 1 capital.

Tranche   An investment slice based on its credit rating that is part of the investment options offered in a mortgage-backed security or collateralized debt obligation transaction.

Notes

Chapter 1: The Mortgage Meltdown

1. Interview with Janet Tavakoli, January 27, 2011.

2. Vikas Bajaj and Christine Haughney, "Tremors at the Door," *New York Times*, January 27, 2007.

3. Interview with Janet Tavakoli, January 27, 2011.

4. Public Law 107–204.

5. Janet Tavakoli, *Dear Mr. Buffet*, John Wiley & Sons, Hoboken, NJ, 2009, p. 81.

6. Charles Gasparino, *The Sellout*, HarperCollins, New York, 2009, pp. 164–66.

7. "O'Neal Ranks No. 5 on Payout List, Group Says," Bloomberg News, November 2, 2007.

8. Jonathan Karp and Miriam Jordan, "How the Subprime Mess Hit Poor Immigrant Groups," *Wall Street Journal*, November 7, 2007, p. A1.

9. Interview with Soario Santos, February 1, 2011.

10. *Allstate Insurance Company et al v. Countrywide Financial Corp. et al.* Complaint, U.S. District Court, Southern District of New York, December 10, 2010, p. 69.

11. *Allstate v. Countrywide*, pp. 67–68.

12. *Allstate v. Countrywide*, p. 70.

13. Mortgage origination data from Inside Mortgage Finance Publications, Bethesda, Maryland.

14. Susan Swain's interview with Janet Tavakoli, C-Span's *Washington Journal*, December 9, 2010.

15. The full name was the Bear Stearns High-Grade Structured Credit Strategies Enhanced Leveraged Fund.

16. The full name was the Bear Stearns High-Grade Structured Credit Fund, shortened here to High-Grade fund.

17. *Securities and Exchange Commission v. Ralph C. Cioffi and Matthew M. Tannin*, U.S. District Court, Eastern District of New York, June 19, 2008, p. 19.

18. Ibid., p. 10.

19. Ibid., p. 15.

20. Ibid., p. 16.

21. Robert Stowe England, "Anatomy of a Meltdown," *Mortgage Banking*, October 2007.

22. Jody Shenn and Bradley Keoun, "Bear Stearns Rivals Reject Fund Bailout in LTCM Redux," Bloomberg News, June 25, 2007.

23. Interview with Michael Youngblood, June 10, 2007. See also: Robert Stowe England, "Anatomy of a Meltdown," *Mortgage Banking*, October 2007.

24. Copy of the "Dear Client" letter from Bear Stearns in possession of the author, July 17, 2007.

25. Landon Thomas, Jr., "A Top Official at Bear Stearns Ousted," *New York Times*, August 6, 2007.

26. Mark Pittman, "Moody's Lowers Ratings on Subprime Bonds, S&P May Cut," Bloomberg News, July 10, 2007.

27. Michael Youngblood, *Structured Finance Insights*, FBR Investments, August 14, 2007.

28. Interview with Mark Zandi, July 27, 2007. See also: Robert Stowe England, "Anatomy of a Meltdown," *Mortgage Banking*, October 2007.

29. Ranking by Inside Mortgage Finance Publications.

30. Interview with Charles Dumas, July 17, 2007. See also: Robert Stowe England, "Anatomy of a Meltdown," *Mortgage Banking*, October 2007.

31. ISDA Market Survey, National Amounts Outstanding at Year-End, All Survey Contracts, 1987-Present, 2010. International Swaps and Derivatives Association.

32. Estimate of $895 billion contained in special report from the Financial Crisis Inquiry Commission, *Credit Derivatives and Mortgage-Related Credit Derivatives*, Preliminary Staff Report, June 29, 2010, pp. 7 and 9.

33. *The Financial Crisis Inquiry Report*, Final Report of the National Commission on the Causes of the Financial and Economic Crisis in the United States, Official Government Edition, January 2011, p. 129.

34. Janet Tavakoli, *Structured Finance and Collateralized Debt Obligations*, Second Edition, John Wiley & Sons, Hoboken, NJ, 2008, pp. 87–88. Tavakoli calculated the total CDO market outstanding in 2006 at $4.7 trillion, counting the unrated tranches. She did not break out how much of the overall market was for CDOs of ABS.

35. The AAA tranches of first-quarter 2007 ABX.HE had fallen only modestly to 95.53.

36. FBR Investment Management's Subprime Weekly Comp Sheet for June 15, 2007.

37. Copy of Mike Perry's e-mail is in the possession of the author.

Chapter 2: The Panic of 2007

1. Stuart Kelly and Elena Logutenkova, "IKB Cuts Profit Forecast Amid Rout in U.S. Mortgages," Bloomberg News, July 30, 2007.

2. Aaron Kirchfeld and Holger Elfes, "Dusseldorf's 'Nippon on Rhine' Is Crimped by WestLB, IKB Woes," Bloomberg News, August 15, 2007.

3. Simon Kennedy, "Central Banks Move to Counter Liquidity Crunch," *MarketWatch*, August 9, 2007.

4. Interview with Doug Duncan, August 15, 2007. See also: Robert Stowe England, "Anatomy of a Meltdown," *Mortgage Banking*, October 2007.

5. Interview with Doug Duncan, August 8, 2007.

6. Interview with Lyle Gramley, September 19, 2007. See also: Robert Stowe England, "Anatomy of a Meltdown," *Mortgage Banking*, October 2007.

7. Jonathan Stempel, "Bank of America Invests $2 Billion in Countrywide," Reuters, August 23, 2007.

8. Sabine Pirone and Shelley Smith, "Northern Rock Customers Crowd Branches, Withdraw Cash," Bloomberg News, September 14, 2007.

9. Fiona Walsh, "Northern Rock Shares Plummet," *Guardian*, September 17, 2007.

10. "Northern Rock Deposits Guaranteed," BBC News, September 17, 2007.

11. Nearly a year later, there was a $146.97 million jumbo prime deal on August 8, 2008, on loans purchased from third parties by the Lehman Brothers conduit program.

12. Gary Gorton, Questions and Answers About the Financial Crisis, Prepared for the U.S. Financial Crisis Inquiry Commission, February 20, 2010, p. 4.

13. Swasi Bate, Stephany Bushweller, and Everett Rutan, *The Fundamentals of Asset-Backed Commercial Paper*, Moody's Investors Service Structured Finance Special Report 57, February 3, 2003, p. 54.

14. Andrew Willis and Boyd Erman, "Credit Crunch Claims Victim in Canada; Coventree Stock Plunges as Investors Balk," *The Globe and Mail*, August 14, 2007.

15. Joe Schneider, "Coventree Misled Investors on Subprime Risk, OSC Says," Bloomberg News, May 12, 2010.

16. Federal Reserve Board, Commercial Paper data base.

17. Patrick Hosking and Siobhan Kennedy, "Cheyne Fund Forced into Receivership as Additional Cash Sought," *The Sunday Times*, September 6, 2007.

18. JPMorgan Chase & Co. is the bank holding company; the investment bank operations are generally referred to as J. P. Morgan, a brand name used by JPMorgan Chase & Co., according to a company spokesman.

19. Eric Dash, "Banks May Pool Billions to Avert Securities Sell-Off," *New York Times*, October 14, 2007.

20. Neil Unmack, "Rhinebridge Commercial Paper SIV May Not Repay Debt," Bloomberg News, October 18, 2007.

21. "Greenspan Warns of Risks with 'Super SIV' Fund," *Wall Street Journal*, October 19, 2007.

22. Michael Shedlock, "Super SIV Bailout Plan Doomed to Fail," Mish's Global Economic Trend Analysis, October 13, 2007. http://globaleconomic analysis.blogspot.com/2007/10/super-siv-bailout-plan-doomed-to-fail.html. Accessed January 20, 2011.

23. Eric Dash and Andrew Ross Sorkin, "Citigroup Sells Abu Dhabi Fund $7.5 Billion Stake," *New York Times*, November 27, 2007.

24. Dan Wilchins, "Banks Abandon Plan for Super-SIV," Reuters, December 24, 2007.

25. Arnold Kling, *Not What They Had in Mind: A History of Policies That Produced the Financial Crisis of 2008*, Mercatus Center, George Mason University, September 2009, p. 26.

26. Gary Gorton, "The Panic of 2007," Paper, August 24, 2008, prepared for the Federal Reserve Bank of Kansas City and for the Jackson Hole Conference, August 2008.

27. Gary Gorton, Q&A for the Financial Crisis Inquiry Commission, p. 2.

28. On the repo markets, see *Research Quarterly,* Vol IV. No. 6 (May 2009), Securities Industry and Financial Markets Association), p. 10, and on the stock market, see "Daily NYSE Group Volume in NYSE Listed" from NYSEData.com *Fact Book.*

29. Gorton, Q&A for the Financial Crisis Inquiry Commission, p. 2.

30. Ibid.

31. Ibid., p. 12.

32. Gary Gorton and Andrew Metrick, "Haircuts," Federal Reserve Bank of St. Louis, November-December 2010.

33. Interview with Andrew Metrick, January 28, 2011.

34. Gorton, 2010, p. 2.

35. Interview with James Rickards, March 30, 2011.

Chapter 3: Seeds of the Disaster

1. CBO's Budgetary Treatment of Fannie Mae and Freddie Mac, Congressional Budget Office, Washington, D.C., January 2010, p. 10.

2. Daniel E. Teclaw and Vandana Sharma, "U.S. Government Cost to Resolve and Relaunch Fannie Mae and Freddie Mac Could Approach $700 Billion," Standard & Poor's, November 4, 2010.

3. Joe Mariano, "Where the Hell Did Billions of Dollars for Reinvestment Come From?" Chapter 2, p. 29 of *Access to Capital: Advocacy and the Democratization of Financial Institutions*, 2002, Gregory Hines, editor. Temple University Press, Philadelphia, 2003.

4. David Walls, *The Workbook* (Summer 1994), "Power to the People: Thirty-Five Years of Community Organizing," pp. 52–53. http://www.sonoma.edu/users/w/wallsd/pdf/Community-Organizing.pdf. Retrieved May 30, 2011.

5. Katharine L. Bradbury, Karl E. Case, and Constance R. Dunham, "Geographic Patterns of Mortgage Lending in Boston, 1982–1987," *New England Economic Review,* Federal Reserve Bank of Boston, Boston, September 1989, pp. 3–30.

6. Allan R. Gold, "Racial Pattern Is Found in Boston Mortgages," *New York Times,* September 1, 1989.

7. Richard Syron would later serve as chairman and chief executive officer of Freddie Mac.

8. Pinto, 2010, p. 51.

9. Alicia H. Munnell, Lynn E. Browne, James McEneaney, and Geoffrey M. B. Tootel, "Mortgage Lending in Boston: Interpreting HMDA Data," Federal Reserve Bank of Boston, Working Paper No. 92–7, October 1992. This study was later published as follows: Alicia H. Munnell, Geoffrey M. B. Tootel, Lynn E. Browne, and James McEneaney, "Mortgage Lending in Boston: Interpreting HMDA Data," *American Economic Review* 86 (March 1996), pp. 25–53.

10. David K. Horne, "Mortgage Lending, Race, and Model Specification," *Journal of Financial Services Research*, Vol. 11, pp. 43–46, 1997. This was a follow-up to an earlier article: David K. Horne, "Evaluating the Role of Race in Mortgage Lending," *FDIC Banking Review*, Spring-Summer, 1994, pp. 1–15.

11. Federal Financial Institutions Reform, Recovery, and Enforcement Act of 1989 (FIRREA).

12. Allen J. Fishbein, "Filling the Half-Empty Glass: The Role of Community Advocacy in Redefining the Public Responsibilities of Government-Sponsored Housing Enterprises," p. 109, *Organizing Access to Capital: Advocacy and the Democratization of Financial Institutions,* edited by Gregory D. Squires (Philadelphia: Temple University Press, 2003), p. 114.

13. Ibid.

14. Ibid.

15. Mortgages purchased by the GSEs in 1993 and 1994, under this agreement, would be evenly split between multifamily and single-family properties.

16. The GSE Act of 1992 was the short version of the law's official title: the Federal Housing Enterprises Financial Safety and Soundness Act of 1992.

17. Interview with Edward Pinto, May 21, 2011.

18. Ibid.

19. Interview with Edward Pinto, September 10, 2010.

20. Ibid.

21. Interview with Edward Pinto, Washington, D.C. June 14, 2010.

22. Robert Stowe England, "Assault on the Mortgage Lenders," *National Review,* December 27, 1993.

23. Vern McKinley reports the vote tally in the following piece: Vern McKinley, "Community Reinvestment Act: Ensuring Credit Adequacy or Enforcing Credit Allocation?" *Regulation* No. 4, 1994, p. 28.

24. England, 1993.

25. Ibid.

26. McKinley, 1994, pp. 25–37.

27. Ibid., p. 25.

28. England, 1993.

29. Ibid.

30. Steve Cocheo, "Fair-lending Pressure Builds," *ABA Banking Journal*, Vol. 86, 1994.

31. Robert S. England, "That's Angelo," *Mortgage Banking*, Vol. 48, No. 10, July 1988, pp. 27–34.

32. Robert Ostrow was a third co-founder of Countrywide, but he left after an early consolidation.

33. Amount of initial investment provided by Angelo Mozilo. See England, 1988, p. 27.

34. "Mortgagestats.com Ranks Countrywide Home Loans No. 1 in Lending to Minorities," press release from PRNewswire, Countrywide Home Loans, Inc., undated.

35. "Case Study: Countrywide Home Loans, Inc.," Fannie Mae Foundation, 2000.

36. CRA Regulation, 1995, p. 22157.

37. England, 1993.

38. Department of the Treasury Office of the Comptroller of the Currency, Federal Reserve System, Federal Deposit Insurance Corporation, Department of the Treasury Office of Thrift Supervision, Federal Reserve System, "Community Reinvestment Act Regulations and Home Mortgage Disclosure; Final," *Federal Register,* May 4, 1995, pp. 22155–22223.

39. Helena Yeaman, "The Bipartisan Roots of the Financial Crisis," *Political Science Quarterly,* Vol. 124, No. 4, 2009–10, pp. 681–696.

40. Yeaman, p. 684.

41. Ben Bernanke, "The Community Reinvestment Act: Its Evolution and New Challenges," Speech at the Community Affairs Research Conference, Washington, D.C., March 30, 2007.

42. National Community Reinvestment Center, *CRA Commitments,* September 2007, p. 8.

43. U.S. Department of Housing and Urban Development, *The National Homeownership Strategy: Partners in the American Dream,* May 1995.

44. William J. Clinton, "Remarks on the National Homeownership Strategy," June 5, 1995.

45. Bryan Boyer, *Cities Destroyed for Cash,* Follett Publishing, New York, 1973.

46. Federal Housing Finance Agency, Table 1, Total Mortgages Held or Securitized by Fannie Mae and Freddie Mac as a Percentage of Residential Mortgage Debt Outstanding, 1990–2009.

47. Bethany McLean, "Fannie Mae's Last Stand," *Vanity Fair,* February 2009.

Chapter 4: The Race to the Bottom

1. The GSE Act of 1992 was the short version of the law's official title: the Federal Housing Enterprises Financial Safety and Soundness Act of 1992.

2. Edward J. Pinto, *Government Housing Policies in the Lead-up to the Financial Crisis: A Forensic Study,* unpublished monograph, November August 14, 2010, Chart 52, p. 148. http://www.aei.org/docLib/Pinto-Government-Housing-Policies-Crisis.pdf. Accessed May 30, 2011.

3. See Edward Pinto's analysis in Exhibit 2 to the Triggers Memo, April 21, 2010, p. 4. http://www.aei.org/docLib/Pinto-Sizing-Total-Federal-Contributions.pdf Pinto, Triggers Memo, 2010.

4. Interview with Edward Pinto, September 30, 2010.

5. Ibid.

6. Edward J. Pinto, *Government Housing Policies in the Lead-up to the Financial Crisis: A Forensic Study,* discussion draft of August 14, 2010. Document in possession of author, Footnote 219, p. 83; Chart 28, p. 89.

7. Freddie Mac defined 660 as an investment-grade score in an industry letter in August 1995.

8. See Fannie Mae Letter LL09-95 to all Fannie lenders from Robert J. Engelstad, "Measuring Credit Risk: Borrower Credit Scores and Lender Profiles," October 24, 1995; and Freddie Mac Industry Letter from Michael K. Stamper, "The Predictive Power of Selected Credit Scores," July 11, 1995.

9. Equifax data in the files of Edward Pinto.

10. Snapshot of Fannie Mae's 1994 credit score data in the files of Edward Pinto.

11. Source for the 2008 FICO score data is Moody's/Economy.com from a document in the files of Edward Pinto.

12. Carol D. Leonning, "How HUD Mortgage Policy Fed the Crisis," *Washington Post*, June 10, 2008.

13. Edward J. Pinto, *Government Housing Policies in the Lead-up to the Financial Crisis: A Forensic Study*, monograph, discussion draft of August 14, 2010, p. 85.

14. Fannie Mae, 1996 Annual Report, (Washington, 1997), p. 40.

15. "1996 Performance of Top U.S. Banking Companies," *American Banker*, March 26, 1997, p. 15.

16. Congressional Budget Office, *Assessing the Public Costs and Benefits of Fannie Mae and Freddie Mac*, May 1996, p. 31.

17. U.S. Department of Housing and Urban Development, "Privatization of Fannie Mae and Freddie Mac: Desirability and Feasibility," Office of Policy Development and Research, July 1996, p. 170.

18. General Accounting Office, "Housing Enterprises: Potential Impacts of Severing Government Sponsorship," May 1996, GAO/GGD-96-120.

19. Consumer Installment Credit, *Federal Reserve Bulletin*, Table 1.55, December 1996, p. A36; Consumer Installment Credit, *Federal Reserve Bulletin*, Table 1.55, March 1993, p. A38.

20. McKinley, p. 6.

21. Ibid., p. 9.

22. HUD, 1996, p. 170.

23. McKinley, p. 9.

24. Ibid., p. 16.

25. "CBO's Answers to Follow-Up Questions from the Hearing on GSE Privatization Studies," June 12, 1996, before the House Banking Committee, Subcommittee on Capital Markets, Securities, and GSEs, undated, p. 2.

26. McKinley, p. 3

27. Inside Mortgage Finance mortgage-backed securities database.

28. Fannie added a loan classification warning statement in its 10-Q filing for the third quarter of 2008. Freddie, in its 10-K for 2008, stated that there is "no universally accepted definition" of Alt-A. Freddie Mac, in its 10-Q for the first quarter of 2008, said that it classified as Alt-A mortgages that originators identified as Alt-A and other loans that had reduced documentation requirements that would indicate they should have been classified as Alt-A.

29. The name of the sender on the memo was Donna Cogswell, a colleague of Andrukonis, but he composed the e-mail.

30. *Adam Kreysar and Tina Kreysar v. Richard Syron et al.*, Class Action Complaint, U.S. District Court, Southern District of New York, January 28, 2009. p. 34.

31. *Financial Crisis Inquiry Report*, p. 180.

32. Ibid., p. 181.

33. Fannie Mae, "Notes to Single Family Conventional Acquisition Report," August 3, 2007; see also Federal National Mortgage Association, Form 10-K for 2006, August 16, 2007 (Filed late).

34. FCIC staff estimates based on data provided by Fannie Mae.

35. Federal National Mortgage Association, Form DEF 14A, November 2, 2007, p. 42; Federal National Mortgage Association, Form 10-K, May 2, 2007, p. 202.

36. "Deepen Segments–Develop Breadth," Fannie Mae Strategic Plan, 2007–2011, June 2007.

37. Enrico Dallavecchia, e-mail to Michael Williams, July 16, 2007.

38. Daniel Mudd, e-mail to Enrico Dallavecchia, "RE: Budget 2008 and strategic investments," July 17, 2007.

39. *Financial Crisis Inquiry Report*, p. 183.

40. Leland Brendsel Political Campaign Contributions, 2002 Election Cycle, CampaignMoney.com.

41. Office of Federal Housing Enterprise Oversight, *Report of the Special Examination of Fannie Mae*, May 2006.

42. Barney Frank had a change of heart about the affordable goals and expressed his new view at a hearing of the House Financial Services Committee on September 29, 2010, where he called them a "mistake."

Chapter 5: The Rise of Private Label

1. Interview with Tom LaMalfa, September 30, 2010.

2. From data collected by Inside Mortgage Finance.

3. In 1995, there was $110.4 billion in Ginnie, Fannie, and Freddie mortgage-backed securities plus another $16 billion in collateralized mortgage obligations and real estate mortgage investment conduits, or REMICs, from the same agencies.

4. In 1998, Russia defaulted on its foreign debt. Long Term Capital Management failed, and the New York Fed arranged for a consortium of banks to do a $3.6 billion rescue of the fund.

5. Alan Greenspan and James Kennedy, "Sources and Uses of Equity Extracted from Homes," Finance and Economics Discussion Series, Federal Reserve Board, Washington, D.C., 2007.

6. Greenspan and Kennedy, 2007, p. 2.

7. These Federal Housing Finance Agency data are compiled from the Department of Housing and Urban Development, the Federal Housing Administration, the Department of Veterans Affairs, and the Rural Housing Service and Inside Mortgage Finance Publications, Table 1, Originations of Single-Family Mortgages, 1990–2009, Conventional and Government-Backed Mortgages, by Loan Type.

8. Inside Mortgage Finance data base.

9. Risk-Based Capital Guidelines; Capital Adequacy Guidelines; Capital Maintenance: Capital Treatment of Recourse, Direct Credit Substitutes and

Residual Interests in Asset Securitization; Final Rules. Department of the Treasury (Office of the Comptroller of the Currency and Office of Thrift Supervision), Federal Reserve System, Federal Deposit Insurance Corporation, *Federal Register* (Vol. 66. No. 230), November 29, 2001, pp. 59614–59667.

10. Kenneth Pinkes, Donald Selzer, Chester Murray, and Thomas Keller, "Moody's Investors Service Response to the Consultative Paper Issued by the Basel Committee on Bank Supervision [titled] 'A New Capital Adequacy Framework,' " March 2000, p. 8.

11. Inside Mortgage Finance data base.

12. Inside Mortgage Finance's *Mortgage Market Statistical Annual*, 2009 edition; compiled by Edward Pinto; from Edward J. Pinto, *Government Housing Policies in the Lead-up to the Financial Crisis: A Forensic Study*, Chart 34, p. 114.

13. Ibid.

14. Ibid., p. 112.

15. Ibid.

16. Edward Pinto, "Memorandum: High LTV, Subprime and Alt-A Originations over the Period 1992–2007 and Fannie, Freddie, FHA and VA's Role," mimeo, February 10, 2010, Table 3. Article in possession of author.

17. Ibid., Table 4.

18. Federal Housing Finance Agency, Home Price Index, Purchase Only, U.S. and Census Divisions (Seasonally Adjusted and Unadjusted).

19. OFHEO stands for the Office of Financial Housing Enterprise Oversight. FHFA is the abbreviation for the Federal Housing Finance Agency.

20. Office of the Comptroller of the Currency, Board of Governors of the Federal Reserve System, Federal Deposit Insurance Corporation Office of Thrift Supervision, National Credit Union Administration, Credit Risk Management Guidance for Home Equity Lending, May 16, 2005.

21. Office of the Comptroller of the Currency, Board of Governors of the Federal Reserve System, Federal Deposit Insurance Corporation Office of Thrift Supervision, National Credit Union Administration, [Proposed] Interagency Guidance on Nontraditional Mortgage Products, December 20, 2005.

22. Ibid.

23. Interview of Susan Bies, FCIC staff, October 11, 2010.

24. Office of the Comptroller of the Currency, Board of Governors of the Federal Reserve System, Federal Deposit Insurance Corporation Office of Thrift Supervision, National Credit Union Administration, [Proposed] Interagency Guidance on Nontraditional Mortgage Products, September 29, 2006.

25. Inside Mortgage Finance data base.

26. Felix Salmon, "Recipe for Disaster: The Formula That Killed Wall Street," *Wired*, Vol. 17 No. 3, February 23, 2009.

27. Robert Stowe England, "The Rise of Private Label," *Mortgage Banking*, October 2006.

28. Council to Shape Change, *Outlook for the Real Estate Finance Industry*, Mortgage Bankers Association, 2006.

29. Inside Mortgage Finance data base.

30. The category, called scratch-and-dent transactions, includes re-performing loans and re-securitized loans from existing MBS and conduit fallout loans.

31. A proper classification and accounting for second liens, which remains to be done, would likely swell the ranks of private-label subprime mortgage securitizations. This category, which was $20.1 billion in 2002, rose to $26.9 billion in 2003.

32. Data from Inside Mortgage Finance Publications

33. Interview with Mike McMahon, September 6, 2006. McMahon worked at the San Francisco office of New York-based Sandler O'Neill & Partners LP.

34. Interview with Angelo Mozilo, October 9, 2001. See also Robert Stowe England, "Fire in the Belly," *Mortgage Banking*, January 2002.

35. "Former Countrywide CEO Angelo Mozilo to Pay SEC's Largest-Ever Financial Penalty Against a Public Company's Senior Executive," press release, Securities and Exchange Commission, October 15, 2011.

36. Gretchen Morgenson, "Lending Magnate Settles Fraud Case," *New York Times*, October 15, 2010. Article cites Equilar as source of information on Mozilo's total compensation.

37. SEC, June 4, 2009.

38. Angelo R. Mozilo, "The American Dream of Homeownership: From Cliché to Mission," John T. Dunlop lecture for the Joint Center for Housing Studies of Harvard University, presented in Washington, D.C., February 4, 2003.

39. *Allstate Insurance Company et al. v. Countrywide Financial Corp. et al.*, Complaint, U.S. District Court, Southern District of New York, December 10, 2010.

40. Ibid., pp. 13–16.

41. Inside Mortgage Finance data base.

42. *Allstate v. Countrywide*, p. 8.

43. Ibid., p. 18.

44. Ibid., p. 19.

45. Ibid., p. 20.

46. Ibid., p. 26.

47. Indymac Bancorp was started by Mozilo and David Loeb in 1985. Loeb served as Indymac's chairman while he also served as Countrywide's chairman until 2003, when he stepped down at Countrywide. He retired as chairman of Indymac in 2003 and died later that year at his home in Sparks, Nevada.

48. Mike Shedlock, "Are You Missing the Real Estate Boom? (Part 2)," August 24, 2005. http://www.safehaven.com/article/3663/are-you-missing-the-real-estate-boom-part-2. Accessed December 24, 2010.

49. Material for Staff Presentation on Housing Valuations and Monetary Policy, Appendix 1 to the Transcript of the Meeting of the Federal Open Market Committee of the Federal Reserve System, June 29, 2005, pp. 172–234.

50. Joshua Gallin (Board of Governors of Federal Reserve System), Andreas Lehnert (Board of Governors of Federal Reserve System), Richard Peach (Federal Reserve Bank of New York), Glenn D. Rudebusch (Federal Reserve Bank of San Francisco), and John C. Williams (Federal Reserve Bank of San Francisco).

51. Ben S. Bernanke, Letter to Mr. Philip Angelides, Chairman, and Mr. William Thomas, Vice Chairman, Financial Crisis Inquiry Commission,

December 21, 2010, p. 2. "On the last point, staff replied that the GSEs were not large purchasers of private-label securities."

52. Ibid., pp. 3–4.

53. Robert Stowe England, "The Rise of Private Label," *Mortgage Banking*, October 2006.

54. Three-year adjustable-rate mortgages have a fixed rate for three years and then adjust in the fourth year. They are also known as 3/27s.

55. Interview with mortgage insurance industry insider, November 19, 2010.

56. Mozilo, February 4, 2003.

57. Interview with Stuart Feldstein, August 17, 2006.

58. SMR Research, *Mortgage Industry Outlook 2006*, September 2005, p. 38.

59. Ibid.

60. Interview with Mark DiRienz, Moody's Investors Service, August 4, 2006.

61. Interview with Robert B. Pollsen, Standard & Poor's, August 2, 2006

62. Interview with Alec Crawford, Greenwich Capital Markets, August 31, 2006.

Chapter 6: Wall Street's Subprime CDO Mania

1. Charles P. Kindleberger and Robert Aliber, *Manias, Panics and Crashes*, Fifth Edition, John Wiley & Sons, Hoboken, NJ, 2005, p. 12.

2. Kenneth Kapner, *Introduction to Collateralized Debt Obligations*, Global Financial Markets Institute Inc., New York.

3. Janet Tavakoli, *Structured Finance & Collateralized Debt Obligations*, Second Edition, John Wiley & Sons, Hoboken, NJ, 2008, p. 2.

4. *The Financial Crisis Inquiry Report*, p. 129.

5. "The CDO Factory," Risk.net, May 1, 2007.

6. Nye Lavalle, "Merrill Lynch's Moronic Godfather of CDOs," Mortgage Servicing Fraud Forum, October 25, 2007.

7. Interview with Wing Chau, FCIC, November 11, 2010, *Financial Crisis Inquiry Report*, p. 350.

8. Joe Donovan, quoted in Michael Gregory, "The 'What If's' in ABS CDOs," *Asset Securitization Report*, February 18, 2002.

9. Interview with Christopher Ricciardi, FCIC, September 15, 2010.

10. *Financial Crisis Inquiry Report*, p. 132.

11. Interview with John Jay, Aite Group, November 15, 2010.

12. Estimate by the staff of the Financial Crisis Inquiry Commission based on data from a survey of CDO managers and underwriters. See *Financial Crisis Inquiry Report*, p. 203.

13. Ibid.

14. Testimony of Thomas Maheras, former Co-CEO of Citi Markets and Banking, Citigroup, Federal Crisis Inquiry Commission, April 7, 2010.

15. Charles Gasparino, *The Sellout*, HarperCollins, New York, p. 191.

16. Michael Lewis, *The Big Short*, W. W. Norton & Company, New York, 2010, p. 11.

17. Lewis, p. 73.

18. Data from Inside Mortgage Finance Publications.

19. S&P's CDO Interface, as reported by Anne Katherine Barnett-Hart, "The Story of the CDO Meltdown: An Empirical Analysis," presented to the Department of Economics in partial fulfillment of the requirements for a Bachelor of Arts degree with Honors, Harvard College, March 19, 2009, mimeo. http://www.hks.harvard.edu/m-rcbg/students/dunlop/2009 -CDOmeltdown.pdf. Accessed May 30, 2011.

20. J. Kyle Bass, Dear Investors, Hayman Capital, Dallas, Texas, July 30, 2007. Letter confirmed as authentic is in possession of author.

21. Testimony of J. Kyle Bass, Managing Partner, Hayman Advisors L.P., U.S. House of Representatives Committee on Financial Services, Subcommittee on Capital Markets, Insurance and Government Sponsored Enterprises, September 27, 2007.

22. Risk-Based Capital Guidelines; Capital Adequacy Guidelines; Capital Maintenance: Capital Treatment of Recourse, Direct Credit Substitutes and Residual Interests in Asset Securitization; Final Rules. Department of the Treasury (Office of the Comptroller of the Currency and Office of Thrift Supervision), Federal Reserve System, Federal Deposit Insurance Corporation, *Federal Register* (Vol. 66. No. 230), November 29, 2001, pp. 59614–59667.

23. Taylor D. Nadauld and Shane M. Sherlund, "The Role of Securitization Process in the Expansion of Subprime Credit," Finance and Economics Discussion Series, Divisions of Research & Statistics and Monetary Affairs, Federal Reserve Board, Washington, D.C., April 22, 2009.

24. See *Federal Register*, Vol. 69, No. 118, Monday, June 21, 2004, Rules and Regulations, p. 29.

25. Nadauld and Sherlund, p. 4.

26. Eric S. Rosengren, "Could a Systemic Regulator Have Seen the Current Crisis?" Federal Reserve Bank of Boston, Seoul, Korea, April 15, 2009.

27. Figures from 10-Ks and SNL Financial from: J. Kyle Bass, managing partner, Hayman Advisors, L.P., Testimony before the Financial Crisis Inquiry Commission, Hearing, January 13, 2010, p. 4.

28. David Li, "On Default Correlation: A Copula Function Approach," *Journal of Fixed Income*, Vol. 9, No. 4, 2000, pp, 43–54.

29. Felix Salmon, "Recipe for Disaster: The Formula That Killed Wall Street," *Wired*, Vol. 17, No. 3, February 23, 2009.

30. Ibid.

Chapter 7: Fast Money and High Stakes

1. The 1999 science fiction thriller *The Matrix* and its two sequels depict a future world where what is believed to be reality is, in fact, simulated by computers.

2. Gillian Tett, *Fool's Gold: How the Bold Dream of a Small Tribe at J.P. Morgan Was Corrupted by Wall Street Greed and Unleashed a Catastrophe*, Free Press, New York, 2009.

3. Tett, p. 46.

4. Frank Partnoy, *Infectious Greed: How Deceit and Risk Corrupted the Financial Markets*, Times Books, New York, 2003.

5. *Financial Crisis Inquiry Report*, p. 142.

6. Laurie S. Goodman, Shumin Li, Douglas J. Lucas, Thomas A. Zimmerman, and Frank J. Fabozzi, *Subprime Mortgage Credit Derivatives*, John Wiley & Sons, Hoboken, NJ, 2008. In 1993, Goodman founded the securitized research department at Paine Webber, which was merged with UBS in 2000.

7. Goodman et al.

8. Mark Twain, "The Celebrated Jumping Frog of Calaveras County," a short story, 1865.

9. Goodman et al., p. 176.

10. Interview with Dow Kim, FCIC staff, September 9, 2010.

11. Ibid.

12. Interview with Wing Chau, FCIC, November 11, 2010, *Financial Crisis Inquiry Report*, p. 203.

13. *Financial Crisis Inquiry Report*, p. 203. Estimate by FCIC staff using Moody's CDO EMS data base.

14. Ibid.

15. Data supplied by Merrill Lynch to the FCIC.

16. Telephone discussion with unnamed attorneys at the SEC with FCIC, September 2, 2010. *Financial Crisis Inquiry Report*, p. 203.

17. Interview with Gregg Lippmann, FCIC staff, May 20, 2010. *Financial Crisis Inquiry Report*, p. 191.

18. *Financial Crisis Inquiry Report*, p. 191.

19. Gregory Zuckerman, *The Greatest Trade Ever: The Behind-the-Scenes Story of How John Paulson Defied Wall Street and Made Financial History*, Crown Business, New York, 2009.

20. Dezhong Wang, Svetlozar T. Rachev, and Frank J. Fabozzi, "Pricing Tranches of a CDO and a CDS Index: Recent Advances and Future Research," October 2006, Working Paper, Mimeo, p. 8.

21. Tavakoli, 2008, p. 5.

22. The FCIC hedge fund survey conducted in 2010 found that from July through December 2006, several hedge funds with average assets under management of $4 billion to $8 billion accumulated positions totaling more than $1.4 billion in mortgage-related CDO equity tranches and almost $3 billion in short positions in mortgage-related CDO mezzanine tranches. FCIC used a Moody's proprietary CDO database to estimate the total mortgage-related CDO equity issuance. The survey did not include hedge funds that closed.

23. Norma CDO I Ltd. Offering Circular, Merrill Lynch & Co., February 28, 2007.

24. Serena Ng and Carrick Mollenkamp, "A Fund Behind Astronomical Losses," *Wall Street Journal*, January 14, 2008.

25. *Cooperatieve Centrale Raiffeisen-Boerenleenbank BA, or Rabobank, vs. Merrill Lynch & Company, Inc.*, 601832/09.

26. Chad Bray, "Bank: Merrill Committed Same Fraud as SEC Claims Goldman Did," *Wall Street Journal*, April 17, 2010.

27. See letter from Rabobank's counsel to Judge Bernard J. Fried of the Supreme Court of the State of New York, May 11, 2010. The letter was not filed with the court because the case was settled.

28. Document of Magnetar Investments in Norma, Attachment G-13 (showing Magnetar purchases of equity tranches in Norma; provided by Merrill Lynch).

29. Letter from Jonathan Pickhardt to Judge Bernard J. Fried, May 11, 2010.

30. Ibid.

31. Jesse Eisinger and Jake Bernstein, "The Magnetar Trade: How One Hedge Fund Helped Keep the Bubble Going," April 9, 2010, ProPublica.org.

32. Dear Magnetar Capital Investor, Magnetar Capital, Evanston, Illinois, April 10, 2010. Copy of letter authenticated and in author's possession.

33. Vikas Bajaj and Christine Haughney, "Tremors at the Door," *New York Times*, January 27, 2007.

34. Mike Shedlock, "Are You Missing the Real Estate Boom? (Part 2)," August 24, 2005. http://www.safehaven.com/article/3663/are-you-missing-the-real-estate-boom-part-2. Accessed December 24, 2010.

35. Goodman et al., p. 142.

36. Ibid.

37. Ibid., p. 143.

38. Mark Pittman, "Bass Shorted 'God I Hope You're Wrong' Wall Street," Bloomberg News, December 19, 2007.

39. Ibid.

40. CNBC, *House of Cards*, February 12, 2009. Documentary available at this site: http://www.cnbc.com/id/28892719.

41. Basel Committee on Banking Supervision, *The Joint Forum: Credit Risk Transfer, Developments from 2005 to 2007*, Bank for International Settlements, Basel, Switzerland, July 2008, p. 20.

42. Basel Committee, 2008, p. 18.

43. Christopher Whalen, "Financial Innovation Meets Main Street: Jefferson County and Municipal Finance in the Wake of the Bubble," Presentation made at the American Enterprise Institute, September 9, 2008.

44. Richard R. Zabel, C.P.A., "Credit Default Swaps: From Protection to Speculation," *Pratt's Journal of Bankruptcy Law*, September 2008.

45. Basel Committee on Banking Supervision, *The Joint Forum: Credit Risk Transfer, Developments from 2005 to 2007*, Bank for International Settlements, Basel, Switzerland, July 2008, p. 9.

46. According to Inside Mortgage Finance Publications, private-label subprime issuance was $194.959 billion in 2003, $362.549 billion in 2004, $465.036 billion in 2005, $448.6 billion in 2006, and $201.547 billion for half of 2007. The amount above the 2003 level for each year is as follows: 2004, $167.59 billion; 2005, $270.077 billion; 2006, $253.641 billion; 2007, first half, $104.068 billion.

47. Private-label subprime issuance was $122.681 billion in 2002. The amount above the 2003 level for each year is as follows: 2003, $72.278 billion; 2004, $239.868 billion; 2005, $342.355 billion; 2006, $325.919 billion; 2007, first half, $140.207 billion.

Chapter 8: American International Group

1. J. Kyle Bass, Managing Partner, Hayman Advisors, L.P., "Testimony before the Financial Crisis Inquiry Commission Hearing of the Financial Crisis," January 13, 2010, Exhibit 2, p. 5.

2. Ibid., p. 2.

3. Michael Shedlock, "Derivatives Catastrophe: Are We Headed for a 'Credit Derivatives Event?' " Whiskey and Gunpowder web site for independent investors, September 12, 2005. http://whiskeyandgunpowder.com/derivatives-catastrophe-are-we-headed-for-a-credit-derivatives-event/. Accessed December 26, 2010.

4. Gillian Tett, *Fool's Gold*, Free Press, New York, 2009, p. 63.

5. Carrick Mollenkamp, Serena Ng, Liam Pleven, and Randall Smith, "Did a Computer Flaw Nearly Wreck AIG?" *The Australian*, November 3, 2008.

6. Ibid.

7. Ibid.

8. AIG Risk Management, document on AIG released by the Federal Crisis Inquiry Commission on July 1, 2010, p. 1.

9. Interviews with Sullivan and Bensinger by the staff of the Federal Crisis Inquiry Commission cited in a memo titled "AIG Risk Management," July 1, 2010, p. 1.

10. Interviews of Sullivan, Bensinger, Robert Lewis (former chief risk officer of AIG), and Elias Habayet (former chief financial officer of AIG Financial Services) by the staff of the Federal Crisis Inquiry Commission cited in memo titled AIG Risk Management, July 1, 2010, p. 1.

11. E-mail titled "Topics to Discuss" from Andrew Forster to Tom Fewings, Sheridan Teasel, Adam Budnick, Gary Gorton; and Alan Frost, July 21, 2005, 06:48:31 a.m.

12. Michael Lewis, *The Big Short*, W. W. Norton & Company, New York, 2010, p. 86.

13. Michael Lewis, "The Man Who Crashed the World," *Vanity Fair*, June 30, 2009.

14. Testimony of Joseph J. Cassano, Financial Crisis Inquiry Commission, June 30, 2010.

15. E-mail from Gene Park titled "CDO of ABS Approach Going Forward—Message to the Dealer Community," to Joseph Cassano, with a copy to Andrew Forster, Alan Frost, Gary Gorton, Sheridan Teasel, Tom Fewings, and Adam Budnick, February 28, 2006, 8:54.29 a.m.

16. Lewis 2010, p. 85.

17. Testimony of Joseph J. Cassano, Financial Crisis Inquiry Commission, June 30, 2010.

18. Andrew G. Simpson, "Greenberg: AIG's Risky Subprime Activity 'Exploded' After He Left," *Insurance Journal*, October 10, 2008.

19. Testimony of Joseph J. Cassano, FCIC, June 20, 2010.

20. Ibid.

21. Comptroller of the Currency, OCC's Quarterly Report on Bank Derivatives Activities, First Quarter 2006, Washington, D.C.

22. Andrew Ross Sorkin, *Too Big To Fail*, Penguin, New York, 2009, pp. 379–380.

23. Rating Action: AIG Casualty Company, Moody's Investors Service, September 15, 2008.

24. Henry M. Paulson, Jr., *On the Brink*, Business Plus, Hachette Book Group, New York, 2010, p. 239.

25. Federal Reserve Board of Directors, Press Release, September 16, 2008, 9:00 p.m. EDT.

26. Office of the Special Inspector General for the Troubled Asset Relief Program, *Factors Affecting Efforts to Limit Payments to AIG Counterparties*, SIG-TARP 10-03, November 17, 2009. http://www.sigtarp.gov/reports/audit/2009/Factors_Affecting_Efforts_to_Limit_Payments_to_AIG_Counterparties.pdf.

27. Janet Tavakoli, "Goldman's Undisclosed Role in AIG's Distress," November 10, 2009. http://www.tavakolistructuredfinance.com/GS3.pdf. Accessed March 9, 2011.

28. Joe Cassano, Collateral Call Status, http://www.cbsnews.com/htdocs/pdf/collateral_b.pdf. Accessed March 9, 2011.

29. Interview with Neil Barofsky, October 5, 2010. See also Robert Stowe England, "Q&A with Neil Barofsky," *Mortgage Banking*, November 2010.

30. Ibid.

31. Ibid.

32. Michael Greenberger, "The Role of Derivatives in the Financial Crisis," Testimony, Federal Crisis Inquiry Commission, June 30, 2010.

33. Manuel Roig-Franzia, "Credit Crisis Cassandra," *Washington Post*, May 26, 2009.

34. Derivatives Regulation § 4.04 [11] at 975 (referencing 7 U.S.C. § 16 (e)(2).

35. Greenberger, p. 17.

Chapter 9: Bear Stearns

1. Alistair Barr, "Bear Stearns Drops on Liquidity Concerns," *MarketWatch*, March 10, 2008.

2. Board of Governors of the Federal Reserve System, Term Securities Lending Facility, March 11, 2008.

3. Gary Matsumoto, "Bringing Down Bear Began as $1.7 Million of Options," Bloomberg News, August 11, 2008.

4. writerjudd (Judd Bagley), "Hedge Funds and the Global Economic Meltdown (Part 1)," March 29, 2009.

5. Kate Kelly, "Where in the World Is Bear's Jimmy Cayne? Playing Bridge," *New York Times*, March 14, 2008.

6. Henry M. Paulson, Jr., *On the Brink*, Business Plus, Hachette Book Group, New York, 2010, p. 93.

7. Ibid., p. 96.

8. Samuel Molinaro, FCIC Testimony, May 5, 2010.

9. Gasparino, pp. 372–73.

10. Paulson, p. 100.

11. Molinaro, FCIC, May 5, 2010.

12. Gasparino, p. 377.

13. Paulson, p. 111.

14. Ibid.

15. Ibid., p. 114.

16. Ibid.

17. Ibid., p. 115.

18. Ibid., p. 120.

19. Molinaro, FCIC, May 5, 2010.

20. Paulson, p. 125.

21. FCIC Transcript, May 5, 2010, p. 163.

22. Ibid., p. 164.

23. Paul Friedman, Testimony Before the Financial Crisis Inquiry Commission, May 5, 2010.

24. Ibid.

25. William D. Cohan, "Inside the Bear Stearns Boiler Room," *Fortune*, March 3, 2009. Excerpt from *House of Cards: A Tale of Hubris and Wretched Excess on Wall Street*, Doubleday Books, New York, 2009.

26. *Financial Crisis Inquiry Report*, p. 154.

27. The law is also known as the Financial Services Modernization Act of 1999.

28. Christopher Cox, Testimony Before the Federal Crisis Inquiry Commission, Hearing, May 5, 2010.

29. FCIC, Transcript, Hearing, May 5, 2010, p. 250.

30. David Einhorn, "Private Profits and Socialized Risk," Grant's Spring Investment Conference, April 8, 2008.

31. Securities and Exchange Commission, Alternative Net Capital Requirements for Broker-Dealers That Are Part of Consolidated Supervised Entities, Final Rule, June 21, 2004.

Chapter 10: Fannie and Freddie

1. All the quotes from Richard Baker are taken from an interview on November 30, 2010.

2. Mr. Brendsel's testimony before the Oversight Subcommittee of the House Ways and Means Committee on September 28, 1989, is recounted in Thomas H. Stanton, *Government-Sponsored Enterprises: Mercantilist Companies in the Modern World*, AEI Press, Washington, DC, 2002, pp. 83–84.

3. OFHEO was authorized under the Federal Housing Enterprises Financial Safety and Soundness Act of 1992, also known as the GSE Act.

4. Bethany McLean, "The Fall of Fannie Mae," *Fortune*, January 24, 2005.

5. Gary Gensler, Testimony, House Banking Subcommittee on Capital Markets, Securities and Government-Sponsored Enterprises, March 22, 1999.

6. "House Passes GSE Reform Bill," *Mortgage Banking*, Vol. 66, No. 3, December 2005.

7. Alan Greenspan, Regulatory reform of the government-sponsored enterprises, Testimony before the Committee on Banking, Housing, and Urban Affairs, U.S Senate, April 6, 2005.

8. E-mail of March 14, 2011, from Alan Greenspan to the author, in response to questions submitted to him by e-mail that same day.

9. H.R. 1461 passed October 26, 2005.

10. Interview with James Lockhart, November 17, 2010. All the quotes from Lockhart in this chapter are from this interview, except where indicated.

11. The Federal Housing Enterprises Financial Safety and Soundness Act of 1992, also the GSE Act.

12. Annys Shin, "Pressure on Fannie, Freddie Increases," *Washington Post*, June 14, 2006.

13. Ibid.

14. The Federal Housing Finance Reform Act of 2007. H.R. 1427 was introduced March 9, 2007.

15. Paul Muolo and Matthew Padilla, *Chain of Blame*, New York: John Wiley & Sons, 2008, p. 112.

16. Office of Federal Housing Enterprise Oversight, "OFHEO, Fannie Mae and Freddie Mac Announced Initiative to Increase Mortgage Market Liquidity," March 19, 2008.

17. Henry M. Paulson, Jr., *On The Brink*, Business Plus, Hachette Book Group, New York, 2010, p. 147.

18. Peter R. Orszag, Congressional Budget Office, CBO's Estimate of the Administration's Proposal to Authorize Federal Financial Assistance for the Government-Sponsored Enterprises for Housing, July 22, 2008.

19. Paulson, p. 152.

20. Ibid., pp. 6–7.

21. Paul Nash, Deputy to the Chairman for External Affairs, FDIC, Letter of October 28, 2010, to Wendy Edelberg, Executive Director, FCIC.

22. Interview of James Lockhart, May 27, 2011.

23. *Jino Kuriakose et al. v. Federal Home Loan Mortgage Company, Richard Syron et al.* U.S. District Court, Southern District of New York, August 15, 2008.

24. Interview with James Lockhart, May 26, 2011.

25. Paulson, p. 1.

26. Ibid., p. 5.

27. Ibid., pp. 9–10.

28. Ibid., p. 11.

29. Ibid., pp. 11–12.

30. Zachary A. Goldfarb, David Cho, and Binyamin Appelbaum, "Treasury to Rescue Fannie and Freddie," *Washington Post*, September 7, 2008.

31. Stephen Labaton and Edmund L. Andrews, "Reinventing Mortgage Giants: A Big Rebuild or a Teardown," *New York Times*, September 9, 2008.

Chapter 11: Lehman Brothers

1. Amit Chokshi, "VIC: Greenlight Capital's David Einhorn—Lehman's a Short," *Seeking Alpha*, November 30, 2007.

2. Josh Fineman and Rhonda Schaffler, "Lehman Remains 'Undercapitalized,' Einhorn Says," Bloomberg News, May 28, 2008.

3. David Einhorn, "Private Profits and Socialized Risk," Grant's Spring Investor Conference, April 8, 2008.

4. Einhorn made his back-of-the-envelope calculation of the capital Lehman needed by requiring 50 to 100 percent capital for investments with "no ready market," 8 to 12 percent for the bank's net assets, 2 percent for the other assets plus a charge for derivative exposure and contingent commitments. This all assumed the fair value of the assets had been accurately stated.

5. In the fourth quarter of 2007, which ended November 30, 2007, Lehman Brothers Holdings Inc. reported $16.9 billion in average tangible common stockholders' equity. See p. 8 of Lehman's press release at http://www.prnewswire.com/news-releases/lehman-brothers-reports-record-net-revenues-net-income-and-earnings-per-share-for-fiscal-2007-58705737.html. Accessed January 13, 2011.

6. Report of Anton R. Valukas, Examiner, *In re Lehman Brothers Holdings Inc., et al., Debtors*; U.S. Bankruptcy Court, Southern District of New York, March 11, 2010, Volume 3 of 9, Section IIIA.4:Repo 105, p. 758.

7. Valukas, 2010, footnote 2848, pp. 723, 733.

8. Ibid., p. 734.

9. Valukas, 2010, footnote 2849, pp. 735–736.

10. Joseph Gentile, Proposed Repo 105/108 Target Increase for 2007, February 10, 2007, p. 1. From Valukas, 2010, p. 738.

11. Valukas, 2010, footnote 2869, p. 738.

12. Ibid., p. 739.

13. Ibid., p. 740.

14. Sorkin, pp. 192–193.

15. *The Financial Crisis Inquiry Report*, Final Report of the National Commission on the Causes of the Financial and Economic Crisis in the United States, Official Government Edition, January 2011, p. 328; also endnote 33 in chapter 18.

16. Sorkin, p. 194.

17. *The Financial Crisis Inquiry Report*, p. 328.

18. William Dudley E-mail of July 15, 2008. http://c0181567.cdn1.cloud files.rackspacecloud.com/2008-07-15_Federal_Reserve_Bank_Email_from _Scott_Alvarez_to_Kieran_Fallon_Re_Lehman_Good_Bank_Bad_Bank_idea _discussed_last_night.pdf, accessed March 15, 2011.

19. "Gameplan and Status to Date," E-mail from Patrick M. Parkinson, August 8, 2008, and follow-ups.

20. Julie Creswell and Ben White, "The Guys from 'Government Sachs,' " TimesDaily.com, October 19, 2008.

21. E-mail from Steven Shafran, August 28, 2011.

22. E-mail of Patrick Parkinson, September 4, 2008.

23. Dennis K. Berman, "Banker leaves Goldman Sachs to Aid Paulson," *Wall Street Journal*, July 21, 2008.

24. Paulson, p. 174.

25. Ibid., p. 175.

26. Ibid., p. 177.

27. *The Financial Crisis Inquiry Report*, pp. 330–331.

28. E-mail of Matthew Rutherford, Treasury Department, September 10, 2008.

29. *The Financial Crisis Inquiry Report*, p. 331, based on an FCIC survey of market participants.

30. Paulson, p. 180.

31. E-mail from Patrick Parkinson, September 11, 2009.

32. E-mail from Jamie McAndrews at the New York Fed, September 11, 2008.

33. *The Financial Crisis Inquiry Report*, p. 332.

34. Paulson, 2010, p. 185.

35. Gary Matsumoto, "Naked Shorts Hint Fraud in Bringing Down Lehman," Bloomberg News, March 19, 2009.

36. Office of Inspector General Office of Audits of the U.S. Securities and Exchange Commission, Practices Relation to Naked Short Selling Complaints and Referrals, March 18, 2009.

37. E-mail from Haley Boesky, New York Fed, September 11, 2008.

38. Paulson, p. 187.

39. Ibid., pp. 189–190.

40. Interview of Ken Lewis, FCIC, October 22, 2010.

41. Paulson, 2010, p. 190.

42. Ibid., p. 193.

43. Ben S. Bernanke, Lessons from the failure of Lehman Brothers, Testimony before the Committee on Financial Services, U.S. House of Representatives, Washington, D.C., April 20, 2010.

44. Paulson, 2010, pp. 201–202.

45. Interview with John Thain, FCIC, September 17, 2010.

46. Paulson, p. 219.

47. E-mail from Christopher T. Tsuboi, New York Fed, September 13, 2011.

48. *The Financial Crisis Inquiry Report*, p. 335.

49. *The Financial Crisis Inquiry Report*, p. 616, identifies the endnotes as follows: Endnote 91: Scott Alvarez, e-mail to Ben Bernanke et al., "Re: Fw: today at 7:00 p.m. w/Chairman Bernanke, Vice Chairman Kohn and Others," September 13, 2008. Endnote 92: Scott Alvarez, email to Mark VanDerWeide, "Re: tri-party," September 13, 2008.

50. Paulson, 2010, p. 206.

51. Interview with Bart McDade, FCIC, August 9, 2010.

52. Paulson, 2010, p. 206.

53. Interview of Robert Diamond, FCIC, November 15, 2010.

54. Ben S. Bernanke, Lessons from the failure of Lehman Brothers, Testimony before the Committee on Financial Services, U.S. House of Representatives, Washington, D.C., April 20, 2010.

55. Paulson, p. 210.

56. Interview with Rodgin Cohen, FCIC, August 5, 2010.

57. Sorkin, p. 353.

58. Interview with Bart McDade, FCIC, August 9, 2010; interview with Alex Kirk of Lehman Brothers, FCIC, August 16, 2010.

59. Thomas C. Baxter, letter to FCIC, October 15, 2010, attaching Exhibit 6, James P. Bergin, e-mail to William Dudley et al., "Bankruptcy," September 14, 2008. Also Interview with Alex Kirk, August 10, 2010.

60. Ibid.

61. Paulson, p. 218.

62. Ibid., p. 219.

63. Interview with Harvey Miller, FCIC, August 5, 2010.

64. Ibid.

65. Ibid.

66. Ibid.

67. Ibid.

68. Ben Bernanke, "U.S. Financial Markets," testimony before the Senate Committee on Banking, Housing and Urban Affairs, September 23, 2008.

69. *The Financial Crisis Inquiry Report*, pp. 340–341.

70. Scott G. Alvarez et al., memorandum, "Authority of the Federal Reserve to Provide Extensions of Credit in Connection with a Commercial Paper Funding Facility (CPFF)," March 19, 2009, p. 7.

71. Allan Melzter, "What Happened to the 'Depression'?" *Wall Street Journal*, August 31, 2009.

72. Interview with James Rickards, March 30, 2011.

73. The uptick rule was also known as Rule 10a-1.

74. Kevin D. Freeman, *Economic Warfare: Risks and Responses*, Cross Consulting and Services LLC, for the Department of Defense Irregular warfare Support Program, June 2009. Copy of study in author's possession.

75. Interview with Kevin Freeman, March 3, 2011.

76. Anuj Gangahar, "It Is Time to Shine Some Light into These Dark Pools" *Financial Times*, July 5, 2008.

77. Laurie Berke, *Dark Pools, Transparency, and Consequences*, TABB Group, November 18, 2009.

78. Interview with Kevin Freeman, March 3, 2011.

79. Interview with James Rickards, March 30, 2011.

Chapter 12: The Panic of 2008

1. In the United States, the OIS are calculated with reference to the federal funds rate, which is an interest rate at which private depository institutions lend portions of their balances held at the Federal Reserve to other depository institutions, usually overnight.

2. Paulson, p. 230.

3. Ibid., p. 228.

4. Gary Gorton and Andrew Metrick, "Haircuts," Federal Reserve Bank of St. Louis, November–December 2010.

5. Ibid.

6. Securities Exchange Commission, Fails-to-Deliver Data—Archive Data.

7. Liz Capo McCormick, "Treasury Traders Paid to Borrow as Fed Examines Repos," Bloomberg News, November 24, 2008.

8. Christopher Condon, "Reserve Primary Money Fund Falls Below $1 a Share," Bloomberg News, September 16, 2011.

9. Bob Ivry, Mark Pittman, and Christine Harper, "Sleep-at-Night-Money Lost in Lehman Lesson Missing $63 Billion," Bloomberg News, September 9, 2009.

10. Paulson, p. 234.

11. Securities and Exchange Commission, Division of Investment Management, Staff No-Action and Interpretive Letters, on or after January 1, 1995.

12. Paulson, p. 251.

13. The following were present: Nancy Pelosi, John Boehner, Barney Frank, Spencer Bachus, Steny Hoyer, Rahm Emanuel from the House; Harry Reid, Mitch McConnell, Dick Durbin, Chris Dodd, Richard Shelby, Chuck Schumer, and Patty Murray from the Senate.

14. David Herszenhorn, "Congressional Leaders Stunned by Warnings," *New York Times*, September 19, 2008.

15. Rep. Paul Kanjorski, Pennsylvania Democrat, who was not in the Congressional briefing from 7 p.m. to 9 p.m., September 18 on Capitol Hill, made a sensational claim that Congressional leaders were told that $550 billion was taken out of money market funds in a matter of hours before 11 a.m. that same day. Kanjorski claimed an alarmed Treasury then closed down money market accounts, an event that did not occur, in order to prevent $5.5 trillion from being withdrawn by the end of the day. Without the Treasury's intervention, the run on money market funds "would have collapsed the entire economy of the United States and within 24 hours the world economy would have collapsed," Kanjorksi said. Source: Interview with Paul Kanjorski, House Economic Stimulus Proposal, C-Span's *Washington Journal*, Host Steven Scully, January 27, 2009. Timeline beginning at 22 minutes and 57 seconds, 5:28 a.m. Pacific Time.

16. Data from Investment Company Institute.

17. *Report of the Money Market Fund Working Group*, Submitted to the Board of Governors of the Investment Company Institute, March 17, 2009, p. 49.

18. In mid-February 2008, the market for auction rate securities froze. These are long-term, variable-rate instruments with interest rates set at periodic auctions. The downgrade of monoline insurers who backed these funds played a role in their demise.

19. The program was known by its abbreviation, AMLF. It expired Feb. 1, 2010.

20. Jon Hilsenrath, Damian Paletta, and Aaron Luchetti, "Goldman, Morgan Scrap Wall Street Model, Become Banks in Bid to Ride Out Crisis," *Wall Street Journal*, September 22, 2008.

21. The Federal Deposit Insurance Corporation Improvement Act of 1991. The systemic risk exemption required the approval of the Treasury secretary, after consulting the President, plus two-thirds of the Federal Reserve Board and two-thirds of the FDIC's board.

22. Interview with Sheila Bair, FCIC, Excerpt 3, November 30, 2010.

23. Ibid.

24. Paulson, p. 323.

25. Keith Fitz-Gerald, "LIBOR OIS Spread Signals Credit Crisis Earthquake," *The Market Oracle*, October 7, 2008. http://www.marketoracle.co.uk/Article6666.html. Accessed January 30, 2011.

26. Paulson, p. 337.

27. Peter Thal Larsen, Jane Croft, Jean Eaglesham, and Kate Burges, "UK to Inject £39bn into Banks," *Financial Times*, October 12, 2008.

28. Joint Statement by Treasury, Federal Reserve, and FDIC, October 14, 2008.

29. The facility was known by its acronym, the CPFF. It expired Feb. 1, 2010.

30. Interview with Neil Barofsky, October 5, 2010.

31. According to the Federal Reserve's term sheet, under the November 23, 2008, arrangement, Citigroup absorbs $29 billion in losses to existing reserves. Losses in excess of that are divided as follows: $5 billion by Treasury (from TARP) and $10 billion for the FDIC. The Federal Reserve funds the remaining pool of assets with a non-recourse loan, subject to 10 percent loss sharing, at a floating rate of overnight index swap (OIS) plus 300 basis points.

32. *Securities and Exchange Commission v. Citigroup, Inc.* Complaint, Case 1:10-cv-0177, July 29, 2010. http://www.sec.gov/litigation/complaints/2010/comp21605.pdf. Accessed March 21, 2011.

33. Ibid., pp. 9–10.

34. Ibid., p. 11.

35. Ibid., pp. 17–18.

36. Ibid., p. 20.

37. Ibid.

38. *Financial Crisis Inquiry Report*, p. 19.

39. Interview of Richard Bowen, FCIC staff, February 27, 2010.

40. Ibid.

41. Interview with Janet Tavakoli, January 27, 2011.

42. Congressional Oversight Panel, *The Final Report of the Congressional Oversight Panel*, March 16, 2011.

43. International Monetary Fund, *Global Financial Stability Report*, April, 2009.

44. International Monetary Fund, *Global Financial Stability Report*, April, 2010.

45. Derek Kravitz, "Number of Underwater Mortgages Rises as More Homeowners Fall Behind," *The Huffington Post*, March 8, 2011.

Index

Varley, John, 186, 189, 190
Vento, Bruce, 48
Veterans Administration (VA), 60, 62

Wachovia Bank, 202
Wall Street firms, 31, 34, 72, 89, 94, 132; CDOs and, 95–104; computer modeling and, 84, 109; new SEC rules and, 107–8, 149–50, 152; "too big to fail," 153; VaR model and, 151–52. *See also* Bear Stearns; Goldman Sachs; Lehman Brothers
Washington Mutual (WaMu), 22, 86, 89, 145, 187; falling share price, 202; FDIC receipt of, 205–6
Wells Fargo, 82–83, 89, 206
WestLB Mellon Asset Management, 21
Whalen, Christopher, 123–24
Whitney, Meredith, 141
Williams, Michael, 70
WMC Mortgage Corp., 5
Wyss, David, 13

Yeaman, Helena, 55
Yellen, Janet, 91
Youngblood, Michael, 11, 13

Zabel, Richard R., 124
Zachary, Mark, 5–6
Zero down payment programs, 77

About the Author

ROBERT STOWE ENGLAND is an author and financial journalist who has specialized in writing about retirement income issues, financial institutions, financial markets, and population aging. From 1999 to 2003, he served as director of research for the Global Aging Initiative at the Center for Strategic and International Studies (CSIS) in Washington, DC. CSIS published three monographs by Mr. England on the impact of global aging on government spending on the elderly, the global economy, and financial markets. In 2005, Praeger Publishers and CSIS jointly published his book *Aging China*, which examines the impact of population aging on China's economic prospects. Mr. England is a senior writer for *Mortgage Banking* and has written for the magazine since 1988. He also writes regularly for the journal *BAI Banking Strategies*. Mr. England was the Washington correspondent for *Plan Sponsor* from 1993 to 2003. He holds a B.A. degree in English from Duke University.